A HISTORY OF

EDUCATION

AMS PRESS

NEW YORK

INTERNATIONAL EDUCATION SERIES

A HISTORY OF
EDUCATION

BY

F. V. N. PAINTER, A.M., D.D.

PROFESSOR OF MODERN LANGUAGES AND LITERATURE IN ROANOKE COLLEGE

AUTHOR OF

"A HISTORY OF ENGLISH LITERATURE," "INTRODUCTION TO AMERICAN
LITERATURE," "GUIDE TO LITERARY CRITICISM," ETC.

REVISED, ENLARGED, AND LARGELY REWRITTEN

NEW YORK
D. APPLETON AND COMPANY
1905

Library of Congress Cataloging in Publication Data

Painter, Franklin Verzelius Newton, 1852-1931.
   A history of education.

   Original ed. issued in series: International education series.
   Bibliography: p.
   1. Education--History. I. Title.
LA13.P2 1972   370'.9   77-137266
0-404-04866-8

Reprinted from the edition of 1905, New York
First AMS edition published in 1972
Manufactured in the United States of America

AMS PRESS INC.
NEW YORK, N. Y.   10003

DEDICATED

TO

The Memory of My Father

EDITOR'S PREFACE

THE present work by Professor Painter takes up the subject from the standpoint of the history of civilization. The educational ideals that have prevailed have been derived from the principles that have controlled nations and religions. Each State has evolved a system of education in conformity with the fundamental idea of its civilization. It may or may not have had a system of schools, but it has possessed instrumentalities for education in the family, civil society, and religious ceremonial, besides its own direct discipline through the laws and their administration and through its public service, civil and military. In religion, whether Christian or "heathen," there is implied a definite fundamental view of the world which is referred to in all concrete relations, and by this there is given a sort of systematic unity to the details of life. The first object of parental government is to train the child into habits of conformity to the current religious view. The government seeks to enforce an observance of regulations that establish social relations founded on the view of the world furnished in religion.

We learn, therefore, to look for the explanation of the system of education in the national ideal as revealed in its religion, art, social customs, and form of government. A new phase of civilization demands a new system of education. The school, originally organized as an instrumentality of the Church, is needed to reenforce the other institutions, and accordingly in modern times gets expansion and modification for this object. It is in this study of the civilization as a whole that we learn to comprehend the organization of the schools of a country.

The attention of the reader is called, first, to the broad contrast between the spirit of education as it existed in Asia and that in Europe. Subjection to authority is the principle on which most stress is laid in the former. The development of the individual seems to be the constantly growing tendency in the latter, and especially in its colonies. Absolute rulers, castes, parental government, and ethical codes, form the chief themes of interest in Oriental education. Personal adventure, its celebration in works of art, the growth of constitutional forms of government that protect the individual from the crushing might of paternalism, free thought, its organization into science— these are the features that attract us in the civilization of the Occident, and which explains its educational systems.

Inasmuch as the element of authority continues throughout all history as a necessary strand of civilization, it follows that Oriental civilization has important lessons for all people, even the most democratic. The net result of the life of the race must be summed up and given to the child, so that he shall be saved from repeating the errors that had to be lived through before the wisdom expressed by the ethical code could be generalized. Implicit obedience has to be the first lesson for the child. How he shall gradually become endowed with self-control, and finally have the free management of all his affairs, is the further problem of the educational system.

After the reader has studied the spirit of the Asiatic systems, he will find his interest in fixing as clearly as possible the spirit of Christianity before his mind. The influence of such an idea as that of the Divine-human God condescending to assume the sorrows and trials of mortal life, all for the sake of the elevation of individual souls, the humblest and weakest as well as the mightiest and most exalted, is potent to transform civilization. That the divine history should be that of infinite tenderness and consideration for the individual, even in his imperfections, acts as a permanent cause to affect the relation of the directing and controlling powers in human society to the masses beneath them. The whole policy of the institutions of civilization—family, State, Church—becomes more and more one of tender nurture and development of individuality as the highest object to be sought by humanity.

In the struggle between the study of the " humanities " and the study of the " moderns " (or science, modern languages, modern literature, and history), we have reached the process that still goes on in our own day unadjusted by the discovery of a common ground that conserves the merits of both tendencies. In Chinese education, with its exclusive training of the memory, in the study of Latin and Greek among modern European nations, and, indeed, in such trivial matters as the study of English spelling, with its lack of consistency and its strain on the mechanical memory, we see the same educational effects obtained. Memory is the faculty that subordinates the present under the past, and its extensive training develops a habit of mind that holds by what is prescribed, and recoils from the new and untried. In short, the educational curriculum that lays great stress on memorizing produces a class of conservative people. On the other hand, the studies that develop original powers of observation, and especially

a scientific mind, devoted to Nature and neglecting human
history, produce a radical, not to say revolutionizing,
tendency. It must be obvious that true progress demands
both tendencies, held in equilibrium.

The study of the wisdom of the race, the acceptance
of the heritage of the past life of the race, is essential to
save the new generation from repeating all the steps traveled on the way hitherto. This necessitates the grounding of education in a study of the humanities. On the
other hand, if this load of prescription is not to be a
millstone that crushes out all spontaneity from the rising
generation, there must be a counter-movement whose
principle is the scientific spirit, approaching the world of
Nature and the world of institutions with the free attitude of science and individual investigation, which accepts
only the results that can be demonstrated or verified by
its own activity, and enjoys therefore a feeling of self-
recognition in its acquisitions. In science, man is doubly
active: on the one hand, seizing and inventorying the
particular fact or event; on the other hand, subsuming it
under a universal principle that involves causal energy
and a law of action. The act of subsumption gives the
mind special gratification because it feels set free from
the limited instance and elevated to the realm of principle,
wherein it sees the energy that creates all instances, and
contains them all potentially within itself. Hence, the
spirit of revolution that is gaining so powerful a hold of
society in the most recent times. The spirit of science
is contagious, and impels toward complete emancipation
from the past. But science has made comparatively little
progress in the social and political departments, and, besides this, no one is born with science, nor is it possible
for one to attain it in early youth. Hence, it is neces-

sary to retain the prescriptive element in education, and to insist upon implicit obedience to prescribed rule at first. There must be a gradual transition over to self-government and free scientific investigation.

W. T. HARRIS.

WASHINGTON, D. C., *September, 1904.*

AUTHOR'S PREFACE

It was in the library of the University of Bonn, many years ago, as I sat before an alcove of educational works and leisurely examined the admirable histories by Raumer and Karl Schmidt, that the thought and purpose of preparing this work were first conceived. In view of the poverty of our literature in educational history, it seemed to me that such a work, by exhibiting the pedagogical principles, labors, and progress of the past, might be helpful to teachers in America.

The history of education, viewed from the standpoint of the philosophy of history, has been traced in its relations with the social, political, and religious conditions of each country. While the results of French and German scholarship in this field have been utilized, the original sources of information whenever accessible have been consulted. As far as was consistent with the limits of this volume, the great teachers of all ages have been allowed to speak for themselves—a method that appeared more satisfactory than to paraphrase or epitomize their views.

Avoiding such matters of detail as serve only to confuse and oppress the memory, I have endeavored to present clearly the leading characteristics of each period, and the labors and distinctive principles of prominent educators. Considerable prominence has been given to

Comenius, Pestalozzi, Froebel, and other educational reformers, who laid the foundations of the scientific methods now coming into general use. In support or illustration of various statements, recognized authorities have been permitted to speak freely.

In preparing this history my position has been, as I believe, that of conservative progress. While what is valuable in educational theory and practise is to be retained, and novelties are to be subjected to rigid scrutiny, it does not seem wise, in view of the fact that the science of education is yet incomplete, to reject summarily all changes and reforms as unnecessary and hurtful innovations. In the sphere of higher education I have not allied myself either to the humanists or the realists, believing that the truth lies between these two extremes. In every department of education I have been able to discover progress, and it is my confident hope that the agitations of the present will issue in a system more nearly perfect than any yet devised.

Thus far the original preface. After seventeen years— nearly double the life of the average text-book—it has been a delight to take up, with the larger resources time has brought, the work of a thorough revision. The result has been practically a new book. Though the original framework, which left nothing to be desired, has been retained, various improvements have been made. Both friendly and unfriendly criticism has been helpful. Most of the book has been rewritten, and subtitles, which will prove useful both to teacher and student, have been introduced. In nearly all cases the original sources of information have been examined; and I wish to express here my obligation to the Commissioner of Education, Dr. W.

T. Harris, through whose kindness I was able to avail myself of the excellent library of the Bureau of Education. Much new matter, especially studies of Richter, Kant, Herbart, Jacotot, Horace Mann, and Herbert Spencer, has been added. The underlying principles of the present movements in education have been considered. A list of authorities has been appended.

In conclusion, I desire to express my gratitude for the cordial reception accorded the original work, and to add the hope that the present revised and enlarged edition will be found still more acceptable and useful.

F. V. N. PAINTER.

SALEM, VA., *September, 1904.*

CONTENTS

A HISTORY OF EDUCATION

INTRODUCTION

DEFINITION.—The history of education is a record of what has been thought and done in all ages and countries in reference to the training of the young. It sets forth the principles and methods that have prevailed at various periods and in different lands. It gives an account of the prominent educators whose theories and achievements have exerted a noteworthy influence upon educational development. It includes an inquiry into the social, religious, and political conditions that have determined the peculiar forms of education, and traces the line of educational progress from its humble beginnings down to the precious heritage of the present.

RELATION TO GENERAL HISTORY.—The history of education is a special department of general history. Education stands in close relation to the civilization of a people, and may be regarded, at the same time, both as an effect and a cause. In setting forth the influences that determine the character of education in any country, educational history becomes to some extent a philosophy of history in general. As such it is a profound study. "The education of a people," says Dr. Henry Barnard, "bears a constant and most preeminently influential relation to its attainments and excellences—physical, mental, and moral. The national education is at once a cause and an effect of the national character; and, accordingly, the history of education affords the only ready and perfect key to the history of the human race, and of each nation in it—an unfailing standard for estimating its advance or retreat upon the line of human progress."

VARIOUS EDUCATIONAL AGENCIES.—It should not be forgotten that, apart from school training, the educational agencies of life are varied and potent. The most important, perhaps, of all educational agencies is the family. It is in the home that the child learns its native language, trains its senses, and acquires the elements of science. It is there that its habits and character are formed in large measure before it passes under the care of special teachers. The social life in which youth is spent is, with its countless interests and activities, a formative influence of great strength. Individual culture is irresistibly promoted by a refined social life, as it is almost irremediably hindered by an environment of ignorance. At the present time the press is an educator of tremendous power. In tracing the influence of schools we should not lose sight of the various educative influences of social environment.

RELIGION AND EDUCATION.—Religion—that ineradicable sense of dependence on a supernatural Being—has always exercised a noteworthy influence on education. At various times religion has determined the character of family life, and also, as among the ancient Jews, the character of social and political life. Both in ancient and modern times the priesthood has often been the educating class. It is religion that has furnished the strongest support of morals and cherished the loftiest ideals of life. The education of the present day in Europe and America is Christian education; for its universality rests on the worth of the individual as a child of God, and the perfection at which it aims is found in the virtues and duties inculcated in the New Testament. The schools of the modern world, with their surpassing excellence and many-sided activities, are directly traceable to religious influences.

NECESSITY OF EDUCATION.—Education in some form is an absolute necessity for each generation. During a considerable period of his early life man is helpless and ignorant; he is without the strength or knowledge to maintain an independent existence. Left to himself in infancy he would quickly perish. The processes of physical and mental growth must therefore be watched over and assisted during the formative periods of childhood and youth. This is the function of education—a function that becomes more complicated and difficult with advancing civilization. There is no more sacred duty resting upon our race than the fostering care and instruction, which at the same time preserve and enrich life. Without some sort of education no generation would be fitted for the duties of maturity, and the progress of humanity would be suddenly and hopelessly arrested.

PREVALENCE OF EDUCATION.—Fortunately for mankind, education is a parental instinct, and in some form or other is as old as our race. Among all peoples, barbarous as well as civilized, each generation has received, often in a very defective and one-sided way, a special training for its subsequent career. When the state of civilization has been low, education has been correspondingly narrow and imperfect. Uncivilized communities do scarcely more than strengthen the body, sharpen the powers of observation, and develop skill in the use of hostile weapons. The beautiful world of science and art is undreamed of.

Among no two nations of antiquity were the theory and practise of education the same. It has always varied with the different social, political, and religious conditions of the people. But, however varied or imperfect its form, education has existed in every nation.

HUMAN PROGRESS.—It is a profound thought of German philosophy that God is leading the world, through a gradual though not uninterrupted development, to greater intelligence, freedom, and goodness. " The mode of this development," says Karl Schmidt, " is the same as that of the individual soul: the same law holds, because the same divine thought rules in the individual, in a people, and in humanity." Like the individual, each nation and our race as a whole have to pass through the successive stages of childhood, youth, and maturity. Each succeeding period inherits the accumulated wisdom of the preceding one, and in its turn adds new treasures of its own. After the lapse of many ages of striving and conflict, mankind has at length reached a stage of development among enlightened nations that seems to accord with the estate of manhood. Intelligence, freedom, morality, and religion, though still far from realizing the dreams of prophetic seers, prevail to a degree unprecedented in the past. With the accumulated forces of knowledge, science, and invention, the rapidity and momentum of human progress at the present time is something startling and unparalleled.

PROGRESS IN EDUCATION.—With improvement in other human interests, there has been unmistakable progress in education. Indeed, the ancient world, as we shall soon see, never succeeded in producing a correct and complete theory of education. If a great thinker now and then approximated the truth, his voice was lost upon the heedless multitude. The practise could hardly be better than the theory. Hence we shall find that education was always defective, usually laying stress upon some particular phase of human culture, to the neglect of others. Sometimes the physical was emphasized, sometimes the intellectual, sometimes the moral, sometimes the religious; but never all together in perfect symmetry. It was reserved for the nineteenth century, so distinguished for its many-sided advancement, to realize an education which leaves, theoretically, no part of man's nature neglected.

NATURE OF EDUCATION.—The essential nature of education is now determined by a consideration of the being to be educated. In the capacities which man has received from his Creator, and in that which he is capable of becoming under favorable circumstances, we find the true ideal of education. Every part of man's nature should receive the development which its innate capacities demand, and without which the human being remains more or less defective and fails in the end of his existence. His innate capacities and powers, though at first existing in a germinal condition, contain within themselves large possibilities and a strong impulse toward development. Through the fostering care of education they should be led to a harmonious realization of their highest possibilities. Viewed in this light, the end of education is seen to be complete human development; and the finished result is a noble manhood or womanhood. The elements of this culture are a healthy body, a clear, well-informed intellect, sensibilities quickly susceptible to every right feeling, and a steady will whose volitions are determined by reason and an enlightened conscience.

" That man, I think," as Professor Huxley has forcibly said, " has had a liberal education who has been so trained in his youth that his body is the ready servant of his will, and does with ease and pleasure all the work that, as a mechanism, it is capable of; whose intellect is a clear, cold logic-engine, with all its parts of equal strength, and in smooth working order, ready, like a steam-engine, to be turned to any kind of work, and spin the gossamers as well as forge the anchors of the mind; whose mind is stored with a knowledge of the great and fundamental truths of Nature and of the laws of her operations; one who, no stunted ascetic, is full of life and fire, but whose passions are trained to come to heel by a vigorous will, the servant of a tender conscience; who has learned to love all beauty, whether of nature or art, to hate all vileness, and to respect others as himself."

OBJECTIVE SIDE OF EDUCATION.—Thus, in its essential nature, education aims at developing a noble type of manhood; but it has also an external relation, which must not be forgotten. Man, as a member of society, has various duties to perform. He must earn a livelihood for himself and perhaps for others; he must discharge the duties growing out of his relations to his fellow men; and as a citizen he must assist in maintaining the government that gives him protection. The numerous duties that thus claim attention in active life require a considerable degree of knowledge and training. As childhood and youth are periods of preparation, it is clear that education, both in its subjects and methods of instruction, should have some reference to the demands of practical life. The individual does not live unto himself alone, and hence the process of human development should be combined with practical wisdom. The school should be a natural introduction to active life, and the transition from academic halls to the duties of manhood or womanhood should be made with as little jar and friction as possible. This is the view of Milton, who has said, in his famous definition: " I call a complete and generous education that which fits a man to perform justly, skilfully, and magnanimously all the offices, both private and public, of peace and war."

Herbert Spencer has presented very forcibly the objective or external relations of education. " How to live," he says, " that is the essential question for us. Not how to live in the mere material sense only, but in the widest sense. The general problem which comprehends every special problem is the right ruling of conduct in all directions under all circumstances. In what way to treat the body; in what way to treat the mind; in what way to manage our affairs; in what way to bring up a family; in what way to behave as a citizen; in what way to utilize all those sources of happiness which Nature supplies; how to use all our faculties to the greatest advantage of ourselves and others; how to live completely. And this being the great thing needful for us to learn, is, by consequence, the great thing which education has to teach. To prepare us for complete living is the function which education has to discharge; and the only rational mode of judging of any educational course is to judge in what degree it discharges such function."

DEVELOPMENT AND KNOWLEDGE.—There are two elements, logically distinguishable but practically inseparable, entering into education. These are the development of the mind and the acquisition of knowledge. Without mental development the individual lacks strength to grapple with the problems of life; and without knowledge he can not wisely employ his power. The great law underlying physical and mental development is self-activity. Every truly educated man is self-made. The various functions

of the mind, whether perceiving, feeling, judging, or willing, must for a long period be called into frequent exercise in connection with objects, facts, relations, and truths,
in order to become active, obedient, and strong. The
basis of this activity is knowledge, which is as necessary
for the development of the mind as food is for the
growth of the body. " As food is indispensable to physical
growth," says Johonnot, " so without knowledge the mind
can not grow. While the mind, from the first, possesses
all the germs of mental power, it is the appropriation of
knowledge alone that converts its latent and apparently
passive capacities into active capabilities." Education is
not creative; it can not give what Nature has withheld.
It is limited by the pupil's individuality, which it can
ennoble but not radically change.

SOURCE OF PRINCIPLES.—Inasmuch as education consists primarily in developing the various innate powers
of man, it is evident that the principles which should
determine educational practise are to be sought in human
nature. The laws of human development must be understood before the methods of training can be accurately
adjusted to the attainment of that end. The leading facts
pertaining to the body must be ascertained before a complete scheme for increasing physical health and vigor can
be devised; the chief principles of intellectual activity
must be understood before the rules for its development
can be fully given. It is true that much may be learned
by actual experiment in teaching, and that many useful
devices may be hit upon; but without a comprehensive
acquaintance with the nature of man the improvements
thus made in the art of education are necessarily fragmentary and uncertain. In its early stages, whether in
individual or national practise, educational effort is lim-

ited to what is experimental and fragmentary; but as education progresses, it seeks to attain those general principles that should determine the character and application of methods.

STUDY OF EDUCATIONAL HISTORY.—The study of educational history, by bringing the whole field within the range of our vision, broadens our views in regard to education. By acquainting us with the views and methods of the past, it spares us the cost of repeating experiments and mistakes. There is no nation of antiquity, no matter how remote in time or space, but has its lessons for us. Furthermore, the history of education reveals the origin and principles of present educational systems, and indicates what is correct in theory and valuable in practise. It inspires educational workers with greater zeal by presenting the examples of self-sacrificing and illustrious teachers in the past. No teacher can study the lives of Luther, Comenius, Pestalozzi, Froebel, and many others— men who, with heroic spirit and achievement, imparted a new impulse to human progress—without perceiving higher possibilities in his vocation, and becoming stronger in his work.

DIVISION OF SUBJECT.—Asia is the birthplace of the human race. The march of progress, following the course of the sun, has been westward through Europe to America. Here many problems of religion, science, government, and education will probably receive their final solution. Following the course of human progress, the history of education naturally divides itself as follows:

I. The Oriental countries, including China, India, Persia, Palestine, and Egypt.

II. The ancient classical nations, Greece and Rome.

III. The Christian education of Europe and America,

which is divided into—(1) the period before the rise of Protestantism and (2) the period after that great movement.

In this classification no account is taken of uncivilized peoples, since education with them consists almost exclusively in training the body for war and the chase. Their education is thus too primitive in its character to bring it within the scope of our present undertaking.

I

THE ORIENTAL NATIONS

GENERAL SURVEY.—A striking fact, which throws great light upon Eastern education, is to be noted in reference to Oriental life. The individual there counts for nothing. A despotic external authority controls his destiny. Education does not aim to develop a perfect man or woman, but to prepare its subjects for their place in the established order of things. It does not aim to beautify the stone, but simply to fit it for its place in the wall. The source of this all-controlling authority varies in the different countries. In China it is fossilized tradition; in India, caste; in Persia, the State; among the Jews, the theocracy. In all the Oriental countries this external authority determines the character of education; and, if this idea is firmly grasped, it will facilitate a thorough understanding of the educational systems of the East.

1. CHINA

CHARACTER OF PEOPLE.—The Chinese empire comprises a fourth part of the population of the globe. Its people belong to the Mongolian race, whose genius is shown in the early invention of paper, printing, gunpowder, and the mariner's compass. Their character presents many points of interest. They are industrious and economical, and in the relations of every-day life they

3   **11**

are polite and kind. Possessed of great patience, they endure oppression and suffering without a murmur. But they are destitute of deep moral convictions. They are hypocritical and dishonest; and, once in authority, they are apt to become tyrannical, and even cruel. Destitute of hope beyond the grave, and incapable of spiritual delights, they are restricted in their aims and aspirations to earthly objects. They are gross in their pleasures; and to acquire wealth, to live in ease, and fill some public office, are the highest aims of their ambition.

SOCIAL RELATIONS.—The idea of filial devotion pervades the social and political institutions of China. From early childhood the duty of reverence and obedience to parents is carefully and persistently inculcated. The State is looked upon as a great family in which the emperor is at once " father and mother." The highest dignitaries fall prostrate before him, and his proclamations invariably end with the words, " Tremble and obey ! " A similar reverence and submission are required from children, and a son guilty of crime against his father is put to death as a national traitor. Chinese civilization is patriarchal in its laws, customs, and social arrangements, and to develop and perpetuate an attitude of filial submission is the fundamental principle of Chinese education.

Woman in China occupies in every way an inferior position. Female infants are sometimes exposed, and, later in life, girls are frequently sold as slaves. In marriage it is expected, to use the words of a Chinese writer, that " the wife be a mere shadow, a simple echo." No matter what may be the husband's conduct or character, she must submit and obey in silence. He alone has the right of divorce, and at will, even for such trifling causes as illness or loquacity, he may put her away. As a consequence of this low esteem, woman has no place in the Chinese system of education.

LACK OF PROGRESS.—Though one of the oldest nations in the world, the Chinese have for many ages made but little progress in civilization. They are very much the same to-day that they were more than two thousand years ago. The collective life of the people has become petrified in fixed forms. Their customs, the relations of the various classes of society, the methods of business and labor, the administration of justice, and the whole circle of thought, have all been stereotyped, and until recent years have been practically unchangeable.

Notwithstanding its evident imperfections, the Chinese regard their civilization with great complacency. They are prone to regard other nationalities as barbarian, and it required the stern arguments of shot and shell, a few decades ago, to induce them to open their cities to foreigners. The preservation of existing institutions is an object of constant care. All deviation from traditional customs is looked upon with jealous disfavor; improvements are hardly tolerated; and the introduction of foreign culture is generally stigmatized as barbarous. With such a national feeling education can have but one end. Its object is to impress upon each generation traditional ideas and customs, and thus prepare it to take its place naturally in the established order of society. It does not aim at a development of the human faculties—it is simply a laborious cramming of the memory.

INTEREST IN EDUCATION.—Among all classes there is a profound respect for learning. Education is frequently and forcibly inculcated in the Chinese classics, and for many centuries parents have regarded it as a sacred duty to instruct their sons as the best means of getting on in the world. All the officers of the Imperial Government are chosen from among those who have completed a long course of study and passed the ordeal of several laborious and rigid examinations. Every community supports one or more primary schools, while the larger towns and cities have academies and colleges. The teachers are generally competent, being prepared for their work by a long course of training. The schools are conducted in rooms destitute of comfort and without furniture, except the chair and table of the teacher and the desks and seats furnished by the pupils themselves. The discipline is severe. The teacher keeps his rattan or bamboo hanging in a conspicuous place, and he uses scolding, castigation, starving, and imprisonment to stir up the diligence of his pupils in their necessarily distasteful tasks.

PRIMARY EDUCATION.—Children are placed under the care of a teacher at the age of six or seven years. The first years of their instruction are devoted to reading and writing; and, as these are very difficult to learn on account of the sign-character of the Chinese language, the great majority never reach any higher attainments. The teaching is wholly by rote: the pupils repeat after the teacher the names of the characters in the book given them to study. After they have learned to pronounce the characters fluently they are taught the meaning, and the moral lessons of the book are impressed upon them. The first book placed in the hands of pupils at school contains such wholesome lessons as the following:

" To bring up and not educate is a father's error."

" To educate without rigor shows a teacher's indolence."

" That boys should not learn is an improper thing. For if they do not learn in youth, what will they do when old?"

HIGHER EDUCATION.—The higher education of the Chinese consists in a knowledge of their ancient classics. The meaning of all difficult or obscure passages has been fixed by law, and any attempt at originality of interpretation on the part of the student is a forbidden impertinence. Those who are able to read the classics may look forward to an official appointment under the government. The inscription over the Peking Academy reads, " Here is taught the art of government." Official advancement generally depends upon new examinations, and this civil-service requirement continually stimulates scholastic activity. In all the large cities there are public examination halls, where in separate cells the candidates, provided only with paper, pencils, and ink, and guarded by sentinels from all outside communication, comment on sacred texts, compose maxims in prose and verse, and write moral and political essays. There is no age limit, and young and old, often to the number of thousands, appear together in these laborious examinations, though as a rule not more than one in a hundred makes his degree.

Every three years an examination for the second or higher degree, conducted by an examiner from Peking, is held in the provincial capitals. To pass this examination is esteemed a great honor, and the successful candidate receives the public congratulations of the magistrates. Three years later he may present himself at Peking for the full doctor's degree, which entitles him to a special dress, precedence in ceremonies, and a high position under the government. These various examinations, which are open to all and conducted with strict impartiality, are no doubt an important factor in the stability of the government.

CHINESE CLASSICS.—The Chinese classics, which form

the basis of higher education, exclude all those studies—geography, history, mathematics, science, and language—which are deemed in the Western world so indispensable to a liberal culture. These classics in their present form are the work of Confucius, the most distinguished of Chinese philosophers and teachers, who lived in the fifth century before Christ. They are in part compilations made by him from older works, and in part his own composition. They treat chiefly of the duties of social and political life, though they are in some measure historical. "I teach you nothing," says Confucius, "but what you might learn yourselves—viz., the observance of the fundamental laws of relation between sovereign and subject, father and child, and husband and wife, and the five cardinal virtues, universal charity, impartial justice, conformity to established ceremonies and usages, rectitude of heart and mind, and pure sincerity."

He confirms the patriarchal organization of society, which may be regarded as the distinctive feature of Chinese civilization. Of filial duty he says: "There are three thousand crimes to which one or another of the five kinds of punishment is attached as a penalty, and of these no one is greater than disobedience to parents. When ministers exercise control over the monarch, then there is no supremacy; when the maxims of the sages are set aside, then the law is abrogated; and so those who disregard filial duty are as though they had no parents. These three evils prepare the way for universal rebellion." The teaching of Confucius is a system of natural morality, from which the ideas of a personal God and future life are excluded. While it has sapped the foundations of all religion, it has fostered a painstaking attention to outward ceremony or etiquette.

CRITIQUE OF CHINESE EDUCATION.—The whole system of Chinese education confines the mind within a narrow circle of ideas, perpetuates the fixed customs of the people, encourages outward morality and ceremony, and renders progress well-nigh impossible. The process of education consists not in a symmetrical development of the intellectual faculties, but in a laborious burdening of the memory with the maxims and usages of the past. Great fields of learning are excluded from the course of study, and, as a result, Chinese scholarship is narrow and provincial. It fosters the pride of ignorance. By employing throughout the principle of authority and discouraging all independent inquiry and effort, it renders the nation unprogressive and feeble in comparison with its great, enterprising competitors of the West. As adapted to perpetuate a traditional state of society the Chinese system may not inappropriately be designated *ancestral education.*

NATIONAL AWAKENING.—But Chinese exclusiveness is becoming a thing of the past. With the commercial activity of the present day no nation can any longer shut itself up in selfish isolation. The leading cities of the " Celestial Empire " have European residents, and stringent immigration laws have not prevented numerous Chinese from making their homes in the United States. There are Chinese counting-houses in New York and London. The indefatigable labors of missionaries, the national humiliation attending the recent Boxer outbreak, and the proximity and influence of Russia and Japan will sooner or later arouse China from its age-long lethargy, and make of it, in all probability, a powerful member in the family of nations. The awakening has already begun. The confidence of the Chinese in the superiority of their civilization has been rudely shaken by defeat; and European schools in the treaty ports, daily newspapers conducted in the modern spirit, and, above all, the aggressive character of commercial and industrial enterprise are rapidly effecting a national transformation.

2. INDIA

LAND AND PEOPLE.—The consideration of education in India ought to possess the greater interest for us since the Hindus are of the same blood as ourselves. As a branch of the great Aryan or Indo-European family of nations they moved southward from their Central Asiatic home, some two thousand years before Christ, into the vast peninsula which extends from the Himalaya Mountains into the Indian Ocean. There they brought into subjection the swarthier aborigines, and, under the influence of a favorable soil and climate, they developed into a very numerous people.

The wealth of the country subsequently became a temptation to the avarice of other nations, and, having lost something of their primeval vigor through climate, religion, and social organization, the Hindus fell an easy prey. The Greeks, the Mohammedans, the Portuguese, and the Dutch successively reached out a covetous hand after the natural and artificial treasures of the country. Last of all, the English, with their insatiable thirst for empire, have brought the whole peninsula under their sway, thereby adding a population of two hundred millions to British dominion.

LANGUAGE AND RELIGION.—The language of the ancient Hindus was Sanskrit, which, as nearly related to Latin, Greek, English, and other Indo-European languages, is of especial interest to the philologist. Though Sanskrit has now given place to dialects, as did Latin after the fall of the Roman Empire, it is still the learned language of the Brahmans. This language is the repository of a literature of great antiquity and surprising magnitude. The Vedas, a collection of religious hymns and heroic poems, were compiled more than a thousand years before Christ, and the Mahabharata is an ancient epic poem, whose length is more than double that of the Iliad, Æneid, and Paradise Lost combined.

The prevailing religion is Brahmanism. In the more intelligent classes this religion is pantheistic, and closely resembles modern philosophic pantheism in Germany. According to Brahmanism, God is an unconscious but all-pervading spiritual presence, which has unfolded from within itself the material and visible universe. As God is thus believed to be in everything as source or cause, the religion of the Brahmans easily and naturally degenerates among the masses into polytheism, in which the various objects of nature are worshiped as divinities.

Brahmanism has, in large measure, determined the life and character of the Hindus. It has made them an eminently contemplative and unprogressive people. " While this pantheistic view of the world dominated the entire life of the Hindu," says Dittes, " his intellect and energy gave place to a mystical contemplation of soul. To become master of his desires, to lay aside every earthly wish, to be lost in the divine even in this world, and through mortifications and penances to prepare for complete absorption in the source of all being—this is the highest wisdom, the true happiness of the Hindu, and the ideal of education."

Buddhism, which rose in the sixth century before Christ

as a sort of protest against Brahmanism, failed after a time to maintain itself in India. As it denies the existence of God and the human soul, it is to be regarded as a system of morals rather than a religion. Its system of morality, in many points comparable to that of Christianity, is based on the twofold foundation of *self-conquest* and *universal charity*. It practically abolished caste, for it taught that men are different from one another, not by the accident of birth, but by their attainments and character. It regards life as an evil, and therefore it makes Nirvana or extinction the highest good. " When man," says Buddha, " is without desire, selfishness, personal feeling, pride, obstinacy, enmity; when the burden of personality is taken from him: then he is in Nirvana, in which will and consciousness are lost in the blissful rest of extinction."

CASTE.—The people of India are divided into four principal classes or castes—the *Brahmans*, or holy teachers; the *Kshatriyas*, or soldiers and princes of the nation; the *Vaisyas*, or farmers and traders; and the *Sudras*, or servants of the three other classes. The three higher castes all enjoy peculiar rights and privileges, though the Brahmans possess the greatest influence, and are the repositories of learning for the whole people. Of the relative position of the several castes, Manu, the reputed author of the most celebrated law-book of the ancient Hindus, says: " Whatever exists in the universe is all in effect, though not in form, the wealth of the Brahman, since the Brahman is entitled to it all by his primogeniture and eminence of birth. . . . The first part of a Brahman's compound name should indicate holiness; of a Kshatriya's, power; of a Vaisya's, wealth; and of a Sudra's, contempt." The moral effects of the caste system have been deplorable, for it has substituted class distinctions and duties for the conception and duties of humanity.

The caste system of India is the controlling factor in education. Every individual is born into one of the four principal castes, and his caste relation determines his instruction and life-work. The Brahmans, by reason of their superiority in birth and training, are the teachers. As education is made to bear some relation to the needs of practical life, the warrior class is exercised in the use of arms, and the working classes are taught agriculture, and the mechanic arts. The Sudras and women are excluded from all literary training. But all classes alike have to learn the privileges, duties, and usages of the several castes, and as these are very numerous, descending to insignificant details in daily life, such instruction forms a large part of the child's education.

PRIMARY EDUCATION.—At the usual age of six or seven years the child is sent to school. This is presided over by a Brahman, who regards it a disgrace to receive a stipulated salary, and who is remunerated by voluntary gifts from his patrons. These gifts range from mere trifles to considerable estates; but, upon the whole, leave the teacher, as elsewhere, poorly paid. He is held in high honor, and pupils render him greater reverence than they show to their parents. He may be indolent and sadly given to sleep, but, to quote a native writer, " he is great on the subject of caste—on what should be eaten, what abstained from; on idolizing the Brahmans and avoiding the pariahs; on his genealogy, his rights, his privileges, and on the mean origin and low position of other castes."

School is usually held in the open air, under the shadow of a friendly tree; but in case of bad weather it is transferred to a thatched shed or other covered building. Along with ceremonial usages and moral instruction, reading, writing, and arithmetic are taught in a primitive, mechanical way. The first exercises in writing are in the sand. The teachers are aided not only by regular assistants, but also by the more mature pupils of the school. The lessons are learned aloud by the whole body of pupils at once. The discipline, in the main, may be regarded as mild, and it is only after admonition has failed that bodily pain is inflicted by the rod, by placing the pupil in an uncomfortable position, or by pouring cold water upon him—a mode of punishment peculiar to India. " Good instruction," says Manu, " must be imparted to the pupil in an agreeable manner, and a teacher who regards virtue must use sweet, gentle words."

HIGHER EDUCATION.—Higher education in India has received, from ancient times, careful attention. Although the higher institutions of learning were destined chiefly for the Brahmans, they were open also to students from the second and third castes. The subjects of study constituted an extensive curriculum, and included grammar, mathematics, history, poetry, philosophy, astronomy, medicine, and law. This course, which required twelve years for its completion, was pursued in its whole extent only by the Brahmans. The students of the warrior caste, from which the civil officers were chosen, and of the trading or agricultural caste, pursued only partial courses, with immediate reference to the wants of practical life. In the science of mathematics the Hindus have made noteworthy progress, and have placed the rest of mankind under obligation for their development of this branch of knowledge.

FUNDAMENTAL DEFECTS.—In the system of India no

provision is made for physical education. The Hindu is naturally averse to physical exertion. A life made up of eating, drinking, and sleeping is his ideal of happiness. He does not feel that exuberant vitality which makes mere existence a conscious enjoyment and wrestling with difficulties a positive pleasure. This is a blessing reserved for the hardier children of the West. The religious side of education lacks the conception of a conscious, personal God, and in practise religion has degenerated into a set of puerile observances. The highest religious aspiration is to be absorbed into the great, unconscious world-spirit. This ideal leads to an intensely selfish subjectivity, which violates, by its idle dreaminess, our fundamental duties to God and man. The intellectual education of the Hindus is not wholly undeserving of commendation. By nature they are a contemplative people, and this natural tendency is constantly fostered by their religion. But, however subtle their intellectual operations may be, the Hindus are wanting in that strong practical energy which is necessary to subdue nature and lift the masses to a high degree of civilization. The name given to the system of India is *Caste Education*.

3. PERSIA

PLACE IN HISTORY.—Persia occupies an important place in history. It attained its highest point of greatness under Cyrus, who freed it from the dominion of the Medes and elevated it into a mighty empire extending from the Indus to Macedonia and Egypt. At this period Persia was the foremost nation in the world, not only in power, but also in civilization. We discover there an individual freedom unknown in either China or India. The individual attains to a self-consciousness and independence in which he recognizes the distinction between the objective and the subjective as a source of authority, and consequently assumes an attitude of freedom in relation to righteousness. Not from the prescription of an external authority, whether tradition or caste, but from a voluntary choice, he sides with Ormuzd in resisting the works of darkness.

RELIGION.—The religion of Persia, founded by Zoroaster in the sixth century before Christ, is interesting in itself, and also in its relation to education. Nowhere else, if we except the Jews, was this relation closer than among the ancient Persians. Zoroaster discovered a dualism running through all nature. The contrast between light and darkness, fruitfulness and barrenness, useful and hurtful animals, fortune and misfortune, life and death, led him to conceive of two spiritual beings, the one good and the other bad, who divide the world into hostile kingdoms. At the head of the kingdom of light is Ormuzd, whose symbol is light; at the head of the other is Ahriman, whose symbol is darkness. In the end the kingdom of good will prevail, and it is the duty of every man to contribute to this triumph. He aids in this work by cultivating the soil, caring for herds, educating children, maintaining physical and moral purity, and opposing whatever is evil and hurtful in the world. " The position of man in the cosmic scheme," says Rawlinson, " was determined by the fact that he was among the creations of Ahura-Mazda. Formed and placed in earth by the Good Being, he was bound to render him implicit obedience and to oppose to the utmost Angro-Mainyush and his creatures. His duties might be summed up under the four heads of piety, purity, industry, and veracity."

GENERAL CULTURE.—The Persians exhibited strength

rather than refinement of culture. They have left no great literature, and in science and art they achieved far less than other empires of the Orient. As they worshiped in the open air they had no need of magnificent temples; but their royal palaces were adorned with sculptured staircases and tall, graceful columns. A graphic picture of the magnificence of the imperial court, as well as of certain social and political customs, is found in the book of Esther. The Zend-Avesta, which purports to be a revelation from Ahura-Mazda to Zoroaster, is about all that remains to us of their literature. It consists of hymns, prayers, and a moral and ceremonial code somewhat resembling the ritualistic parts of the Pentateuch. It teaches that the future destiny of man is fixed by the preponderance of good or evil in his life, and in some of the hymns and prayers we find a deep aspiration after holiness and personal communion with God. " We praise all good thoughts," says one of the hymns, " all good words, all good deeds which are or shall be; and we likewise keep clean and pure all that is good."

DOMESTIC LIFE.—As in all Asiatic nations, the women were slavishly subordinate, and excluded, as a rule, from the advantages of education. Every morning the wife was required to kneel at the feet of her husband and ask, " What do you wish that I should do?" And having received his reply, she must humbly withdraw to obey his commands. Children were objects of parental pride, and as they were looked on as the source of the future power and prosperity of the State, the king was accustomed to show special favors to the heads of the largest families. The utmost care was exercised in the training of children. Up to the age of seven they were left beneath the parental roof under the care of the mother, but after that age they were regarded as belonging to the State, and were educated in public institutions.

PUBLIC TRAINING.—Till the age of fifteen this education was physical and moral. The body was strengthened and hardened by temperate habits in eating and drinking, by gymnastic and military exercises, and exposure to heat and cold. The moral nature of the child was developed with assiduous attention. As far as possible it was preserved from contact with vice, while the virtues of self-control, truthfulness, and justice were constantly enjoined and practised. Ingratitude and lying were considered the most shameful vices, while truthfulness was looked on as the highest virtue. At about fifteen the boy passed to youth's estate, and at this critical period of life he was subject to strict supervision and wholesome restraint. Through severe military discipline he was prepared for the hardships of war, while the wise instruction of overseers or governors fitted him for the civil service of the State. The teachers were the ripest and worthiest men of the country. At the age of fifty the Persian was exempt from military service. It was from among these men of advanced age and ripe experience that the instructors of youth were chosen, and they were expected to be patterns of the virtues that they inculcated by precept.

MAGI.—The Magi were an important class in Persia. They had charge of all the religious ceremonies, and were the learned class, being at once both priests and philosophers. So great was their reputation that people from distant countries came to receive instruction at their hands. The learning of Pythagoras, which gave him such eminence among the Greeks, is said to have been borrowed in large measure from the Magi. The king was required to pass some time under their instruction in order to learn the principles of governing and the right way to worship the gods. After ascending the throne he did not determine any important undertaking without consulting them. From this circumstance they were regarded as the directors of princes.

SUMMARY.—The one-sidedness of Persian education is evident. The State, which was absolutely despotic, was the controlling influence. As physical strength and moral rectitude were held to be the qualities of greatest utility, the one fitting for war and the other for the administration of justice, they alone were emphasized in the long period of public training. Intellectual culture was wholly neglected in the school training. Reading and writing, if they formed any part of instruction at all, were taught only in a very limited measure. The higher branches of knowledge, as philosophy, astronomy, and medicine, were pursued only by the Magi. The system of Persia has been aptly denominated *State education*.

4. THE PEOPLE OF ISRAEL

SEMITIC RACE.—The Semitic race, including the Babylonians, Assyrians, Phœnicians, and especially the Children of Israel, unites profound contemplation with great practical wisdom. For many centuries it played an important part in the world's history, founding mighty and warlike kingdoms. Great cities arose in the valleys of the Euphrates and Tigris, remarkable progress was made in the arts and sciences, manufactures and commerce flourished, and a considerable degree of culture was attained. The forces of nature, particularly the sun and the moon, were worshiped as divinities. A kind of picture-writing

4

in cuneiform or wedge-shaped characters was employed, and books, consisting of square clay tablets written on both sides and treating of geography, history, mathematics, astronomy, and law, were collected in public libraries.

The Phœnicians were for a long time the leading maritime nation of antiquity, and, next after the Jews, they have exerted the widest influence upon the Western world. They were the inventors of our alphabet, which, with certain modifications, was transmitted to us through the Greeks and Romans. Much light has recently been thrown upon the early civilization of these Semitic peoples through the discovery of written records in long-buried cities and long-forgotten tombs. Some of these records carry us back to a time fully four thousand years before Christ. A great background of unsuspected history and culture has been found for the civilization of the Jewish people. But, further than these general statements, it is not necessary to speak of education in Babylonia, Assyria, and Phœnicia.

ANCIENT JEWS.—The ancient Jews, whose literary remains have been pretty fully preserved in the Scriptures, deserve further study. This people has occupied a unique position in the world's history. It was the divinely appointed office of the Jews to develop and preserve, in the midst of polytheistic nations, a knowledge of the true God, and to furnish at last, in the fulness of time, the great Teacher of our race. For a long period God was recognized as the immediate ruler and lawgiver; and even after a formal kingdom had been established under Saul, the sovereigns were so controlled by the law previously given to Moses and by the prophets who were raised up at particular junctures that the theocratic principle continued dominant for many centuries.

The history of this strange people extends through nearly four thousand years. It has experienced alike the joys of prosperity and the pains of adversity. But whatever the character of its outward circumstances, whether exercising a wide dominion from a splendid capital or wandering among all nations as a by-word and reproach, it has clung with the utmost tenacity to its national feeling and customs. The power of education has never been better exemplified. The influence which the Jewish race has exerted upon the world is incalculable. It has supplied the basis of all true theology; in the Decalogue it has laid the foundation of a faultless morality; and in Christianity it has provided the most perfect form of religion.

EDUCATIONAL HISTORY.—The educational history of this people has varied with its political and social condition. In this study attention is directed to the most important and typical period. The Jewish nation reached its highest point of development—its golden age—under the reigns of David and Solomon. Its educational practise at this time marks an advance upon the systems already considered. Though the individual is still subject to an external authority, it is no longer tradition, caste, or State, but Jehovah himself. It is this fact that gives the Jews their unique place in educational history.

THEOCRATIC INFLUENCE.—Among the Jews the theocracy controlled both the theory and the practise of education. If it gave education a very one-sided tendency, it yet laid stress upon an important and hitherto neglected principle. The end of education among the ancient Jews was to make faithful and obedient servants of the living God. It aimed at preparing each succeeding generation to fulfil faithfully its part in the grand work assigned

to that people. The divine Lawgiver himself prescribed
the principal subjects and methods of instruction. The
law, whether moral, ceremonial, or judicial, was to be
carefully studied. " Therefore shall ye lay up these my
words," are the Lawgiver's instructions, " in your heart
and in your soul, and bind them for a sign upon your
hand, that they may be as frontlets between your eyes.
And ye shall teach them your children, speaking of them
when thou sittest in thine house, and when thou walkest
by the way, when thou liest down, and when thou risest
up. And thou shalt write them upon the door-posts of
thine house, and upon thy gates." [1] From this passage
it appears that the ability to read and write was general
among the ancient Jews, and in this particular they
probably surpassed every other nation of antiquity.

NATURE OF EDUCATION.—Education was restricted to
the family, in which the father was the principal teacher.
There were no popular schools nor professional teachers.
Yet the instruction of the Jew, as is evident from the
Pentateuch, embraced a vast number of particulars. His
whole life under the theocracy was hemmed in with minute
regulations, and ignorance was not accepted as a valid
excuse for transgression. The various kinds of food were
prescribed; the principles that were to govern the relations
of the people to one another were specifically given; directions for the treatment of strangers and servants were mi-
nutely laid down; the facts of their wonderful history and
the precepts of the moral law had to be carefully studied;
and the burdensome ritual of the tabernacle and temple
had to become thoroughly familiar. At the basis of their
education lay the great principle, " Behold, the fear of the
Lord, that is wisdom; and to depart from evil is understanding."

---

[1] Deut. xi, 18–20.

ANNUAL FESTIVALS.—Among the potent educational agencies of the Jews the national festivals merit consideration. These festivals, three in number, required every adult male to present himself annually before the tabernacle or temple at Jerusalem. Commemorating important national events, they kept the people acquainted with their past history. The passover recalled the delivery from Egyptian bondage; the pentecost, the terrific splendors that attended the giving of the law; the feast of tabernacles, the hardships and miraculous preservation in the wilderness. These frequent reunions not only contributed to national and religious unity, but they also exerted a strong educating influence upon the people.

LEARNED CLASS.—The Jews officially established what in some sense may be regarded a learned class. These were the priests and Levites, whose especial duty it was to study and preserve the law, to act as judges and genealogists, and in general to fulfil the functions of historian and theologian. " As the priests and Levites were to test the accuracy of weights and measures," says Jahn, " of which there were several models preserved in the sanctuary, it was necessary that they should understand something of mathematics; and as they were to determine and announce the movable feasts, new moons, years, and intercalary years, they had occasion for the study of astronomy. The priests were to instruct the people in religion and law, and to solve questions which might arise upon these subjects."

MUSIC.—Music was evidently a part of education among the Hebrew people. The word psalm itself indicates a lyric to be sung to the accompaniment of a stringed instrument. A variety of musical instruments, as may be seen from the last Psalm, were in common use. As we learn from 1 Chronicles (xxiii, 5), David appointed no fewer than four thousand Levites to praise the Lord with instruments of music in connection with the temple service. There was also a large choir specially trained for singing. The music appears to have been rather crude in character, volume of sound counting for more than melody or harmony.

SCHOOLS OF PROPHETS.—The schools of the prophets, of which there are only scanty notices in the sacred books, seem to have been private institutions for the study of poetry, medicine, and, in particular, the law. They were presided over by men venerable for their age and ability, and patronized by ambitious youths and adults. They corresponded, in some degree, to the modern university, the Mosaic law, however, overshadowing all other studies. The influence of these schools can not have been otherwise than favorable to Jewish culture. They were in a flourishing condition under the reign of David, and it is not improbable that the " sweet singer of Israel " himself had profited by their instruction. It was at this period that religious poetry reached its zenith. The Psalms of David, as portraying the deepest and most varied religious experience, have never been superseded. After a lapse of nearly three thousand years they are still regarded as an invaluable poetic and literary treasury, and some of its beautiful gems are set in the memory of each passing generation.

GENERAL ESTIMATE.—The educational system of the ancient Jews had evident defects. It made no provision for physical training, though the Mosaic law carefully enforced some laws of hygiene. On its purely intellectual side it was unquestionably weak and produced no lasting works of art. Even in building the temple Solomon found it necessary to import a skilled superintending artificer from Tyre. Yet, in not a few particulars, Jewish education gave admirable results. The domestic life of the Hebrew people was far more beautiful than that of other Oriental countries. According to the story of creation in Genesis, with which every Jewish child was made familiar, woman was created not to be the slave of man, but "a helpmeet for him." Though this lofty ideal was far from being realized in the life of the people, woman often occupied a place of honor, as in the case of Miriam and Deborah, and the admirable picture of a model housewife, as given in the last chapter of Proverbs, must have been frequently approximated. Jewish education produced great poets, prophets, and kings; and the literature it has bequeathed to us—history, biography, dramas, lyrics, practical ethics, and inspired eloquence— is an inestimable treasure for our race.

The name given to the ancient Jewish system is *theocratic education.*

5. EGYPT

EGYPTIAN CIVILIZATION.—In Egypt, which Herodotus called "the gift of the Nile," we have perhaps the oldest civilization in the world. Recent historical investigations carry the political history of the country back to fully four thousand years before Christ, and the great Pyramids, which exhibit a high degree of intellectual and mechanical development, antedate our era by at least two millenniums. The ancients looked upon Egypt as a school of wisdom. Greece sent thither illustrious philosophers and lawgivers—Pythagoras and Plato, Lycurgus and Solon—to complete their studies, and Herodotus, to whom we are indebted for many particulars, spent some time there gathering materials for his history. In the Scripture, which incidentally furnishes numerous details, it is said in praise of Moses that he "was learned in all the wisdom of the Egyptians."

MECHANIC ARTS.—At an early period Egypt made high attainments in the mechanic arts. Great perfection was reached in spinning and weaving; glass was manufactured, and some of the secrets of coloring it have baffled modern ingenuity; iron and steel, together with the common agricultural and mechanical implements made from them, were in use. Magnificent ruins still make a profound impression upon the beholder, while single specimens of art have been transported over distant seas to adorn the public places of great modern cities. The temple of Karnak, from its massive forms and brilliant decorations, has been pronounced the most magnificent of man's architectural works.

LITERATURE.—The literature of Egypt, of which recent discoveries have furnished us noteworthy specimens, embraced the whole circle of knowledge of ancient times. Libraries existed as early as the sixth dynasty. The most ancient papyrus we possess, dating from the eleventh dynasty, or more than two thousand years before Christ, contains, not unlike the book of Proverbs, maxims of practical wisdom, in which personal and social virtues are inculcated. "Love thy wife," the husband is told, "and cherish her as long as thou livest; be not a tyrant; flattery acts upon her better than rudeness." "If thou art wise," it is said again, "bring up thy son to fear God. If he obey thee, walking in thy steps, and caring for thy goods as he ought, then show him favor. Yet thy foolish son is also thine own offspring; estrange not thine heart from him, but admonish him." The chief monument of religious literature is the Book of the Dead, which contains the funeral ritual of the Egyptians. The poetic literature, which in structure resembles Hebrew poetry, consists of both lyrics and epics.

SPHINX AS TYPE.—In spite of their evident culture and progress in civilization the Egyptians did not arrive at complete intellectual freedom. " The Sphinx," says Hegel, " may be regarded as a symbol of the Egyptian spirit. The human head looking out from the brute body exhibits spirit as it begins to emerge from the merely natural—to tear itself loose therefrom and already to look more freely around it, without, however, entirely freeing itself from the fetters Nature had imposed. The innumerable edifices of the Egyptians are half below the ground and half rise above it into the air. The whole land is divided into a kingdom of life and a kingdom of death."

CASTE SYSTEM.—The Egyptians were mild in disposition and gentle in manners. Woman was held in higher honor than in Persia, India, or China; she appeared freely in public unveiled, was honored by her husband, and had the right to ascend the throne. Like the people of India, the Egyptians were divided into castes, the highest of which was composed of the priests. The priests possessed immense wealth and influence, were supported by the State, and held one-third of the land free of tax. Egypt has been called the land of priests. They were the chief representatives of learning and the recognized intellectual leaders of the people. The military class ranked next to the priests. The rest of the population was divided into three general classes—the first included the farmers and boatmen; the second, the mechanics and tradesmen; the third, herdsmen, fishermen, and common laborers.

FUNCTIONS OF PRIESTHOOD.—The priests not only attended to the duties of religion, but likewise filled the civil offices that required learning. "They therefore," says Jahn, "devoted themselves in a peculiar manner to the cultivation of the sciences. This learned nobility, so to speak, was strictly hereditary, and no one from another tribe could be received among its members. They studied natural philosophy, natural history, medicine, mathematics (particularly astronomy and geometry), history, civil polity, and jurisprudence. They were practising physicians, inspectors of weights and measures, surveyors of land, astronomical calculators, keepers of the archives, historians, receivers of the customs, judges, and counselors of the king, who was himself a member of their tribe. In short, they—like Raguel, the priest of Midian, and Melchizedek, the priest and king of Salem—formed, guided, and ruled the people by establishing civil regulations, performing sacred services, and imparting religious instruction."

ELEMENTARY EDUCATION.—The foregoing facts prepare us for a better understanding of Egyptian education. This great interest was under the absolute control of the priests. The education of the lower classes was of the most elementary nature. The youth destined for business pursuits were commonly taught reading, writing, and arithmetic, while the rest learned from parents or relatives the manual occupations to be followed through life. The method of teaching seems to have anticipated some of our modern methods, inasmuch as numbers were taught in the concrete by means of plays. There were two species of writing in common use—the demotic, which seems to have been a hybrid between hieroglyphic and syllabic writing, was employed by the common people; while the hieratic, which was more purely hieroglyphic, was employed by the priests. The bark of the papyrus-reed, which grew in jungles along the Nile, was used instead of paper.

The children were early trained in good manners and morals. The Egyptians knew, says Plato, " that children ought to be early accustomed to such gestures, looks, and motions as are decent and proper, and not to be suffered either to hear or learn any verses and songs other than those which are calculated to inspire them with virtue; and they consequently took care that every dance and ode introduced at their feasts or sacrifices should be subject to certain regulations."

HIGHER EDUCATION.—The priestly and warrior castes enjoyed the greatest educational advantages. At Thebes, Memphis, and Heliopolis there were institutions for superior instruction which were open to these two classes. The course of study embraced language, mathematics, geometry, astronomy, natural science, and religion, though the most advanced instruction was reserved for the priesthood alone. The annual overflow of the Nile, which in many cases destroyed landmarks, made a knowledge of mathematics, particularly of geometry, of high importance, and hence this subject received especial attention. Gymnastics and music were excluded from the general means of culture. " It is not the custom in Egypt," says Diodorus, " to learn gymnastics and music; it is believed that the former is dangerous to the youth, and that the latter is not only useless, but even hurtful, because it renders men effeminate." Yet in Chemnis gymnastics were taught, and music was employed in connection with religious services. Reverence for the priesthood and religion, and respect for the usages handed down by tradition, were carefully and effectually inculcated.

CONCLUSION.—The Egyptian system, as it existed before the intermixture of Grecian elements, has been designated *priestly education.* " Egypt loves only the past," says Karl Schmidt, " and its national monument is the pyramid, that is, a Titanic grave. We easily understand the influence which the priests must exercise upon such a land; it is made for them, or rather, it is made by them. No chain is stronger in the hand of priests, in order to keep a people in bondage, than an infinitely complicated ritual. The priesthood constituted the really human element among the Egyptians. Their power was limited only by the absolute power of the high priest, namely, the king."

II

THE ANCIENT CLASSICAL NATIONS

INTEREST AND PROMINENCE.—The ancient classical nations, Greece and Rome, are surrounded with a peculiar charm. They are the earliest representatives of European civilization, and as such they have placed us under great and permanent obligations. Though the stream of culture has broadened and deepened since their glory waned, receiving in particular the mighty tributaries of Christianity and modern science and invention, it must yet trace its origin to the renowned cities of Athens and Rome. They have left us a rich heritage in the domains of science and government; they have transmitted heroic deeds of patriotism that have never been surpassed; in architecture and sculpture they have furnished models and inspiration for all time; and in the most important departments of literature—in poetry, history, oratory, and philosophy—they have produced works of exalted genius and perpetual worth. These nations must always retain a prominent place in the history of the world.

PLACE IN EDUCATION.—These two nations naturally occupy a prominent place in the history of education. They have left us tolerably complete records of their thought and achievements. In education they mark an obvious advance upon the defective systems of the Orient. The individual comes into a certain prominence. He is not crushed beneath the weight of some relentless external power, but attains at length to a degree of personal freedom. To some extent at least the worth of the individual is appreciated, and within certain limits he is left to himself in the pursuit of wealth and happiness. Education becomes the subject of careful, scientific thought, and enlarged views of its nature and obligations are promulgated. Plato, Aristotle, Cicero, and Quintilian—these are honored names in educational history. Beautiful results, as exhibited in the physical and intellectual life of the people, are obtained. No other nations have exerted such immeasurable influence upon the world.

1. GREECE

LAND AND PEOPLE.—Greece, the older of the ancient classical nations, is about half the size of Pennsylvania, and possesses a mild climate and rich diversity of surface. Its numerous coast indentations give it peculiar facilities for commerce. These facts are worthy of mention, for they were not without influence upon the well-endowed and versatile inhabitants. As a branch of the Aryan family the Greeks are of the same blood as the leading nations of Europe. In ancient times Greece was divided into a considerable number of little States. This gave occasion to almost incessant strife, during which one and another of the States, according to the skill of its leaders or the number of its allies, gained the ascendency. In the history of education, however, only two States, or rather two cities, are worthy of consideration. These are Sparta and Athens. It is here alone, so far as the records have descended to us, that a complete system of education was developed.

THE HEROIC AGE.—During the heroic age, to which

belongs the immortal siege of Troy, education possessed but a single character in all Greece. It was patriarchal. The father trained his sons to physical strength and filial piety, and the mother trained her daughters to household duties and domestic virtues. In the language of Schiller, " to throw the spear and honor the gods " was the end of male education. At a later date, when Greece had attained its highest power, when Leonidas defended Thermopylæ, and Miltiades won the field of Marathon, the educational systems of Sparta and Athens were in striking contrast and contributed no little to perpetuate and embitter the feud existing between these two proud cities.

A. Sparta

SOCIAL CONDITION.—This city was inhabited by the Dorians, a hardy and warlike race of Greeks, who held tenaciously to old customs and sternly set themselves in opposition to the highest forms of culture. In the ninth century before Christ, Lycurgus prepared a constitution for Sparta corresponding to the Doric character and the peculiar circumstances of the State. The Spartans, including only about nine thousand families, were but a small part of the population of Laconia, though they were the conquering and ruling class. There were two other classes still more numerous and sorely discontented with Spartan domination; these were the Periœci, who lived as freemen in the towns adjacent to Sparta, and the Helots, who were bound to the soil as serfs. In order to maintain their supremacy in the midst of this hostile population it was necessary for the Spartans to be constantly vigilant and strong.

SYSTEM OF LYCURGUS.—The system of Lycurgus, harsh

and repulsive in nearly all its features, aimed at training a powerful body of soldiers. It transformed Sparta into a perpetual training-camp. Lycurgus made a new distribution of land; he made iron the circulating medium of the country, and he required the male portion of the population to live in common at public tables. By these sweeping regulations he struck down many evils in the commonwealth. With the abolition of wealth and commerce, pride, avarice, and luxury were destroyed. The sternest simplicity prevailed. "The most masterly stroke of this great lawgiver," says Plutarch, "by which he struck a yet more effectual blow against luxury and the desire of riches, was the ordinance he made that they should all eat in common, of the same bread, of the same meat, and of kinds that were specified, and should not spend their lives at home, lying on costly couches at splendid tables, delivering themselves up into the hands of their tradesmen and cooks to fatten them in corners, like greedy brutes, and to ruin not their minds only, but their very bodies, which, enfeebled by indulgence and excess, would stand in need of long sleep, warm bathing, freedom from work, and, in a word, of as much care and attendance as if they were continually sick."

PHYSICAL EDUCATION.—The education of Sparta was chiefly physical. The children were regarded as the property of the State. The new-born babe was brought before the body of judges, and, unless it was approved of as a strong and promising child, it was destroyed. Up to the age of seven years the child remained under the care of its natural guardians. After that time the boys were placed in public educational establishments, where they were subjected to a rigorous discipline. Their fare was coarse and meager, their clothing scanty, and their beds were piles of rushes plucked with their own hands from the banks of the river. "After they were twelve years old," says Plutarch, our principal authority, "they were no longer allowed to wear any undergarments; they had one coat to serve them a year; their bodies were hard and dry, with but little acquaintance with baths and unguents—these human indulgences they were allowed only on some particular days in the year. They lodged together in little bands upon beds made of the rushes, which grew by the banks of the river Eurotas, which they were to break off with their hands without a knife; if it were winter, they mingled some thistledown with their rushes, which it was thought had the property of giving warmth." They were encouraged to supplement their daily allowance of food by theft. If detected, they were severely whipped for their want of skill. In order to strengthen and harden the body they were continually trained in gymnastic exercises, the chief of which were jumping, running, wrestling, spear-throwing, and quoits.

LITERARY CULTURE.—In the system of Lycurgus but small provision was made for literary culture. Reading and writing were taught only to a very limited extent. The absence of formal intellectual training, however, was partly compensated by the constant association of the young with the old, from whom they imbibed lessons of practical wisdom. At the public tables they were instructed in State affairs by the conversation of leading men; they learned to converse in an intelligent and agreeable manner; and by a natural spirit of imitation they early acquired a dignified bearing and practical wisdom beyond their years. Their judgment was cultivated by frequent questions requiring well-considered answers. A sententious mode of speech was carefully inculcated.

Lycurgus himself, if we may judge by certain anecdotes related of him, affected a curt and energetic style. To a Spartan who urged the establishment of a democracy in Lacedæmon, he said: "Begin, friend, and set it up in your family." To another who asked why he permitted such trivial sacrifices to the gods, he replied: "That we may always have something to offer them."

MORAL EDUCATION.—The moral education of Sparta presented many admirable points. The Spartan youth were taught to maintain an absolute control over their appetites and to observe temperance in all their habits. Drunkenness was looked upon as a shame. A modest and retiring manner was inculcated until the moment for action came; then the Spartan youth were quick, aggressive, and strong, ready to purchase victory with their lives. Obedience to parents and reverence for established usages were carefully cultivated. The respect entertained for age was so great that it was said to be a pleasure to grow old in Sparta. This respect was shown by saluting the aged, rising up in their presence, making place for them in company, and, above all, by receiving with submissive spirit their advice and reproofs.

An old man once entered a theater at Athens too late to get a seat. As he stood hesitating a moment, he was beckoned by a group of young Athenians. When he had made his way to them they retained their seats, and thus exposed the old man to ridicule. As he withdrew in confusion he came to the benches occupied by the Lacedæmonian ambassadors, who rose in a body to receive the old man among them. The Athenians, suddenly struck by this display of characteristic Spartan virtue, burst forth in applause; whereupon the old man exclaimed, "The Athenians know what is right, but the Spartans practise it."

MUSIC.—The musical education of the Spartans has been well described by Plutarch. " Nor was their instruction in music and verse," he says, " less carefully attended to than their habits of grace and good breeding in conversation. And their very songs had a life and spirit in them that inflamed and possessed men's minds with an enthusiasm and ardor for action; the style of them was plain and without affectation; the subject always serious and moral; most usually it was in praise of such men as had died in defense of their country, or in derision of those that had been cowards—the former they declared happy and glorified, the life of the latter they described as most miserable and abject."

FEMALE EDUCATION.—The girls were not neglected. They were under the training of the women, as the boys were of the men. The ideal was to fit them to be the wives of warriors. In the interests of a hardy race they were encouraged to engage in gymnastic exercises, in . which the claims of modesty were often forgotten. This physical training was not without perceptible results, and the Spartan women became the admiration of all Greece for their development, strength, and beauty. They cherished a passionate love of country. Nothing appeared to them so shameful as cowardice, and the Spartan mother could hear unmoved of sons and husbands slain in battle, if they died facing the enemy.

GENERAL SUMMARY.—Though crude in form, and destructive of the best instincts of our nature, the system of Sparta admirably subserved its purpose. It made the Spartans a powerful band of warriors, secured them continual supremacy in Laconia, and raised them for a time to the leadership of Greece. It produced Leonidas. " The Spartan education," to quote Thirlwall's excellent summary, " was simple in its objects; it was not the result of any general view of human nature, or of any attempt to unfold its various capacities; it aimed at training men who were to live in the midst of difficulty and danger, and could be safe themselves only while they held rule over others. The citizen was to be always ready for the defense of himself and his country, at home and abroad; and he was, therefore, to be equally fitted to command and to obey. His body, his mind, and his character were formed for this purpose, and for no other; and, hence, the Spartan system, making directly for its main end, and rejecting all that was foreign to it, attained, within its own sphere, to a perfection which it is impossible not to admire."

We may call the system of Sparta *martial education*.

B. Pythagoras

BIOGRAPHICAL FACTS.—Pythagoras is an interesting character, whether we regard the keen penetration of his intellect, his moral excellence, his system of education, or the influence exerted by him upon his contemporaries. In spirit, though not by birth, he was allied to the Dorians —a fact that makes it proper to notice his labors at this point. As he left no written records, not a few mythical stories have been connected with his origin, and many of his teachings are involved in obscurity. He was born about 580 B. C. on the island of Samos. After spending many years in private study, during which he counted the sages Bias and Thales among his teachers, he sought to increase his store of knowledge by travel in the East. He is said to have visited Chaldea and India. In Egypt he came into possession of the wisdom of the priests, by which his subsequent teachings were perceptibly influenced. "The spectacle of Egyptian habits," says Grote, "the conversation of the priests, and the initiation into various mysteries or secret rites and stories not accessible to the general public, may very naturally have impressed the mind of Pythagoras, and given him that turn for mystic observance, asceticism, and peculiarity of diet and clothing, which manifested itself from the same cause among several of his contemporaries, but which was not a common phenomenon in the primitive Greek religion."

SCHOOL AT CROTONA.—Subsequently he founded a school at Crotona, in southern Italy, which attained to wide influence and celebrity. Unlike the institutions of Sparta, it was entirely independent of the State, and aimed at the perfection of the individual rather than of the citizen. Pythagoras resolutely set himself against the idle luxury and moral degeneracy that prevailed about him, and urged the intellectual culture and moral excellence that distinguish man from the lower animals. He was careful to receive only students of character and ability. They lived together as one family or brotherhood, the expense being defrayed from a common fund. The course of study, which was comprehensive, was divided into two parts, distinguished as *exoteric* and *esoteric*. It was only after the satisfactory completion of the former preliminary course, which occupied three years, that the student was admitted to the profounder studies of the esoteric course and to a freer and closer fellowship with the great master himself.

IDEA OF EDUCATION.—Pythagoras was not very far from grasping the true idea of education. The keynote of his system was harmony. "Virtue and health and all good and God," he said, "are in harmony." He wished to introduce into human life the harmony which he discovered in the universe at large, and which produced the music of the spheres. He aimed at harmony of body and soul; harmony between parents and children; harmony in social life; harmony between man and God. He recognized the innate evil tendencies of our nature which generate discord; and in education he sought a remedy. " At birth," says Karl Schmidt, in summarizing the views of Pythagoras on this point, " man is very imperfect, and naturally inclined to arrogance; through an uninterrupted education, lasting throughout the whole life, he must be freed from these innate evils, and be elevated to purity of heart and mind. Early training to abstinence in eating, sleeping, and speaking, to temperance in all particulars, to mutual improvement through hearty friendship and profound scientific culture, lead in this direction. The work of man on earth is to attain to true knowledge —to knowledge of those subjects which in their nature are unchangeable and eternal. And wisdom has no other end than to free the human spirit through instruction from the slavish yoke of sensual desires, to conduct it to a likeness with God, and to make it worthy to enter hereafter into the fellowship of the gods. As for all things, so also for men, harmony is the end of life."

COURSE OF STUDY.—The course of study in the school of Pythagoras embraced mathematics, astronomy, geography, and music or harmony. Especial prominence was given to mathematics, which he regarded as the noblest science. Number, in fact, lay at the basis of the Pythagorean philosophy. The great unity from which all things proceed is God. Number governed the creative processes in the beginning, and is involved in all cosmical motion and phenomena. The relations of all things, whether material or immaterial, are expressed by numbers. The devotion of Pythagoras to this science was not fruitless. He guessed the existence of an antipodal continent, and divined the movement of the earth—a fact that encouraged Copernicus in working out the true idea of the solar system. To him we owe the discovery of the geometrical truth that the square of the hypotenuse of a right-angled triangle is equal to the sum of the squares of the other two sides. Next to mathematics music, was the favorite study of the Pythagoreans. They ascribed to it a softening effect upon the passions, and believed that by suitable melodies and harmonies they could transform and elevate the soul. At night the cares of the day were banished by song, and in the morning song gently incited to the duties of the day.

RELIGION.—Religion formed the basis of moral action. Pythagoras, by a profound insight into nature, reached the conception of one God, the universal Ruler. Him it is the duty of man to serve. Religious ceremonies were prominent in the school at Crotona; and morning, noon, and night, offerings were regularly made. Temperance, courage, obedience, fidelity, and moral purity were among the virtues constantly enforced by precept and exacted in practise. Pythagoras believed in the metempsychosis or transmigration of the souls of deceased men into the lower animals. On one occasion, seeing a dog beaten and hearing him howl, he desired the striker to desist, saying, "It is the soul of a friend of mine, whom I recognize by his voice." A strict watch was to be kept over the daily life; and a disciple, in the spirit of his master, recommends:

Let never sleep thy drowsy eyelids greet
Till thou hast pondered, with reflection meet,

The day's full course. What good or mischief done?
What duty fairly met or basely shunned?
From first to last thy record ponder o'er ;
In all the good rejoice, the base deplore.

CRITIQUE.—The method of instruction was dogmatic.
The assertion of Pythagoras was held as a sufficient test
of truth. This circumstance gave rise to the expression
ipse dixit—he himself said it—which put an end to all
discussion. In many particulars the system of Pythagoras
showed its affinity with the Doric spirit. It was strict in
morals, severe in discipline, partial to physical training,
authoritative in method, and aristocratic in tendency. It
was this last fact that brought the school into disfavor,
and then into open conflict with the masses of Crotona.
At length the building in which Pythagoras taught was
set on fire by a mob, and whether he escaped by flight or
perished in the flames is uncertain. This was the end
of the school which for a considerable period had exerted
a strong moral, intellectual, and political influence in
southern Italy.

C. Xenophon

BIOGRAPHICAL FACTS.—Xenophon, who was born at
Athens in 445 B. C., was distinguished as a general, historian, and philosopher. He joined the expedition of the
younger Cyrus against the King of Persia, and after the
disastrous battle of Cunaxa he conducted the famous
retreat of the ten thousand Greeks, of which he has
given an interesting account in the Anabasis. He was
for some years a pupil of Socrates, many of whose views
he adopted, and in the Memorabilia he has beautifully
described the character and teachings of the Athenian

philosopher. Banished from Athens for some political offense, he took up his residence within the district of Sparta, where he spent twenty years in leisured retirement. His numerous writings belong to this period. He was a man of practical insight rather than of profound speculation.

THE CYROPÆDIA.—Though an Athenian by birth, Xenophon was a Spartan both by natural sympathy and long residence. In his Cyropædia, which is a historical romance rather than a sober history, he presents his views of education in the ideal training he ascribes to Cyrus. He was more or less acquainted with the affairs of Persia, and in the education of Cyrus he has embodied, as will be seen, some elements of Persian training; but, upon the whole, the system of Xenophon corresponds to that of Sparta, in which his own children were brought up.

EDUCATION BY THE STATE.—According to Xenophon, education is a duty belonging to the State. In the passage that follows he seems to have intended a contrast between Athens and Sparta. " Most states," he says, " let each one bring up his sons as he pleases, and further permits the older youth to live as they choose; only they forbid them to steal, to rob, to enter a house by force, to strike in secret, to commit adultery, and disobey the civil authority. If any one commits such a misdeed they subject him to punishment. The Persian laws, on the contrary, take the initiative, and exercise a care that the citizens from the beginning on have no inclination to a wicked or shameful deed."

MORAL TRAINING.—The moral side of education seemed to Xenophon of especial importance. Morality was taught practically rather than theoretically. " The boys went to school," he says, " to have their sense of justice awakened and developed. Therefore the masters spent the day especially in holding court among the boys, who, after the manner of men, brought indictments against each other for theft, violence, cheating, offensive language, etc., not only the convicted prisoners but also the false accusers being punished. Ingratitude was punished with especial severity, for the Persians hold that the ungrateful can love neither the gods, their parents, their fatherland, nor their friends, since with ingratitude shamelessness is always united, and this latter is the most prolific source of all vices."

An incident attributed to Cyrus illustrates Xenophon's idea of the practical teaching of law and morals. When Cyrus, then a boy of twelve years, was brought to the court of his grandfather Astyages, he was asked by his mother, " My child, how will you learn justice at this despotic court, since your teachers are at home? " Cyrus answered, " Mother, I understand justice very well already. For my teacher, since I showed an eagerness for learning, often placed me as judge over others; and only once was I beaten for giving a wrong decision. One time a large boy with a small coat compelled a little boy with a large coat to exchange with him. I decided that it was better for both, because each had the coat that fitted him best. Then I was beaten, and told that my decision would have been right if the question had been whom the coat fitted; but since the question had been who was the lawful owner of the coat, I ought to have inquired to whom the coat really belonged, and whether taking a thing by force rendered its possession lawful."

MILITARY TRAINING.—Xenophon would have the virtues of temperance and self-control carefully instilled. To this end the youths should be accustomed to simple

and frugal fare, and drilled in habits of strict obedience
to their superiors. They should acquire military experience in acting as guards for the city. Hunting was
esteemed a helpful training for military service. " It
accustoms them," says Xenophon, " to rise early in the
morning and to bear heat and cold; it exercises them in
long marches and in running; it necessitates them to use
their bow against the beast that they hunt, and to throw
their javelin wherever he falls in their way; their courage
must of necessity be oftenest sharpened in the hunt, when
any of the strong and vigorous beasts present themselves,
for they must come to blows with the animal if he comes
up to them, and must be upon their guard as he
approaches; so that it is not easy to find what single
thing, of all that is practised in war, is not to be found
in hunting."

SERVICE OF THE STATE.—After this period of youthful
training, covering about ten years, the young man enters
upon full manhood. The next twenty-five years are given
to the service of the State. The full-fledged citizen serves
as soldier in times of war and as magistrate in times of
peace. Arriving at the age of fifty or a little more, he
becomes an elder. " These elders," says Xenophon, " no
longer go on any military service abroad, but, remaining
at home, have the dispensation of public and private justice; they take cognizance of matters of life and death,
and have the choice of all magistrates; and if any of the
youth or full-grown men fail in anything enjoined by the
laws, the several magistrates of the tribes, or any one
that chooses, gives information of it, when the elders
hear the cause and pass sentence upon it, and the person
that is condemned remains infamous for the rest of his
life."

DEMOCRATIC ELEMENT.—A democratic element entered into Xenophon's system of education. All parents were free to avail themselves of the educational advantages provided by the State, and no one was excluded from the highest positions of honor on account of lowliness of birth. But only those who pursued the educational course in its entirety passed, step by step, to the dignity and responsibility laid upon the elders. Those who gave themselves in early life to trade were obliged to remain content with the pecuniary rewards they might obtain. "The order of elders," says Xenophon, "stands composed of men who have pursued their course through all things good and excellent."

WOMAN'S EDUCATION.—In his Economics Xenophon has given us his idea of woman's education. It is of a purely domestic character, fitting her to perform the duties of wife and mother. "The gods," he says, "have plainly adapted the nature of woman for works and duties within doors, and that of man for works and duties without doors." The queen bee is to his mind the type of wifely virtue and duty. The wife must watch over the rearing of children, guide the servants, keep everything in its place, and watch over what her husband provides. "Whatever is brought into the house," Ischomachus tells his docile and sensible wife, "you must take charge of it; whatever portion of it is required for use, you must give it out; and whatever should be laid by, you must take account of it and keep it safe, so that the provision stored up for a year, for example, may not be expended in a month. Whenever wool is brought home to you, you must take care that garments be made for those who want them."

D. Athens

ATTICA.—Attica was a small but beautiful district in Central Greece. In size it was hardly equal to one of our counties; and, at the time of its greatest prosperity, it did not number more than half a million people, of whom nearly four hundred thousand were slaves. Though insignificant in size and population, it was in Athens, the capital of Attica, that the restless and brilliant genius of the Greek wrought out the most perfect form of heathen civilization. Nowhere else in Greece did education, both in its theoretical and practical aspects, attain so high a development.

AIM OF EDUCATION.—The beautiful was an object of constant endeavor in Athenian life. The taste was highly cultivated. The city was filled with model statuary; the drama received a frigidly chastened form; the Acropolis was crowned with architectural magnificence. A beautiful soul in a beautiful body—this was the chief end of Attic education. It was attained by a harmonious union of physical and intellectual culture. This conception of the purpose of education is indeed incomplete; but it has the merit of laying stress upon important elements that in other ages and countries have been too often neglected. The educational system of Athens produced results that are worthy of admiration. Nowhere else do we find braver warriors, wiser statesmen, greater artists, nobler writers, or profounder thinkers. Miltiades, Phidias, Æschylus, Plato, Aristotle—these are imperishable names; and the heroism displayed at Marathon, Salamis, and Platæa still move the heart like martial music.

SOLON.—The prosperity of Athens dates from the time of Solon, who lived in the sixth century before Christ.

He was counted among the seven sages of Greece, and was the lawgiver of Athens, as Lycurgus was of Sparta. Appointed to draft a constitution to replace the cruel code of Draco, he established laws noted for their wisdom and humanity. Parents were forbidden to sell or pawn their children—an unnatural and barbarous custom previously tolerated. Education was encouraged. In addition to intellectual training, the youth were required to learn a business or trade that would serve as a means of livelihood. Any father who neglected to give his sons a practical training forfeited all claims upon their support in his old age. This measure of Solon's laid a solid foundation for the prosperity of the State, and brought labor into honor at a time when it was generally held dishonorable.

AGE OF PERICLES.—But we pass to the time of Pericles, the golden age of Greece, for the closer study of Attic education. The social condition of Athens, Pericles himself has portrayed in his famous funeral oration. " We enjoy," he says, " a form of government which does not copy the laws of our neighbors; but we are ourselves rather a pattern to others than imitators of them. In name, from its not being administered for the benefit of the few but of the many, it is called a democracy; but with regard to its laws, all enjoy equality, as concerns their private differences; while with regard to public rank, according as each man has reputation for anything, he is preferred for public honors, not so much from consideration of party as of merit; nor, again, on the ground of poverty, while he is able to do the State any good service, is he prevented by the obscurity of his position. . . . Moreover, we have provided for our spirits the most numerous recreations from labors by celebrating games and sacrifices through the whole year and by maintaining elegant private establishments, the gratification daily received from which drives away sadness. Owing to the greatness, too, of our city, everything from every land is imported into it; and it is our lot to reap with no more peculiar enjoyment the good things which are produced here than those of the rest of the world likewise."

EDUCATION A PRIVATE INTEREST.—In Attica only the freemen, who constituted about one-fifth of the population, were allowed the advantages of education. Female education was neglected. The wife was servilely subject to the husband. As a rule, it was only women without character who sought to increase their charms by intellectual culture. The State had no further connection with education than to maintain a general supervision over the schools and to provide gymnasia for the physical training of the youth. Education was an individual interest, and it was left to the wisdom or ability of the father to determine what culture his sons should receive. But, as the popular sentiment was highly favorable to the cause of learning, education was general among the freemen. Even those who received no formal school-training were not left wholly without culture, for, in the democratic city of Athens, the people mingled freely together, and the numerous works of art had an elevating influence.

THE FESTIVALS.—The great festivals of the Greeks, though originally religious institutions, exerted a noteworthy influence upon the education and culture of the people. The four principal festivals—the Olympian, the Pythian, the Nemean, and the Isthmian—were celebrated with extraordinary splendor. They drew together immense crowds from all parts of Greece. To athletic sports of all kinds—running, wrestling, boxing, discus-throwing, and horse-racing—were added contests in music, poetry, and history. To be a victor in any of these contests and to wear the crown of olive, ivy, or laurel was esteemed an honor that exalted not only the fortunate contestant, but the city from which he came. His name was celebrated in poetry and his figure perpetuated in marble or bronze. The inevitable effect upon Grecian life was to stimulate at once the highest degree of physical and intellectual culture.

DOMESTIC TRAINING.—The education of the Athenian youth extended through eighteen years, which were divided into three nearly equal periods. The first period included the domestic training. Among the poor, the mother was the teacher; but among the wealthy, nurses were employed. These had entire supervision over the child, and were its constant companions. It is interesting to know that the children of Athens more than two thousand years ago were entertained by the same devices in use to-day, among which may be named rattles, dolls, swings, balls, stick-horses, little wagons, and toy houses and ships.

PRIMARY EDUCATION.—The boyhood education began with the seventh year. The boy was then removed from the nurse's care, and placed under the charge of a pedagogue, usually an aged and trustworthy slave, under whose care he remained throughout the rest of his education. The pedagogue performed the important functions óf servant, guardian, counselor, and moral censor. He attended his charge in walks and amusements, and accompanied him to and from school. Instruction was given by private teachers. The better class occupied comfortable rooms in which they received their pupils; while those without means imparted instruction in public places, receiving but little remuneration. Reading and writing were the subjects first studied. In teaching reading the Athenian instructor employed the alphabetic system, and encountered all the difficulties growing out of the dissimilarity between the names of the letters and their sounds as combined in words and syllables. A wax tablet and stylus were the earliest writing-materials. The pupil imitated a copy set by the teacher. After these elementary studies were sufficiently mastered, arithmetic, grammar, and literature were taken up. The Iliad and the Odyssey were among the earliest reading-books of the Greek. These, with other poetical and prose works, were carefully studied, extended portions being copied with the pen and memorized for declamation. Geography was learned chiefly from the second book of the Iliad, which contains the well-known catalogue of ships, and describes the various districts from which the Grecian forces came.

SECONDARY INSTRUCTION.—At the age of twelve or fourteen the sons of the poor usually relinquished study in order to learn a trade or engage in work, while the sons of the wealthy entered upon a higher course, embracing grammar, poetry, music, rhetoric, mathematics, and philosophy. Much of this higher instruction was given in the gymnasia, which, at first, places of physical exercise only, became at length centers of intellectual culture also. The two principal gymnasia in Athens were the Lyceum and the Academy, to which only youth of pure Athenian blood were admitted.

MUSIC.—Music formed an important part of education. It was believed to exert a very ennobling influence upon the mind and character. Poems were set to music and sung. The principal musical instrument was the cithara, a stringed instrument corresponding to the modern guitar, to which it has given name. The flute, though always

6

used at banquets and public festivals, was less popular, because it distorted the face and was unsuited to vocal accompaniment. "He who followed music as a profession," says Falke, "was looked upon as a mere laborer, and enjoyed but little respect; but, as a part of education and culture, singing and playing the cithara were an ornament to the freeman. Already, in Homer's day, Achilles sang and played; and to Epaminondas, the disciple of philosophers, the victorious leader of State and army, it was imputed as an honor that he was a good musician, and even dancer. Music was not introduced into the schools as a means of pleasure and amusement; but it was supposed to have a purifying and educating power. It was studied for the elevating influence which it exerted upon the soul."

PHYSICAL CULTURE.—A gymnastic training ran parallel with mental culture through its whole extent. This training was given by private teachers in their own or in public gymnastic schools. The elementary gymnastic schools, designed exclusively for boys, were called *palæstra.* Here the exercise consisted in running, jumping, wrestling, and other similar sports. The art of swimming was almost universal. "He knows neither the alphabet nor swimming," was a Greek expression for an ignoramus. The later physical training was received in the State gymnasia. The exercises assumed a more manly character, and consisted of leaping, running, wrestling, throwing the javelin, and hurling the discus or quoit. This was the classic course of gymnastics, and is known by the name *pentathlon.* The gymnastic discipline of Athens had a different purpose from that of Sparta. The Athenian sought beauty of body, and with what success, the model forms of Grecian statuary bear lasting witness.

The Spartan aimed at strength and endurance, but, in connection with these qualities, he often developed a coarseness that appeared to the refined Athenian taste almost brutal.

MORAL PURPOSE.—The moral purpose underlying this system of education has been presented by Plato in his Protagoras. The passage is well worth quoting for the insight it gives into Athenian education. " As soon as any one understands," he says, " what is said, nurse, mother, pedagogue, and the father himself, vie with each other in this, how the boy may become as good as possible; in every word and deed teaching and pointing out to him that this is just, and that unjust; this is honorable, and that base; this is holy, and that unholy; and this you must do, and that you must not do. And if the boy obeys willingly, it is well; but if not, like a tree twisted and bent, they make him straight by threats and blows.

" After this they send him to masters, and give them much more strict injunctions to attend to the children's morals than to their reading and music; and the masters do attend to this, and when the boys have learned their letters and are able to understand what is written, as before words spoken, they place before them on their benches to read, and compel them to learn by heart, the compositions of good poets, in which there are many admonitions, and many details and praises, and encomiums of good men of former times, in order that the boy may imitate them through emulation and strive to become such himself. Again, the music-masters, in the same way, pay attention to sobriety of behavior, and take care that the boys commit no evil; besides this, when they have learned to play on the harp, they teach them the compositions of other good poets, and those lyric, setting them to music, and they compel rhythm and harmony to become familiar to the boys' souls, in order that they may become more gentle, and being themselves more rhythmical and harmonious they may be able both to speak and act; for the whole life of man requires rhythm and harmony.

" Moreover, besides this, they send them to a teacher of gymnastics, that, having their bodies in a better state, they may be subservient to their well-regulated mind, and not be compelled to cowardice, through bodily infirmity, either in war or other actions. And these things they do who are most able; but the richest are the most able, and their sons beginning to frequent masters at the earliest time of life leave them latest. And when they are set free from masters, the State still further compels them to learn the laws, and to live by them as a pattern, that they may not act at random after their own inclinations."

CITIZENSHIP.—At eighteen the youth entered the military service of the State. They were placed as guards at frontier posts, and were subject to severe discipline. Two years later they were formally enrolled among the voters and admitted to the privileges of full citizenship. The oath administered on this occasion was as follows: " I will not bring reproach upon our sacred arms, nor desert the comrade at my side, whoever he may be. For our sanctuaries and laws I will fight alone or with others. My country I will leave, not in a worse, but in a better condition. I will at all times submit willingly to the judges and established ordinances, and will not consent that others infringe or disobey them. I will honor the established religious worship. The gods be my witness! "

THE SOPHISTS.—After the Persian war education in Athens declined. The teachers of philosophy and rhetoric, who professed to give their pupils a liberal education and to fit them for civic life, frequently degenerated into sophists. They exercised their disciples not in the discovery of truth, but in specious forms of argumentation. They cultivated the art of making " the worse appear the better reason." This unmanly and dishonorable insincerity provoked the hostility of the philosophers. Socrates delighted in puncturing their fallacies; and Aristotle defined a sophist as " an impostrous pretender to knowledge, a man who employs what he knows to be fallacy for the purpose of deceit and of getting money."

SUMMARY.—Athenian education, though far above any system preceding it, is by no means ideal. Its fundamental idea is not correct. The beautiful, as an esthetic conception, is not the supreme end of life. The moral and the useful are of higher significance. The worth of man was not fully grasped in Attica. Slaves were excluded from all education, and women were held in servile subordination. Education in Athens was particularistic. Its aim was not a manhood of typical and universal perfection, but the beautiful Athenian; and hence it had not breadth enough to become the educational system of our race.

The system of Athens has been called *esthetic education.*

E. Socrates

BIOGRAPHICAL FACTS.—Socrates, one of the most distinguished of Greek philosophers, was born at Athens, 469 B.C. His father was a sculptor. Socrates pursued the same occupation for some years with success, but subsequently relinquished it to devote himself to study. His personal appearance was unattractive, but he possessed a strong body and was capable of great endurance. He took part in the Peloponnesian war as a heavy-armed soldier, and won the admiration of his associates by his strength and courage. His wife Xantippe was a notorious scold, for which no doubt she had too much occasion; but he endured her shrewishness with a truly model patience and resignation.

HIS TEACHING.—Socrates left no writings; but Plato and Xenophon, two of his most distinguished disciples, have given full accounts of his teaching. He did not establish a private school, but frequented the gymnasia and public walks, conversing with whoever was willing to listen to him. He diverted attention from the material to the moral and intellectual interests of life. He did not lose himself in empty transcendental speculations, and for this reason it was said of him by the ancients that he brought philosophy from heaven down to earth. "Socrates," says Xenophon, "continued discussing human affairs; investigating what is piety? What is impiety? What is the honorable and the base? What is the just and the unjust? What is temperance or the unsound mind? What is courage and cowardice? What is a city? What is the character fit for a citizen? What is authority over men? What is the character befitting the exercise of such authority? and similar questions. Men who knew these matters he accounted good and honorable; men who were ignorant of them he likened to slaves."

HIGH MORAL CONCEPTIONS.—At the basis of the thought and teaching of Socrates lay high moral conceptions. He taught and practised a temperance in eating and drinking, by which he lived "in good spirits and uninterrupted health." He combated the idea that happiness consists in luxury and extravagance, and declared that "to want nothing is to resemble the gods." He inculcated habits of industry, maintaining that "to be busy is useful and beneficial for a man, and that to be unemployed is noxious and ill for him." Upright living seemed to him the worthiest object of endeavor. "When some one asked him," as Xenophon relates, "what object of study he thought best for a man, he replied, 'Good conduct.'" He was a man of profound piety, and in the midst of a dominant polytheism he rose to the clear conception of one supreme Being. "Then shalt thou, my Aristodemus," he says, "understand that there is a Being whose eye pierceth throughout all nature, and whose ear is open to every sound; extended to all places, extending through all time, and whose bounty and care can know no other bound than those fixed by His own creation." He believed in the immortality of the soul. "It is necessary," he said, "that one should venture himself upon this thought and delight himself with this hope. Let him take confidence in his soul, he who has renounced as foreign the pleasures of the body, he who has loved science, he who has adorned his soul with its true beauty—temperance, justice, strength, liberty, truth; and let him hold himself ready for departure from the world against the hour when destiny shall call for him." When he had been unjustly condemned to death, he spent the last hours of his life discoursing to his disciples upon this high theme.

SOCRATIC METHOD.—Apart from his noble ethical instruction, the principal significance of Socrates in a history of pedagogy is found in his method of teaching. He is the inventor, or at least the chief representative, of the developing method. Without an elaborate and fixed system of philosophy he made truth the object of his inquiry. He plied his interlocutor with skilful, persistent questions, forcing him to careful definition and fundamental principles. In this method of question and answer, as practised by Socrates, a negative and a positive side are clearly distinguishable. In the former case he places himself in the attitude of an inquirer after knowledge, seemingly accepts for a time the instruction of the disciple, and then, through unexpected deductions or evident contradictions, brings the latter to confusion and forces him to recognize his ignorance. This process, often insidious and exasperating, is known as *Socratic irony*. Socrates delighted in using it against the sophists.

The positive side of the Socratic method was inductive. It led, through progressive and well-directed interrogation, to the recognition of truths that had not been previously grasped with clearness. This phase of his method Socrates characterized as *maieutic*. " I myself," he says, " produce no wisdom, and it is correctly thrown up to me that I ask others questions without answering anything myself, as if I were incapable of proper replies. The reason is, that God compels me to help others bring forth, while withholding that power from me. Hence, I am by no means a wise man, and have no wisdom as the product of my own spirit to show. But those who have been with me have made incredible progress, as appears to them and to others. And so much is certain, that they have never learned anything from me, but have only themselves discovered very much that is beautiful, and have held it fast. In this production God and I have helped."

XENOPHON'S ESTIMATE.—Xenophon concludes his Memorabilia of Socrates with these words: "Of those who knew what sort of a man Socrates was, such as were lovers of virtue, continue to regret him above all other men, even to the present day, as having contributed in the highest degree to their advancement in goodness. To me, being such as I have described him, so pious that he did nothing without the sanction of the gods; so just that he wronged no man even in the most trifling affair, but was of service, in the most important matters, to those who enjoyed his society; so temperate that he never preferred pleasure to virtue; so wise that he never erred in distinguishing better from worse, needing no counsel from others, but being sufficient in himself to discriminate between them; so able to explain and settle such questions by argument; and so capable of discerning the character of others, of confuting those who were in error, and of exhorting them to virtue and honor—to me, I say, he seemed to be such as the best and happiest of men would be. But if any one disapproves of my opinion, let him compare the conduct of others with that of Socrates, and determine accordingly."

F. Plato

BIOGRAPHICAL FACTS.—The most distinguished pupil of Socrates was Plato. This philosopher, born in the year 429 B. C., traced his descent to Solon, and Codrus, an ancient king of Athens. In youth he received a careful education, and devoted himself for a time to poetry; but, after becoming acquainted with Socrates in his twentieth year, he gave himself up wholly to the study of philosophy. In pursuit of knowledge, he traveled in Egypt, and then in Italy, where he visited the school of

Pythagoras. At length, after many changes of fortune, he returned in his fortieth year to Athens, his native city, and devoted himself to gratuitous teaching. With his philosophy, which was idealistic, we have nothing to do.

REPUBLIC AND LAWS.—To Plato belongs the honor of first subjecting education to a scientific examination. He has discussed the subject at length in his Republic and in his Laws. The former is a picture of an ideal State with a Utopian system of education; the latter, in regard to both the State and education, is more closely conformed to existing conditions in Athens and Sparta. The Republic introduces the caste system, but the Laws favors a kind of socialism. " The first and highest form of the State," it is there said, "and of the government and law, is that in which there prevails most widely the ancient saying that friends have all things in common." Such a State, whether inhabited by gods or men, will bring to all, in the opinion of Plato, the highest degree of happiness.

IDEA OF EDUCATION.—Plato has repeatedly given expression to his conception of education, in which the moral element is always prominent. " A good education," he says in the Laws, " is that which gives to the body and to the soul all the beauty and perfection of which they are capable." Elsewhere he defines education as a training of youth in that manner of life which is prescribed by the laws of the State and approved by the worthiest men, and which develops in the young that hatred of evil and that love of virtue which they will cherish in maturity. Accordingly education appears to Plato as the highest of all pursuits. It is through education that man, exalted above brutish instincts, is brought nearest to God. Instruction in money-making arts, physical training, or manual knowledge of any kind, does not deserve the name of education unless it is accompanied by intelligence and morality.

BASIS OF HIS SYSTEM.—Plato thought he discovered a resemblance between the individual and the commonwealth. The individual, as he points out, possesses *intelligence*, having its center in the head; *courage*, having its seat in the breast; and *appetite*, having its lodgment in the stomach. The individual well-being depends upon the harmonious control and cooperation of these different factors. "The duty of education," he says, "is to control the appetite, and so to balance the other elements of the soul that each may tend to the perfection of the other."

Pursuing this fancied analogy between the individual and the State, Plato provides for three corresponding classes or castes. The first class includes the philosophers, who, by their superior intelligence, were to exercise the functions of government. They were to be characterized by truthfulness, temperance, magnanimity, and gentleness. The second class or order embraced the warriors, whose office was the defense of the State, and who were to receive a training suited to their vocation. The third caste comprehended the tradesmen, farmers, and mechanics, whose duty was to provide for the support of the State, and who were excluded from any but a primary education. When these three orders of citizens performed harmoniously and faithfully their several functions the highest civic welfare would be promoted. "If the magistrates are wise," says Plato, "if the warriors are courageous, and if the artisans are temperate, the State will be just. Everything will be in its place; the necessary subordination of the classes, resulting from the variable dignity of function, will be respected."

STATE EDUCATION.—It will be observed that Plato made education the business of the State, reminding us of the Persian and Spartan systems. All interests, whether of the family or of the individual, were subordinated to the State. A community of wives, children, and property was advocated. Plato understood the influence of a wholesome environment; and hence, he says, " we ought to seek out artists who by the power of genius can trace out the nature of the fair and the graceful, that our young men, dwelling, as it were, in a healthful region, may drink in good from every quarter, whence any emanation from noble works may strike upon their eye or their ear, like a gale wafting health from salubrious lands, and win them imperceptibly from their earliest years into resemblance, love, and harmony with the true beauty of reason."

COURSES OF STUDY.—The system of Plato provided an elementary and a higher course of instruction. The former began in childhood and lasted till the student was twenty. It consisted first of physical and moral training, and afterward of reading, writing, mathematics, and astronomy. This course was designed especially for the warrior class. Plato clearly recognized the evils of excessive physical training. " Let a man apply himself to gymnastics," he says, " and become trained, and eat much, and wholly neglect music and philosophy, and at first his body will become strengthened; but if he does nothing else, and holds no converse with the muses, though his soul have some natural inclination to learn, yet if it remains uncultivated by acquiring knowledge by inquiry, by discourse, in a word, by some department of music, that is, by intellectual education, it will insensibly become weak, deaf, and blind. Like a wild beast, such a man will live in ignorance and rudeness, with neither grace nor politeness."

The higher course of instruction began at twenty and lasted till thirty-five. It was reserved alone for the philosophic or ruling class, and included especially geometry, music, and dialectic. These studies were pursued, not in a utilitarian, but in an abstract and disciplinary way. Their purpose was to train the mind in abstract thinking; to lead it away from the sensuous or phenomenal to the ideal or universal. The crown of this higher course of training was dialectic, which attains to universal truth without the intermediation of the senses. "When a person," says Plato, "starts on the discovery of the absolute by the light of reason only, and without any assistance of sense, if he perseveres by pure intelligence, he attains at last to the idea of the good and finds himself at the end of the intellectual world."

MUSIC.—Plato attached special importance to music. He maintained that intellectual culture reacts favorably upon the body. "My belief is," he says, "not that the good body improves the soul, but that the good soul improves the body." Elsewhere he inquires: "Is it not, then, on these accounts that we attach such supreme importance to a musical education, because rhythm and harmony sink most deeply into the recesses of the soul, bringing gracefulness in their train and making a man graceful if he be rightly nurtured; but if not, the reverse? and also because he that has been duly nurtured therein will have the keenest eye for defects, whether in the failures of art or in the misgrowths of nature; and feeling a most just disdain for them, will commend beautiful objects, and gladly receive them into his soul, and feed upon them, and grow to be noble and good; whereas he will rightly censure and hate all repulsive objects, even in his childhood, before he is able to be reasoned with, and when reason comes he will welcome her most cordially who can recognize her by the instinct of relationship, and because he has thus been nurtured?" Dramatic and epic poetry Plato would exclude from his ideal republic as injurious to religion and morality. To lyric poetry he was more favorable, though he would limit it to the reverent praise of gods and heroes.

EDUCATION OF WOMAN.—Plato insisted that women should have the same training in gymnastics and literary culture that men received. In this he showed his sympathy with Sparta rather than with Athens. He based his argument for the higher education of woman on her native endowments, which do not essentially differ from those of men, and also on the security and welfare of the State. "If it should happen," he says, "that enemies from without, whether Greeks or barbarians, should fall upon the State in great force, and put everybody under the necessity of fighting for his own fireside, would it not be a great fault in the government if the women were so badly brought up that they were not disposed to die and to expose themselves to the greatest dangers for the safety of the country, as we see birds fight for their little ones against the most ferocious animals; and that, at the least alarm, they should run to seek refuge in the temples in order to embrace the altars and statues of the gods, impressing in that way upon the human species the stigma of showing itself more cowardly than any other species of animal?"

SUMMARY.—The system of Plato is a State education. The individual does not exist for himself, but for the State. No doubt he profits by the training that is provided for him, but it deprives life of all individual freedom. The system is a despotism, which the human race has never voluntarily adopted. While abounding in wise suggestions and profound thoughts, the education urged by Plato has remained in the realms of the imagination.

G. Aristotle

BIOGRAPHICAL FACTS.—Aristotle, whom an able German writer calls "the Alexander of the intellectual world," was born at Stagira, in Macedonia, 384 B. C. In youth he went to Athens, where he was a member of Plato's school for twenty years. His eminent abilities soon became the subject of remark, and he was called by the philosopher "the intellect of his school." Unlike his great theorizing teacher, Aristotle was a careful and practical investigator, and he succeeded by his genius and industry in compassing the whole circle of knowledge as it then existed. He created the science of logic, and made valuable contributions to many other departments of learning.

At the age of forty-seven, when his fame as a philosopher had become established, he was appointed teacher of Alexander the Great. He enjoyed the highest esteem both of Philip and Alexander, and received at their hands many marks of distinguished favor; among these may be mentioned the restoration of his native town, Stagira, which had been destroyed by war, and the erection there of a gymnasium for his philosophical lectures. Though having the royal pupil under his charge less than four years, he did much in molding his mind and character, and the effects of his teaching were afterward discernible in the conqueror's life.

THE LYCEUM.—When about fifty Aristotle returned to Athens and taught at the Lyceum. He lectured to a circle of disciples as he walked about the shady avenues, and this fact has given to his school of philosophy the name *Peripatetic*. In the morning he gave to select pupils a lecture upon some abstruse subject; in the afternoon he delivered a popular lecture to a wider circle of hearers. "In his works," says Ritter, "we see him the calm and sober inquirer, who does not, like Plato, pursue a lofty ideal, but keeps carefully in view the proximately practicable, and is not easily misled into any extravagance, either of language or of thought. His principal object is to examine truth under all her aspects, never to step beyond the probable, and to bring his philosophical system in unison with the general opinions of men, as supported and confirmed by common sense, observation, and experience."

EDUCATION AND THE STATE.—Aristotle recognized three legitimate forms of government—the monarchy, the aristocracy, and the republic. The latter he regarded as the least liable to abuse, and therefore the best; and it is for the training of citizens in a republic that he elaborates, in the Politics, his educational system. He rejects the communistic ideas of Plato, and recognizes the family as the basis of social organization. He regards the moral training of children as specially important, and to this end he would have them kept from every contaminating influence, and early placed under the charge of wise and capable pedagogues or guardians. Aristotle's views did not differ materially from the current practise of Athens, and the immediate practical end of education was, to his mind, the service of the State. But the happiness of the individual was likewise considered, which was to be found at last in a life of cultured leisure and contemplation.

AIM OF EDUCATION.—The supreme aim of education, according to the conception of Aristotle, is the practise of virtue. This principle excludes, on the one hand, practical utilitarianism, and on the other a specialized or professional skill. A life of refined and meditative leisure is his ideal of the noblest life. " Every work," he says, " is to be esteemed mean, and every art and every discipline as well, which renders the body, the mind, or the understanding of freemen unfit for the habit and practise of virtue. For which reason all those arts which tend to deform the body are called mean, and all those employments which are exercised for gain; for they take off from the leisure of the mind, and render it sordid. There are also some liberal arts which are not improper for freemen to apply to in a certain degree, but all sedulous endeavor to acquire a perfect skill in them is exposed to the faults I have just mentioned."

ADAPTATION TO CAPACITY.—Aristotle recognized three steps in the process of human development, and therefore adapted his training to the capacity and needs of the child. The first stage of development pertains to the body; the second, to the instincts; and the third, to the reason. The exercises and studies of the child are to be determined by these three fundamental facts of its life. This principle gives us the idea of a progressive education based on nature, and so anticipates, in some measure, the views of later educational reformers. Until the age of seven the child is to be left under the care of its parents; but after that time it is to be under public instruction. " For where education is neglected," he says, " it is hurtful to the city."

COURSE OF STUDY.—Aristotle approved of the subjects usually employed in the education of Athenian children.

7

Reading was to be taught as a thing useful in itself and helpful in acquiring knowledge. Drawing was commended for its esthetic results in enabling a man better to judge the productions of the fine arts. Like Plato, he reprobated excessive gymnastic training. "What is fair and honorable," he says, "ought to take the foremost place in education; for it is not a wolf, nor any other wild beast, that will brave any noble danger, but rather a good man. So that those who permit boys to engage too earnestly in these exercises, while they do not take care to instruct them in what is necessary to do, render them too mean to speak the truth, and accomplished in only one duty of a citizen, but in every other respect good for nothing, as reason evinces."

Music.—Aristotle advocated a musical training not only as a means of softening the passions, but also as a resource in elegant leisure. "It is clear," he says in an interesting passage, "that there are branches of learning and education which we must study with a view to the enjoyment of leisure, and these are to be valued for their own sake; whereas those kinds of knowledge which are useful in business are to be deemed necessary, and exist for the sake of other things. And therefore our fathers admitted music into education, not on the ground either of its necessity or utility, for it is not necessary nor, indeed, useful in the same manner as reading and writing, which are useful in money-making, in the management of a household, in the acquisition of knowledge, and in political life, nor like drawing, useful for a more correct judgment of the works of artists, nor again like gymnastics, which give health and strength; for neither of these is to be gained from music. There remains, then, the use of music for intellectual enjoyment in leisure, which appears to have been the reason of its introduction, this being one of the ways in which it is thought that a freeman should pass his leisure."

SUMMARY.—Notwithstanding his greatness, Aristotle was hemmed in by the limitations of his time and country. The end of education with him was the useful and happy citizen. Though recognizing, in some degree, the rights of the family and of the individual, he gave, as Plato had done, an undue importance to the State. He failed to grasp the worth of the individual in its fulness, and consequently his system of education contemplated only the freemen or ruling class of the commonwealth. The slaves and artisans, as well as the women, were excluded from its advantages. Though containing, as we have seen, beautiful ideals and high ethical aims, the educational system of Aristotle was content to leave a large part of the population in ignorance and degradation.

2. ROME

HISTORY.—Ancient Rome, founded 754 B. C., has a history extending through more than a thousand years. Beginning as a single city, it gradually extended its power until it embraced all the countries bordering upon the Mediterranean. From a condition of weakness and barbarism it rose to be the imposing mistress of the world and the chief representative of human progress. It finally gathered into its arms the elements of Grecian and Oriental culture, and, as its end drew nigh, freely scattered them over the rest of Europe. Rome has been the bearer of culture to the modern world. As a matter of course education varied during this long period of development. It will be sufficient in our present inquiry to speak first of the earlier and more austere type of Roman education, and afterward to discuss more at length the educational system in the age of Augustus, when the imperial city produced its richest fruits in literary culture.

CHARACTER.—Roman character, which lies at the basis of Roman history and culture, deserves a passing word. It is in striking contrast with Grecian character. Both are interesting, but one-sided and defective. The Greek, with his restless, lively, emotional nature, was esthetic, worshiping the beautiful; the Roman, with his rugged strength, was practical, reverencing the useful. These types of character are complementary of each other; and when united and ennobled by Christianity they present the highest form of manhood. To the Roman, life was serious; his manner was stately and grave. The finest feelings of humanity, the domestic and social affections, the refined pleasures of literature and art, were sacrificed for the sterner duties of framing laws, constructing aqueducts and highways, declaring wars, and leading armies. The spirit of conquest characterized the Romans, and made them utilitarian in all their views and aims. Utilitarianism determined education. "The children of the Romans," says Cicero, "are brought up that they may some time be useful to the country, and hence they should be taught the nature of the State and the regulations of our forefathers. Our country has borne and educated us on the condition that we consecrate to its service the best powers of our spirit, talent, and understanding; therefore we must learn the arts through which we can serve the State, for I hold that to be the greatest wisdom and the highest virtue."

FAMILY LIFE.—The family life of Rome marked a notable advance over that of Greece and the Oriental countries. The worth of woman began to receive proper recognition. Polygamy was not tolerated. In theory, the husband was unlimited master, and even held the right of life and death over his children; but, in practise, the wife, by her virtues and tact, softened the sternness of his authority and arrived at undisputed control in the household. The type of womanhood produced in the best days of Rome was admirable. Its leading traits were attractive dignity, strong motherly instincts, and lovely domestic virtues. Not diamonds or pearls, but her two rosy-cheeked boys, were Cornelia's most precious jewels. The Roman matron managed her household tastefully and frugally, and found delight in caring for her children. For the first six or seven years she was their only teacher; and with the utmost fidelity she formed their language, ideas, and moral sentiments. It was not till the age of degeneracy had set in that Roman mothers intrusted their children to nurses and pedagogues.

EARLIER PERIOD.—The earlier period of Roman education admitted but a small literary element. Education was thoroughly utilitarian, fitting the young Roman to fulfil the various duties of householder, citizen, and soldier. It was not an education for cultured retirement, but for efficient activity in the State. Its method was that of correct example. "The method of the old Roman education," says Monroe, " is essentially that of the apprentice system; the youth learns by observation and direct imitation of the master in the army, at the farm, in the courts and the forum. To this training is added a small amount of instruction by the parent or by the master. In the latter period the school supplants the home and the camp and forum, and this early training gives place to the formal instruction of the rhetorical school."

The elder Cato may be regarded as the embodiment of this earlier Roman spirit. He used his influence to repress the influx of Grecian learning. He wrote to his son: "Believe me, as if a prophet had said it, that the Greeks are a worthless and incorrigible race. If this people diffuse their literature among us, it will corrupt everything." His fears, not of the literature of the Greeks, but of their vices, were only too well founded; and as has happened at later periods in the world's history, brilliant culture went hand in hand with deep moral degradation. The educational practise of this earlier period is well exemplified by Cato. As Plutarch tells us, this sturdy Roman taught his son to read, "although he had a servant, a very good grammarian, called Chilo, who taught many others; but he thought not fit, as he himself said, to have his son reprimanded by a slave, or pulled, it may be, by the ears when found tardy in his lesson; nor would he have him owe to a servant the obligation of so great a thing as his learning; he himself, therefore, taught him his grammar, law, and his gymnastic exercises. Nor did he only show him, too, how to throw a dart, to fight in armor, and to ride, but to box also, and to endure both heat and cold, and to swim over the most rapid and roughest rivers. He says, likewise, that he wrote histories, in large characters, with his own hand, that so his son, without stirring out of the house, might learn to know about his countrymen and forefathers; nor did he less abstain from speaking anything obscene before his son, than if it had been in the presence of the sacred virgins, called vestals."

PRIMARY EDUCATION.—In the age of Augustus a

clearly defined system of schools had been developed. Elementary instruction began with the seventh year, and embraced reading, writing, and arithmetic. The teacher of the primary school was called *literator*. The general custom was to teach the names and order of the letters before their forms—a method that Quintilian properly criticizes. In connection with spelling and reading, great care was bestowed upon pronunciation. By degrees the easier poets were read and explained, and choice passages were learned by heart. Writing was taught by inscribing a copy on a waxen tablet or board, and allowing the pupil to follow the outline of the letters with the stylus. After reading and writing came the art of reckoning, to which importance was attached because of its value in business. The fingers and an abacus of pebbles were extensively employed; and, through repeated mental exercises, the pupil was accustomed to compute with rapidity.

SECONDARY EDUCATION.—The primary training of the child ended with the twelfth year, when he was handed over to the *literatus* in order to receive more advanced instruction. The Greek language was taken up, and grammar was carefully studied. For the culture of the understanding, the best writers, particularly the poets, were employed, among whom may be mentioned Homer, Virgil, Æsop, and Cicero. Poems and orations were committed to memory. Especial importance was attached to history, and several Romans have won celebrity by the extent and accuracy of their historical knowledge. Poetry, oratory, philosophy, and criticism were other subjects studied under the *literatus*.

HIGHER EDUCATION.—At fifteen or sixteen the young Roman assumed the dress of manhood, known as the *toga virilis*. It devolved upon him to choose his calling, and to direct his subsequent studies in reference to it. Agriculture, arms, politics, law, and oratory were open to him. In his choice the young Roman, with his utilitarianism, was determined more by the prospect of accumulating wealth than by the dignity of the calling. Agriculture, which was held in great esteem, was selected by those who lacked ability to achieve success in other pursuits. The art of war was acquired in the field; politics, law, and oratory were learned in the forum, courts, and senate, under the guidance of some distinguished patron. Eloquence, as the surest road to popularity and success, was studied with assiduity. Theory and practise were combined. A wide course of reading was pursued in this connection; for, according to a saying of Cicero's, the orator ought to know everything.

Schools Private.—The schools were private enterprises. The teachers of the primary schools did not stand in high esteem, as the *literator* was often a person who had failed in other callings. The *literati*, however, were frequently able to attain to wealth and distinction, especially if they were called to the instruction of the imperial princes. The public schools were not generally patronized by the higher classes of society. The moral tone of these schools was low; and the vitiated air, with which the rooms were filled, was felt to be prejudicial to health. Hence it was common to employ private tutors; or, as in the case of Æmilius Paulus, the conqueror of Macedonia, to keep Greek teachers permanently attached to the house.

Discipline.—The school regulations were exacting, and the discipline was sufficiently severe. Obedience and modesty were looked upon as important qualities. The pupils were required to be neat in dress and cleanly in person, and to observe a quiet decorum. On entering the school-room they greeted the teacher with a respectful salutation. Corporal punishment was employed. The ferule was the ordinary instrument of punishment; but, in case of grave faults, the rod or whip was also used.

A passage from the Epigrams of Martial presents an interesting picture of the discipline and order maintained in some of the Roman schools. " What right," he exclaims, " have you to disturb me, abominable schoolmaster, object abhorred alike by boys and girls? Before the crested cocks have broken silence you begin to roar out your savage scoldings and blows. Not with louder noise does the metal resound on the struck anvil, when the workman is fitting a lawyer on his equestrian statue; nor is the noise so great in the large amphitheater when the conquering gladiator is applauded by his partisans. We, your neighbors, do not ask you to allow us to sleep for the whole night, for it is but a small matter to be occasionally awakened; but to be kept awake all night is a heavy affliction. Dismiss your scholars, brawler, and take as much for keeping quiet as you receive for making a noise."

EDUCATION OF HORACE.—In his sixth satire Horace gives a description of his early education, and incidentally of the school-life of Rome in his day. " If no one," he says, " can truly lay to my charge avarice, meanness, or the frequenting of vicious haunts; if my life is pure and innocent, and my friends love me, I owe it all to my father. He, though not rich, for his farm was a poor one, would not send me to the school of Flavius,[1] to which the first youths of the town, the sons of the cen-

---

[1] A schoolmaster of Venusia, the poet s birthplace.

turions, the great men there, used to go, with their bags
and slates on their left arm, taking the teacher's fee on
the Ides of eight months in the year; but he had the
spirit to carry me, when a boy, to Rome, there to learn
the liberal arts which any knight or senator would have
his sons taught. Had any one seen my dress, and the
attendant servants, so far as would be observed in a
populous city, he would have thought that such expense
was defrayed from an old hereditary estate. He himself
was ever present, a guardian incorruptible, at all my
studies. But why should I multiply words?—he preserved me chaste (which is the first honor of virtue) not
only from every actual guilt, but likewise from every foul
imputation; nor was he afraid lest any should turn it to
his reproach if I should come to follow a business
attended with small profits, in capacity of an auctioneer
or (what he was himself) a tax-gatherer."

GENERAL SUMMARY.—Roman education was preeminently *practical*. It was determined not by any speculative views of beauty or of human nature, but by the
actual needs of life. "A clear and direct perception of
his relation to the outer world," says Laurie, "not as a
dwelling-place for the gods, but as a world to subdue and
reduce to order, was the characteristic of the Roman."
The education of Rome, though treated as a private
interest, often gave admirable results. Its orators, poets,
and historians are surpassed in the ancient world only
by the Greeks. Though the Roman might be lacking in
originality, he showed himself especially capable in organ-
izing and leading armies and in framing and administer-
ing laws. "The Roman men of affairs," says Merivale,
"were generally men of well-trained understandings.
Their soldiers could speak and write as well as command,

Their knowledge of ideas and letters was wide in its range, though perhaps their views had little depth, and still less originality. But there is something very remarkable in the ease with which they could turn from the active to the literary life, from study to composition, from speaking to speculation."

A. Cicero

BIOGRAPHICAL FACTS.—Cicero, the distinguished orator, statesman, and philosopher, was perhaps the best representative of his age, combining in himself the highest Roman and Grecian culture. Born in the year 106 B. C., of a noble family, he was educated at Rome under the best teachers of his time, among whom was the poet Archias. At sixteen he assumed the manly gown, and studied law, oratory, and philosophy. He afterward traveled in Greece and Asia for the purpose of study. At Rhodes he studied oratory with Apollonius, a celebrated rhetorician, at whose request he once delivered a declamation in Greek. When he had finished, the auditors were profuse in their praises; but Apollonius, after maintaining a sorrowful silence for a time, said: " You have my praise and admiration, Cicero, and Greece my pity and commiseration, since those arts and that eloquence, which are the only glories that remain to her, will now be transferred by you to Rome." After his return to Italy he filled several important offices, among them the consulship, in which his services were so eminent that he received at the hands of his grateful countrymen the proud title of " father of his country." At last, after many changes of fortune, he was murdered by emissaries of Antony, against whom he had delivered a series of philippics.

GENERAL VIEWS OF EDUCATION.—During his later years Cicero employed his leisure in writing several philosophical works, in which, especially in his Offices and Orator, he set forth more or less completely his views of education. He held that education should begin with the earliest childhood, and that during this sensitive period the amusements and surroundings should be favorable to refinement and culture. He demanded of teachers that they should be just, and neither too mild nor too severe. Punishment should be resorted to only after other means of discipline had failed; it should have nothing degrading in its form, and should never be administered in anger, as it is then impossible to observe moderation. The pupil should be made to feel that correction springs from the desire to do him good. The ethical side of education was strongly emphasized. The widest culture, including history, literature, and philosophy, was earnestly advocated, not however to grace a life of leisure, but to give greater efficiency in social service. The memory, Cicero maintained, should be carefully cultivated; and, to this end, extracts from Grecian and Roman writers should be learned by heart. In choosing his life-work a young man should be guided by his tastes and abilities.

ELOQUENCE.—Eloquence was with Cicero the consummate flower of education. His ideal for the orator was very high, and in comparison with it modern practise often appears quite superficial. "A knowledge of a vast number of things is necessary," he says, "without which volubility of words is empty and ridiculous; speech itself is to be formed not merely by choice, but by careful construction of words; and all the emotions of the mind which nature has given to man must be intimately known; for all the force and art of speaking must be employed in allaying or exciting the feelings of those who listen. To this must be added a certain portion of grace and wit, learning worthy of a well-bred man, and quickness and brevity in replying as well as in attacking, accompanied with a refined decorum and urbanity. Besides, the whole of antiquity and a multitude of examples are to be kept in the memory; nor is the knowledge of laws in general, or of the civil law in particular, to be neglected."

NATURE TO BE FOLLOWED.—Cicero recognized the differences of temperament and talent among men, and maintained that every one should carefully follow out his peculiar character or individual bent. "For we ought to manage," he says, "so as never to counteract the general system of nature; but having taken care of that, we are to follow our natural bias, insomuch that, though other studies may be of greater weight and excellence, yet we are to regulate our pursuits by the disposition of our nature. It is to no purpose to thwart nature or to aim at what you can not attain. We therefore may have a still clearer conception of the graceful I am recommending from the consideration that nothing is graceful that goes (as the saying is) against the grain, that is, in contradiction and opposition to nature."

TWO ERRORS IN LEARNING.—In the pursuit of knowledge Cicero pointed out two errors: the first consists in jumping at conclusions, and the second in wasting time over obscure or trifling subjects. He held that knowledge is "but solitary and barren" unless it can be made serviceable to mankind. "All of us," he says, "are impelled and carried along to the love of knowledge and learning, in which we account it glorious to excel, but consider

every slip, mistake, ignorance, and deception in it to be
hurtful and shameful. In this pursuit, which is both
natural and virtuous, two faults are to be avoided. The
first is the regarding things which we do not know as if
they were understood by us, and thence rashly give them
our assent. And he that wishes, as every man ought to
wish, to avoid this error must devote both his time and
his industry to the study of things. The other fault is
that some people bestow too much study and pains upon
things that are obscure, difficult, and even immaterial in
themselves. When those faults are avoided, all the pains
and care a man bestows upon studies that are virtuous
in themselves, and worthy of his knowledge, will be
deservedly commended."

LITERATURE.—Cicero set a high value on literature,
both poetry and prose. In defending the Roman citizenship of his early teacher Archias, he exclaims: " Let then,
judges, this name of poet, this name which no barbarians
even have ever disregarded, be holy in your eyes. Rocks
and deserts reply to the poet's voice; savage beasts are
often moved and arrested by song; and shall we, who
have been trained in the pursuit of the most virtuous
acts, refuse to be swayed by the voice of poets?" Literature in general he praised as an encouragement to virtue,
an aid to intellectual culture, and a source of refined and
permanent enjoyment. " Even if there were no such
great advantages to be reaped from it," he says, " and
if it were only pleasure that is sought from these studies,
still I imagine you would consider it a most reasonable
and liberal employment of the mind; for other occupations are not suited to every time, nor to every age or
place; but these studies are the food of youth, the delight
of old age; the ornament of prosperity, the refuge and

comfort of adversity; a delight at home, and no hindrance abroad; they are companions by night, and in travel, and in the country."

PHILOSOPHY.—A follower of Plato and Socrates, Cicero made an earnest plea for the study of philosophy, which had hardly, in his day, been fully naturalized in Rome. No other branch of study appeared to him more noble or more useful in the conduct of life. " By the gods," he exclaims, " what is more desirable than wisdom? What is more excellent? What is worthier for mankind? If we seek intellectual entertainment and recreation from care, is there anything comparable to philosophy, which always investigates what pertains to a happy life? Or if we aim at equanimity in life and virtue, then philosophy is the art through which it is to be obtained, or there is none. If there is any school of virtue, where shall we seek it but in this kind of knowledge? "

B. Seneca

BIOGRAPHICAL FACTS.—The philosopher Seneca lived during a period of great moral degeneracy—a fact that renders the purity of his teachings all the more remarkable. He was born at Cordova, in Spain, two years before the beginning of the Christian era. When quite young he was taken by his father, a man of no mean ability, to Rome, where he was initiated in the study of eloquence. After traveling some time in Greece and Egypt he returned to Rome and pleaded in the courts of law with eminent success. He was subsequently banished to Corsica for eight years, which period he spent in philosophical studies. " There is no land," he beautifully wrote at this time, " where man can not dwell—no land where he can not uplift his eyes to heaven; wherever we are, the distance of the divine from the human remains the same." Upon his recall to Rome he was appointed tutor to Nero; but, in spite of the excellence of his instruction, he was unable to control the depraved passions of his pupil. He was finally condemned to death, on a charge of conspiracy, in the year 65 A. D.—a standing testimony to the injustice and corruption of his age.

PHILOSOPHICAL VIEWS.—Seneca held exalted views of man, whom he regarded as an efflux of the divine Being and as an object of divine love and care. He did not believe in the blind fate of the Stoics; to his mind fate was the divine world-plan, and remained unchangeable, because God can will only what is best. Within this divine order of the universe large room is left for the exercise of man's free will. The truly wise man is the one who knows how to bring his will into harmony with the divine.

This high philosophy, which bears a striking resemblance to Christianity, lies at the foundation of Seneca's educational views as contained in his moral writings. Believing that it is the soul, and not outward station, which gives the individual worth, he felt esteem not only for the nobility, but also for the slave. "Wherever a *man* is," he says, "there is room for doing good." But he perceived the weakness and imperfection of human nature, which it is the function of education, as far as possible, to render perfect. For this reason the teacher occupies a high office and, no less than the legislator, renders an important service to the State.

THE TEACHER.—Seneca naturally recommended care in the selection of a teacher. He would have the teacher to be a man of moderation, who through gentle means would work upon the mind and character of his pupil, and so lead him to virtue. It was only when gentle means had failed that punishment was to be resorted to, and then with due reflection without anger. The teacher, he maintained, ought to adjust his methods and his instruction to the character of his pupil. "It is surely impossible," he says, "to change nature, and the temperament with which one is born can not be altered, but improved." Wisdom is needed to lead the pupil along the right paths of development without doing violence to his nature. "The spirit grows," Seneca says, "when it is not restricted; but through slavish treatment it is weakened." The teacher, therefore, should observe the golden mean between laxness and severity of discipline. Wise precept was to be reenforced by correct example. "The road by precept," he says, "is long; by example, it is short and sure."

STUDIES RESTRICTED.—With a vigorous, practical sense, Seneca wished to remove from instruction such studies as were distracting or useless. "Do not scatter your efforts too much," he says, "for he is nothing who is everything. Those make a mistake who think to further their culture by reading as many books as possible, for a multitude of books distracts the mind. We should hold only to the best writers, and from them daily learn some truth. The study of an author should have regard to three points—its grammatical structure, its historical references, and finally its deeper philosophic truth, which should be applied to the mind and heart."

He repeatedly condemned the minute and trifling scholarship which seems to have been fashionable in his day, and of which he was himself, perhaps, a victim in his youth. "Didymus the grammarian," he says, "wrote

8

four thousand books; I should pity the man who read so much rubbish. In these books are debated such questions as these: What was Homer's country? who was Æneas's real mother? whether Anacreon had a stronger taste for wine or women? whether Sappho was chaste? and other like matters, which, if thou didst know, thou shouldst unlearn."

LIBERAL STUDIES.—Yet Seneca was not a gross or inconsiderate utilitarian. In his estimate of studies he showed something of the Athenian spirit. " Thou desirest to know," he says, " my opinion of liberal studies. Of those things whose end is gain I admire none; I number none among those things that be good. Handicrafts may be profitable, nay, even useful, if they prepare but do not engross the mind. For we must exercise ourselves therein only so long as the mind can perform nothing greater; they must be our essays, not our works. Thou seest why certain are called liberal studies, because they be worthy of a free man. But one study there is which is liberal indeed, namely, that which makes a free man. Such is the study of wisdom, which is a high, valiant, and magnanimous thing; other things be petty and childish."

PHILOSOPHY.—The chief of studies with Seneca was philosophy, because it teaches true wisdom. Rising above the petty details of learning, it concerns itself with the world at large, with the principles of things, with truth and righteousness. " The mind is made perfect," says Seneca, " by one thing, namely, by the unchangeable knowledge of good and bad things, for which alone philosophy is competent. But no other art inquireth about good and bad things." Elsewhere he says again: " It is philosophy that gives us a veneration for God, a charity for our neighbor; that teaches us our duty to heaven, and exhorts us to an agreement one with another. It unmasks things that are terrible to us, assuages our lusts, refutes our errors, restrains our luxury, reproves our avarice, and works strangely upon tender natures."

LEARNING AND CHARACTER.—With his deep ethical sense Seneca placed character above learning. Right living seemed to him more important than recondite scholarship. " We take a great deal of pains," he says, " to trace Ulysses in his wanderings, but were it not time as well spent to look to ourselves that we may not wander at all? Are we not ourselves tossed with tempestuous passions, and both assailed by terrible monsters on the one hand, and tempted by sirens on the other? Teach me my duty to my country, to my father, to my wife, to mankind. What is it to me whether Penelope was virtuous or not? Teach me to know how to be so myself, and to live according to that knowledge. What am I the better for putting so many parts together in music, and raising a harmony out of so many different tones? Teach me to tune my affections, and to hold constant to myself. Geometry teaches me the art of measuring acres; teach me to measure my appetites, and to know when I have enough; teach me to divide with my brother, and to rejoice in the prosperity of my neighbor."

C. Quintilian

BIOGRAPHICAL FACTS.—Quintilian, the celebrated writer on rhetoric, was born at Calahorra, in Spain, about the year 42 A. D.; and, like most other great men of his time, he was educated at the metropolis. He devoted himself for a time to the practise of law, in which he achieved considerable success; but he finally abandoned this calling to become a teacher of oratory, in which he won a high and enduring reputation. He was invested by Vespasian with consular dignity, and granted an allowance from the public treasury. He was the first Roman teacher that was salaried by the State and honored with the title "professor of eloquence." He taught in Rome for twenty years, and numbered among his pupils many distinguished names.

INSTITUTES OF ORATORY.—In his later years he wrote his Institutes of Oratory, in twelve books, in which he presented a complete scheme of education—the most valuable treatise on the subject that has come down to us from antiquity. "The first book," he says in outlining his plan, "will contain those particulars [of primary education] which are antecedent to the duties of the teacher of rhetoric. In the second we shall consider the first elements of instruction under the hands of the professor of rhetoric, and the questions which are asked concerning the subject of rhetoric itself. The five next will be devoted to invention (for under this head will also be included arrangement), and the four following to elocution, within the scope of which fall memory and pronunciation. One will be added, in which the orator will be completely formed by us, since we shall consider, as far as our weakness shall be able, what his morals ought to be, what should be his practise in undertaking, studying, and pleading causes; what should be his style of eloquence, what termination there should be to his pleading, and what may be his employments after its termination."

EARLY ENVIRONMENT.—Quintilian entertained a favorable opinion of the native capacities of children, and admonished parents to cherish the best hopes of their offspring. Nurses should speak correctly and have good morals, as they have charge of children at the most impressible period. "We are by nature," he says, "most tenacious of what we have imbibed in our infant years; as the flavor, with which you scent vessels when new, remains in them; nor can the colors of wool, for which its plain whiteness has been exchanged, be effaced; and those very habits, which are of a more objectionable nature, adhere with the greater tenacity; for good ones are easily changed for the worse, but when will you change bad ones into good? Let the child not be accustomed, therefore, even while he is yet an infant, to phraseology which must be unlearned."

PRIMARY EDUCATION.—The pedagogues subsequently chosen for the children should either be men of acknowledged ability, which Quintilian greatly preferred, or they should at least be conscious of their want of learning, and thus remain themselves docile. Children should begin with the Greek language, as they would naturally acquire Latin; yet the study of the vernacular should not be long deferred, lest a pure pronunciation be lost. Education should not be postponed, as was customary at that time, till the seventh year, but should begin with the earliest childhood. Something can be learned during this early age; "and whatever is gained in infancy," says Quintilian, "is an acquisition to youth." Amusements should be utilized as means of instruction. Care should be exercised not to give the child a distaste for learning through undue urging or excessive tasks. "I am not so unacquainted with differences of age," he says, "as to think that we should urge those of tender years severely or exact a full complement of work from them; for it will

be necessary, above all things, to take care lest the child
should conceive a dislike to the application which he can
not yet love, and continue to dread the bitterness which
he has once tasted, even beyond the years of infancy.
Let his instruction be an amusement to him; let him
be questioned and praised; and let him never feel pleased
that he does not know a thing; and sometimes, if he is
unwilling to learn, let another be taught before him, of
whom he may be envious."

The forms and names of the letters should be learned
simultaneously; and whatever devices in the way of playthings might facilitate this knowledge should be employed.
Writing should be learned by following copies cut in wood
or inscribed in wax. In learning to read, the child should
advance slowly, mastering the elements fully.   Public
schools should be preferred to private instruction; for,
without exposing pupils to any greater danger, they supply the stimulating influence of association, friendship,
and example.   The disposition and ability of each pupil
should be studied. Precocity is often deceptive, lacking
solidity and endurance. Integrity and self-control should
be taught early. " That boys should suffer corporal punishment," Quintilian says, " I by no means approve; first,
because it is a disgrace, and a punishment for slaves;
. . . secondly, because if a boy's disposition be so abject
as not to be amended by reproof, he will be hardened,
like the worst of slaves, even by stripes; and, lastly,
because, if one who regularly exacts his tasks be with
him, there will not be the least need of any such chastisement."

SECONDARY INSTRUCTION.—Under the *literatus* the
pupil should pursue grammar, composition, music, geometry, astronomy, and literature. Greek and Latin authors

should be read with judicious criticism and all necessary historical explanations. Lastly, the student should pass to the rhetorician to complete his course. Special regard should be had to the moral character of the teacher and to his qualifications. The teacher of eminent abilities is the best to teach little things as well as great things, and he is likely to have a better class of pupils. Severity in criticism should be avoided. "I used to say," Quintilian tells us, "with regard to some compositions, that I was satisfied with them for the present, but that a time would come when I should not allow them to produce compositions of such a character." The natural tastes and capacities of pupils should be regarded, though not to too great an extent. We should strengthen what is weak and supply what is deficient.

ETHICAL FACTOR.—To Quintilian, as to the other great educational theorists of the ancient world, the ethical factor of education seemed of preeminent importance. He defined an orator as "a good man skilled in speaking." "I say not only that he who would answer my idea of an orator must be a good man," he argues, "but that no man, unless he be good, can ever be an orator. To an orator discernment and prudence are necessary; but we can certainly not allow discernment to those who, when the ways of virtue and vice are set before them, prefer to follow that of vice; nor can we allow them prudence, since they subject themselves, by the unforeseen consequences of their actions, often to the heaviest penalty of the law, and always to that of an evil conscience. But if it be not only truly said by the wise, but always justly believed by the vulgar, that no man is vicious who is not also foolish, a fool assuredly will never become an orator."

D. Plutarch

BIOGRAPHICAL FACTS.—Plutarch, the celebrated biographer and moralist, was born at Chæronea, in Bœotia, about 50 A. D. After studying at Delphi under a distinguished teacher, he took up his residence at Rome, where, during the reign of Domitian, he became a popular teacher of philosophy. In later years the emperor Hadrian, his friend and pupil, appointed him magistrate in his native city, where he died about 120 A. D. He was a man of excellent native ability and of wide scholarship. He is best known for his Parallel Lives, which has always enjoyed a high degree of popularity, and for his Morals, in which, among many other essays, is found his famous treatise On the Training of Children. Though the authenticity of this treatise has been questioned, no one doubts that it presents the views of the Greco-Roman philosopher.

HEREDITY.—Plutarch begins his essay by insisting on good heredity. The parents who would not transmit a taint to their offspring should live chastely and soberly. " Such children as are blemished in their birth," he says, " either by the father's or the mother's side, are liable to be pursued as long as they live with the indelible infamy of their base extraction, as that which offers a ready occasion to all that desire to take hold of it, of reproaching and disgracing them therewith." But to be well born naturally imparts a loftiness and gallantry of spirit. The faults or imperfections of nature, Plutarch held, may in a measure be made good by education. " As a good natural capacity," he says, " may be impaired by slothfulness, so dull and heavy natural parts may be improved by instruction; and whereas negligent students arrive not at the capacity of understanding the most easy things, those who are industrious conquer the greatest difficulties."

EARLY SUSCEPTIBILITY.—Mothers should care for their children. Hired nurses, who are without natural affection, show less tenderness and care for them. The manners of children should be formed from the beginning by proper example. "Childhood," Plutarch says, "is a tender thing, and easily wrought into any shape. Yea, and the very souls of children readily receive the impressions of those things that are dropped into them while they are yet but soft; but when they grow older they will, as all hard things are, be more difficult to be wrought upon. And as soft wax is apt to take the stamp of the seal, so are the minds of children to receive the instruction imprinted on them at that age."

PEDAGOGUES AND TEACHERS.—When the child arrives at the proper age a pedagogue should be selected with great regard to character. Plutarch censured the careless course of his contemporaries, who frequently selected the least competent and trustworthy of their servants to watch over their children. "If they find any slave that is a drunkard or a glutton, and unfit for any other business, to him they assign the government of their children; whereas a good pedagogue ought to be such a one in his disposition as Phœnix,[1] tutor to Achilles, was."

Of still more importance seemed to him the proper selection of a teacher. He should be a man of experience, and especially of irreproachable character. The fathers are worthy of contempt who, through ignorance or carelessness, place their children under the tuition of incompetent or rascally men. "We are to look," he says, "after

---

[1] See Iliad, book ix, 619-627 (Munford).

such masters for our children as are blameless in their lives, not justly reprovable for their manners, and of the best experience in teaching. For the very spring and root of honesty and virtue lie in the felicity of lighting on good education." Learning appeared to him as the highest possession—better than riches, glory, or physical strength. For " learning alone, of all things in our possession, is immortal and divine."

DISCIPLINE AND OVERSIGHT.—Children should be led to study by gentleness and reason rather than by stripes. Harshness is not the best method of dealing with slaves, much less with children. " Praise and reproof," he says, " are more effectual upon free-born children than any such disgraceful handling; the former to incite them to what is good, and the latter to restrain them fror⌐ what is evil." Parents ought to look after the progress of their children even after they have been placed under the care of the pedagogue. " Even that sort of men," he says, " will take more care of the children when they know that they are regularly to be called to account. And here the saying of the king's groom is very applicable, that nothing made the horse so ⌐t as the king's eye."

POINTS OF TRAINING.—Plutarch advocated physical training as a means of building up a good constitution and fortifying the body for military service. " Children must be sent to schools of gymnastics," he says, " where they may have sufficient employment that way also. This will conduce partly to a more handsome carriage, and partly to the improvement of their strength. For the foundation of a vigorous old age is a good constitution of the body in childhood." The memory was to be diligently cultivated by exercise. Memory was made the mother of the muses to indicate its fundamental relation to learning. Children were to be disciplined in chaste speech and courteous manner. They were to live simply, refrain from anger, and bridle their tongues. In reference to the last point he says: "Experience shows that no man ever repented of keeping silence; but many that they have not done so."

GENERAL EDUCATION.—Plutarch, beyond all other writers of antiquity, advocated general education. The lower classes were not to be excluded from its privileges and benefits. "It is my desire," he says incidentally, "that all children whatsoever may partake of the benefit of education alike; but if yet any persons, by reason of the narrowness of their estates, can not make use of my precepts, let them not blame me that give them, but Fortune which disableth them from making the advantage by them they otherwise might. But even poor men must use their utmost endeavor to give their children the best education; or if they can not, they must bestow upon them the best that their abilities will reach."

III

CHRISTIAN EDUCATION BEFORE THE RISE OF PROTESTANTISM

1. BRIEF SURVEY OF THE PERIOD

IMPERFECT DEVELOPMENT.—The first period of Christian education extends to the sixteenth century. During this long period Christianity did not completely control society and education. Always encountering determined opposition, and having weak and fallible men as its representatives, it has never achieved faultless results. At first its violent contrast with existing customs and morals, and afterward its union with the State, gave it one-sided tendencies and crippled its efficiency.

WHAT WAS ACCOMPLISHED.—Notwithstanding unfortunate tendencies in the Church during the first period of Christian education, indispensable work was accomplished. The greatest political power of the earth was brought under the influence of Christianity. The young and vigorous nations of the north of Europe, which at a later time were to be the representatives and bearers of Christian culture, were converted to Christianity. The relics of ancient literature, which were to perform an important office in quickening and forming modern Christian culture, were preserved in the monasteries, and multiplied by tireless copyists. The beginnings of popular education were made. A thirst for knowledge was disseminated

among the higher classes, and universities were founded
as centers of intellectual culture. In part, the course of
study, both for primary and secondary education, was
fixed; and the mistakes and one-sidedness of educational
effort have remained for our instruction.

THE TEUTONIC RACE.—The Teutonic race, which received the precious boon of civilization from falling
Rome, possessed at the beginning of our era certain characteristics that brought it into sympathy with Christianity, and prepared it for the hearty adoption of the new
faith. As compared with the Romans in point of culture,
those brave German tribes ranked as barbarous; but, in
force of character, purity of morals, and nobility of feeling, they were far above the Romans. They recognized,
in a high degree, the worth of the individual, and were
warm defenders of personal freedom. They possessed a
deep religious nature and great reverence and love for
the truth. Women were held in high esteem. Their
respect for marriage and their purity of morals were portrayed by Tacitus, in order to shame the licentiousness
of Rome. In addition to all this, the Teutonic races
possessed great physical and intellectual vigor, which
fitted them to take up the world's development at the
point where antiquity, with strength exhausted, had left
it. They were to become, in due time, the leaders in art,
science, commerce, government, religion, and culture, in
all which they made new and extended conquests. It
is the Teutonic nations that are chiefly to claim our
attention hereafter. They are the great leaders in education, as they are in every other weighty human interest.

2. THE RELATION OF CHRISTIANITY TO EDUCATION

THE NEW ERA.—Though much in the education of pagan antiquity was admirable, it still remained defective. It was controlled by wrong principles and confined within too narrow limits. It did not grasp the worth of the individual in all its fulness, and never freed itself from the narrowness of national boundaries. Grecian education, as we have seen, aimed at forming the beautiful Greek; Roman education, at forming the practical Roman. If philosophers sometimes rose to larger and juster views, their teachings remained without practical results in the education of their day. But, with the advent of Christ into the world, there came a new era in history. New truths were thrown into the world which were destined to change its character and culture. With his coming mankind started upon the period of its final development; for when the truths announced by him have been fully realized the kingdom of heaven will cover the earth.

CHRISTIANITY AND EDUCATION.—The wide-reaching influences of Christianity have profoundly affected education. Christianity has placed education upon a new and immovable foundation. In teaching that God is the common Father of all men, it removes from education the fetters of national limits and prejudices. It gives the world the great thought of the brotherhood of mankind—a thought whose benign effects have not yet been fully realized. In making every one a child of God, stamped with the impress of the divine image, Christianity attaches due importance to the individual. It makes him the object of redemption, the steward of God, the heir of eternal life. He is made to possess an endless worth in himself. Christianity teaches that all men are alike before God, who " is no respecter of persons." With this mighty truth it sweeps away the false distinctions of class and caste which have weighed so heavily upon Oriental countries. It abolishes slavery. In enforcing the law of brotherly love, Christianity seeks to overthrow the injustice and oppressions of society. Inculcating the duty of personal holiness, it seeks to abolish vices which were sanctioned by the philosophy, religion, and society of the ancient world, and which polluted and undermined Grecian and Roman civilization. It elevates marriage into a divine rite. It makes the wife the friend and companion of her husband, their union symbolizing that of Christ with his Church. Children are looked upon as the gift of God. Christ took them up in his arms and blessed them. So far from having the right to expose his children to death, according to the universal custom among pagan nations, the parent is required to " bring them up in the nurture and admonition of the Lord." These are some of the great truths of Christianity which have changed the character both of civilization and of education.

3. THE FOUNDER OF CHRISTIANITY

GRANDEUR OF HIS LIFE.—The life of Christ, apart from its religious significance in the world's redemption, is well worth a careful study. It is now more than nineteen centuries since his birth. During this vast period the world has moved forward in its gigantic process of development. The sum of human knowledge has been immeasurably increased, new arts and sciences have arisen, yet the life of Christ stands forth in unapproachable beauty. The greatest minds of modern times, with the docility of the Galilean fishermen, have paid him the tribute of reverent admiration. The brilliant and skeptical Rousseau acknowledged that " the life and death of Jesus Christ are those of a God." The great German, Herder, said, " Jesus Christ is in the noblest and most perfect sense the realized ideal of humanity." No one will deny the intellectual greatness of Napoleon, yet he has said of Christ: " His birth and the story of his life, the profoundness of his doctrine, which overthrows all difficulties, and is their most complete solution; his gospel, the singularity of his mysterious being, his appearance, his empire, his progress through all centuries and kingdoms—all this is to me a prodigy, an unfathomable mystery. I defy you to cite another life like that of Christ."

HIS TRAINING.—As the Jewish system of education had changed but little, the domestic circle at Nazareth was probably his only school. From Joseph he received formal instruction in the Jewish law, while the gentleness and piety of Mary were not without influence in molding his character. He profited, no doubt, by the weekly synagogue service, and, on his annual visits to the holy city, dwelt fondly upon its wondrous associations. He studied the Scriptures of the Old Testament in the original Hebrew, and stored his memory with their historical facts, moral precepts, and inspired prophecies. Unlike the professional religious teachers of his day, he penetrated beneath the surface of temporary forms and took his stand on self-evidencing and eternal truth.

The results of this training, with its deep religious significance, are apparent throughout Christ's subsequent career. At twelve years of age he confounded the doctors in the temple; afterward he repulsed the repeated assaults of Satan in the wilderness; he vindicated his Messiahship by the testimony of the prophets; he baffled the cunning of the Pharisees by his profound acquaintance with Scripture. When he taught the people he called forth the testimony that "never man spake as this man." He announced new and profound spiritual truths. In a word, he raised himself above all others whom millions yet to-day regard as their grandest teachers. Buddha, Confucius, Mohammed—to say nothing of Greek and Roman sages—are not worthy to be compared with Christ.

METHOD OF TEACHING.—In his manner of instructing his disciples and the multitudes that gathered around him Christ has given us valuable lessons in method. His heart goes out toward his hearers in the tenderest sympathy; he "was moved with compassion toward them, because they were as sheep not having a shepherd." His teaching is adapted to the capacity of his hearers, and is usually connected with some outward circumstance that renders it more impressive. He observes the order of Nature, and seeks only a gradual development—" first the blade, then the ear, after that the full corn in the ear." With his disciples, he insists chiefly upon the practical and fundamental truths of religion, building, as it were, a substantial framework in the beginning, which the Holy Spirit was to conduct afterward to a harmonious and beautiful completion. " One finds in his program," says Paroz, " neither literary studies nor course of theology. And yet, strange as it may seem, when the moment of action arrives, the disciples—those unlettered fishermen— have become orators that move the multitudes and confound the doctors; profound thinkers that have sounded

9

the Scriptures and the human heart; writers that give to the world immortal books in a language not their mother-tongue."

SUMMARY.—Both in his life and his teaching Christ has profoundly influenced the education of the world. He has set up a new spiritual ideal as the object of human attainment; for we are to be "perfect even as our Father in heaven is perfect." In his own person he has become the moral exemplar of our race. With him the supreme factor in education is ethical culture, by which we are brought to recognize and discharge our duties to God and man. Truth is made the breath of life, and the highest attainment of human effort is spiritual harmony with Him who has "made all things and upholds them by the might of his power."

The testimony of Karl Schmidt is striking and emphatic. "By word and deed," he says, "in and with his whole life Christ is the teacher and educator of mankind. Henceforth there is no higher wisdom than that exhibited by Christ, that God is a spirit, and that they that worship him must worship him in spirit and in truth; no greater truth than this, that God dwells essentially in man, that God is the true, divine being of man; no diviner duty than this: 'Thou shalt love the Lord thy God with all thy heart, and with all thy soul, and with all thy mind. This is the first and great commandment. And the second is like unto it, Thou shalt love thy neighbor as thyself.' That is absolute truth, doctrine for all time, in the appropriation and realization of which lies the task of mankind, while in the person of Christ himself the absolute example is given as to whither this truth leads, what it accomplishes, and how it appears in taking form."

4. EDUCATION IN THE EARLY CHURCH

PRIMITIVE CHRISTIAN LIFE.—We shall discover among the primitive Christians an unmistakable incompleteness in educational training; but, at the same time, we shall find the highest purity of life and the most self-sacrificing devotion that have been manifested, perhaps, in the history of our race. After contemplating the vicious society of heathen countries, and turning even from our own more cultured civilization, it is delightful to consider the beautiful characteristics of the primitive Christian life. With the early Christians the adoption of Christianity meant the complete exemplification of its precepts in the life. Says Justin Martyr, who was born about the end of the first century, himself one of the most distinguished Christians: "We who once delighted in lewdness now embrace chastity; we who once embraced magical arts have consecrated ourselves to the good and unbegotten God; we who loved above all things the gain of money and possessions now bring all that we have into one common stock, and give a portion to every one that needs; we who once hated and killed one another now pray for our enemies, and endeavor to conciliate those who unjustly hate us. Now, whosoever are found not to live as Christ taught, let it be publicly known that they are not Christians, though they should profess with their tongues the doctrines of Christ."

MARRIAGE.—The marriage relation was almost ideal in its beauty. According to apostolic injunction, marriage between believers only was allowed. Again we let one of the Church fathers speak. Tertullian, who lived in the second century, says: "How intimate the union between believers! Their hopes, their aspirations, their desires, all the same. They are one in faith and in the service of their Lord, as they are also in flesh and in heart. In mutual concord they read the Scriptures, and fast and pray together, aiding and sustaining each other by mutual instruction and encouragement. They go in company to the house of the Lord; they sit together at his table. In persecution and in want they bear their mutual burdens and participate in each other's joys. They live together in mutual confidence, and in the enjoyment of each other's society. In the freedom of mutual confidence they administer to the sick, relieve the needy, distribute their alms, and each freely engages in his religious services without concealment from the other. Unitedly they offer their prayers to God, and sing his praise, knowing no rivalry but in these acts of devotion. In such scenes of domestic bliss Christ rejoices and adds his peace. To two so united he grants his presence; and where he is no evil can abide."

EDUCATION A DUTY.—The education of children was regarded as a sacred duty. The Apostolic Constitutions, dating from the third century, admonish parents to the education of their children, and also point out its general character. "Whoever neglects to admonish and educate his son," says this ancient document, "hates his own child. Teach your children the Word of God, make them earnest and obedient, even with stripes, from their infancy, teaching them the Holy Scriptures, which are Christian and divine, and delivering to them every sacred writing, not giving them such liberty that they may get the mastery, and act against your opinion, not permitting them to club together for a treat with their equals. For so they will be turned to disorderly courses; and if this

happens by the carelessness of their parents, those that
begot them will be guilty of their souls. For if the
offending children get into the company of dissolute persons by the negligence of those that begot them, they will
not be punished alone by themselves, but their parents
also will be condemned on their account."

OPPOSITION TO PAGAN EDUCATION.—There was naturally and inevitably opposition on the part of Christian
leaders to the traditional pagan education. The ends to
be attained, as contemplated in Christian and in pagan
education, were radically different. Furthermore, after
the beginning of the Christian era, the pagan schools had
degenerated. The teachers were, in large measure, mer-
cenary men, and their instruction was, in many cases,
superficial and worthless. The moral tone of much of
the literature taught in the schools of paganism was
repugnant to the lofty ideals of purity and goodness
entertained by the fathers of the Church. Therefore it
is not strange to find the Apostolic Constitutions, in harmony with a general sentiment, prohibiting heathen learning: "Abstain from all the heathen books. For what
hast thou to do with such foreign discourses, or laws, or
false prophets which subvert the faith of the unstable?
For what defect dost thou find in the law of God that
thou shouldest have recourse to those heathenish fables?
For if thou hast a mind to read history, thou hast the
books of the Kings; if books of wisdom or of poetry, thou
hast those of the prophets, of Job, and the Proverbs, in
which thou wilt find greater depth of sagacity than in
all the heathen poets and sophisters, because these are
the words of the Lord, the only wise God. If thou desirest something to sing, thou hast the Psalms; if the
origin of things, thou hast Genesis; if laws and statutes,

thou hast the glorious law of the Lord God. Do thou therefore utterly abstain from all strange and diabolical books."

PURPOSE AND MANNER OF EDUCATION.—The purpose of these early Christian parents, as of the ancient Jews, was to train up their children in the fear of God. In order that the children might be exposed as little as possible to the corrupting influence of heathen associations, their education was conducted within the healthful precincts of home. As a result, they grew up without a taste for debasing pleasures; they acquired simple domestic tastes; and, when the time came, they took their place as consistent and earnest workers in the Church.

SUMMARY.—Such was the character of education among the primitive Christians. It is defective, indeed, subordinating and even sacrificing the intellectual to the moral and religious elements of our nature; but the type of character it frequently produced was admirable. The beauty of this character, with its purity, charity, and righteousness, made a deep impression on an age notorious for its vice.

A. Catechetical Schools

ORIGIN AND NATURE.—The catechetical schools, which sprang up naturally in this primitive period, were designed to prepare candidates for Christian baptism. In the apostolic period new converts to Christianity were received into the Church by baptism after a very brief course of instruction and upon a very simple profession of faith. The Ethiopian eunuch, for example, received at most only a few hours' instruction as he rode along in his chariot, and was baptized upon the confession, " I believe that Jesus Christ is the Son of God." But as Christianity spread, and converts from among the Jews and heathen became more numerous, it was found advisable, for the sake of greater unity, purity, and intelligence in the Church, to give candidates for baptism more extended instruction. This instruction, which extended from a few months to three years, was given by a special Church officer under the name of catechist, and embraced the fundamental truths and doctrines of Christianity. The candidates, called catechumens, or learners, studied the ten commandments, the Lord's prayer, and other portions of Scripture, as well as a short confession of faith containing the chief articles of Christian belief. The instruction was at first imparted privately at some convenient place, but afterward in the church or school-buildings.

SCHOOL OF ALEXANDRIA.—The most celebrated of the catechetical schools was that of Alexandria, founded in the second century. It was in this city that Christianity came into closest contact with heathen culture. Many of the candidates applying for admission into the Church were representatives of heathen learning. In preparing them for baptism it was necessary that the instruction assume a more complete and scientific form. In addition to this, the Alexandrian school devoted itself to the education of Christian teachers. It became, in fact, a theological seminary of high order, in which, along with specifically Christian instruction, philology, rhetoric, mathematics, and philosophy were studied. The attitude of this school toward heathen learning is thus expressed by Clement, one of its earliest and most distinguished teachers: "The Mosaic law and heathen philosophy do not stand in direct opposition to each other, but are related like fragments of a single truth, like the pieces, as it were, of a shattered whole. . . . Both prepared the way, but in a different manner, for Christianity." The school had no public buildings, and the teachers, several of whom were very distinguished, taught in their private houses. They received no fixed salary, but were supported by gifts from their pupils. Alexandria was the birthplace of scientific Christian theology.

5. EDUCATION DURING THE MIDDLE AGES

ASCETICISM.—It is necessary to notice a peculiar tendency in the Church which exerted for nearly a thousand years an important influence upon education. This was the ascetic tendency, which disdains the present world in the interests of the world to come. This tendency has been forcibly characterized by George Eliot as "otherworldliness." It fails to grasp the great truth that human life is an organic unity; that eternal life is but a continuation of temporal life; and that on earth, as well as in heaven, we are in the presence and service of God. Asceticism, which manifested itself in various forms of self-abnegation or physical torture, was based upon the idea that the body is the seat of sin. Hence it was concluded that by imposing restraints and suffering upon the body, by which its natural force was weakened, the soul was enabled to attain to a higher degree of sanctity. The two principal classes of ascetics were the hermits, who withdrew from society to live in solitude, and the monks, who lived together in monasteries under the vow of poverty, chastity, and obedience. The latter was by far the more numerous class, and its existence has been perpetuated to the present.

ORIGIN AND RESULTS.—Traces of the ascetic spirit are to be found in the primitive Church; but it was not till late in the fourth century that it reached a complete development. It then remained dominant throughout the middle ages. Perhaps it was a phase of human development necessary in the zigzag march of progress, and indispensable to the ultimate attainment of truth. At all events it was a natural one. The heathen world had long been attaching too much relative importance to the earthly life. By a natural reaction the Church, when it came to assert itself in opposition to prevailing beliefs and customs, unduly contemned the present world in magnifying the world to come.

"In the first stage of its development," profoundly observes Karl Schmidt, in speaking of the Church, "it was religion especially that dominated all intellectual interests. The religious impulse in Christianity was so powerful and weighty that the human spirit found in it and its exemplification complete satisfaction. There was a great withdrawal of man within himself, into that part of his nature that unites him to God, and that belongs, not to the perishable, but to the imperishable; not to the visible, but to the invisible world. The supernatural laid hold of men's minds with mighty energy. Man, as the son of heaven, became a stranger upon this earth, and esteemed the splendor of this world as of little value. The world in all its beauty had been tested by antiquity, and had not afforded the lasting peace promised of it. Heaven now took its place, and the citizen of heaven displaced in a measure the citizen of earth. This one-sided apprehension of man as a heavenly being, this complete sway of the transcendental, forms the leading characteristic of the world before the Reformation, in which period

Christianity appeared as an abnegation of the world. Only the world of religion is truth. The natural world is destitute of worth, and escape from it is the end of life. Hence the world-disowning asceticism, fasting, celibacy."

VIEWS OF THE CHURCH FATHERS.—This ascetic, transcendental movement very soon found advocates among the most influential of the Church fathers. Says Chrysostom, who lived in the fourth century: "Mothers ought to care for the bodies of their children, but it is necessary also that they inspire their offspring with love for the good and with fear toward God. And fathers will not limit themselves to giving their children an earthly vocation, but will interest themselves also in their heavenly calling. The most beautiful heritage that can be given children is to teach them to govern their passions. Never ought they to hear licentious conversation at home. Let us take care to develop modesty in them, for nothing torments youth so much as what is contrary thereto. Let us have for our children the same fear that we have for our houses when servants go with a light into places where there is inflammable material, as hay or straw. They should not be permitted to go where the fire of impurity may be kindled in their hearts and do them an irreparable injury. A knowledge of the Scriptures is an antidote against the unreasonable inclinations of youth and against the reading of pagan authors, in which heroes, the slaves of every passion, are lauded. The lessons of the Bible are springs that water the soul. As our children are everywhere surrounded with bad examples, the monastic schools are the best for their education. Bad habits once contracted can not be got rid of. This is the reason God conducted Israel into the wilderness, as into a monastery, that the vices of the Egyptians might be unlearned. And yet the Israelites were continually falling into their old habits! Now our children are surrounded by vice in our cities and are unable there to resist bad examples. In the monasteries they do not see bad examples; they lead there a holy life in peace and tranquillity. Let us take care of the souls of our children that they may be formed for virtue, and not be degraded by vice."

The ascetic tendency found an ardent representative in St. Augustine, who has been called the Paul of the fifth century. With great vehemence he rejected all heathen science in Christian education. " Those endless and godless fables," he says, " with which the productions of conceited poets swarm, by no means accord with our freedom; neither do the bombastic and polished falsehoods of the orator, nor finally the wordy subtleties of the philosopher. God forbid that trifles and foolishness, windy buffoonery, and inflated falsehood, should ever be properly called science!" Again he says: " A young man exclaims, in reading a scene of Terence, ' What! is it not permitted us to do what the gods dare to do?' This reasoning is carried on by many young people. We learned beautiful words in our authors, but we learned more easily to commit bad actions. Intoxicated pagan masters made us drink in the cup of error, and beat us when we refused. Was there then no other means to teach us our language and to cultivate our mind?"

It would be a mistake, however, to suppose that all the fathers of the Church shared this narrow spirit. There were not wanting those who held broader and juster views, and who advocated an education that comprehended the valuable elements of heathen culture. For example, Basil the Great, of the fourth century, says: " In the combat which we have to deliver for the Church we ought to be armed with every resource, and to this end the reading of poets, historians, and orators is very useful. . . . We may compare the lessons of holy Scripture to the fruits of a tree, and the productions of pagan wisdom to the foliage which shelters the fruit and gives grace to the tree. . . . Moses cultivated his intelligence by studying the science of the Egyptians, and Daniel adorned his mind with that of the Chaldeans. . . . But there is a choice to be made among pagan authors. It is necessary to close the ear to bad reading, as Ulysses did to the seductive songs of the sirens. The habit of reading bad actions leads to doing bad acts. It is necessary to reject the shameful stories of the gods, as we are to shun the voluptuous music of the pagans."

In his old age Augustine recovered from the extreme views of his earlier years, and in his Christian Doctrine, written after he had passed three score and ten, he favored the adoption of whatever in heathen learning might be excellent and available for higher uses. He laid down the great, comprehensive principle, so often forgotten in the centuries since his day, that truth is of God wherever it may be found.

A. Monastic Schools

THE CHURCH AND EDUCATION.—During the period under consideration the Church attained to great power. Rome became the capital of a new ecclesiastical empire. It always regarded education as one of its exclusive functions. When the darkness of the barbarian invasions settled over Europe it was not indifferent to the instruction of the people. The prevalence of ignorance was lamented by not a few enlightened ecclesiastics, and the necessity of establishing schools, especially for religious instruction, was recognized. "In the year 859," says Neander, "the Council of Langres and the Council of Savonnières decreed that, wherever God raised up able men for teachers, all suitable efforts should be made to found public schools, so that the fruits of both kinds of knowledge, spiritual and secular, might grow in the Church; for it is a lamentable fact, and a most disastrous evil, that the true understanding of Scripture has already become so far lost that the lingering remains of it are now scarcely to be found."

MONASTERIES.—Under the impulse of asceticism, reenforced by the unsettled social condition of Europe, monasteries were rapidly multiplied. By the seventh century they were scattered throughout all the countries that had once composed the Roman Empire. The Benedictine order, founded in the sixth century, was the largest and most influential brotherhood. Their monasteries for long ages continued to be in many respects sources of blessing to the world. They became asylums for the oppressed; fortresses against violence; missionary stations for the conversion of heathen communities; repositories of learning; homes for the arts and sciences. They preserved and transmitted to later ages much of the learning of antiquity.

COURSE OF INSTRUCTION.—As the heathen schools had now disappeared, the monasteries engaged in educational work. Under the existing conditions it was but natural that nearly all instruction should have a theological or ecclesiastical aim. Purely secular studies were pursued only in the interests of the Church. The course of instruction in the convent or monastic schools embraced the so-called seven liberal arts, which were divided into two classes: the *trivium* included Latin grammar, dialectic or logic, and rhetoric; and the *quadrivium,* arithmetic, geometry, astronomy, and music. Reading and writing were included in grammar, and arithmetic and music were sometimes substituted for the other studies of the *trivium,* which was the first and most popular course. Seven years were devoted to the completion of the course in liberal arts.

Latin, the language of the Church, was made the basis of education, to the universal neglect of the mother-tongue. The works of the Church fathers were chiefly read, though expurgated copies of the Latin classics were used. Dialectic or logic was based on the writings of Aristotle and gave rise to a class of scholars called the schoolmen. The works of Quintilian and Cicero, or later works based upon them, were used in rhetoric. Arithmetic was imperfectly taught, importance being attached to the supposed secret properties of numbers. Geometry was taught in an abridged form, while astronomy did not differ materially from astrology. The study of music consisted chiefly in learning to chant the hymns of the Church.

RELATION TO THEOLOGY.—The relation in which these liberal studies stood to theology is clearly pointed out by Rhabanus Maurus, an educational writer of the ninth century, in his admirable treatise on the Education of the Clergy. "Grammar teaches us," he says substantially, "to understand the old poets and historians, and also to speak and write correctly. Without it one can not understand the figures and unusual modes of expression in the holy Scriptures, and consequently can not grasp the right sense of the divine Word. Even prosody should not be neglected, because so many kinds of versification occur in the Psalms; hence, industrious reading of the old heathen poets and repeated exercise in the art of poetic composition are not to be neglected. But the old poets should be previously and carefully expurgated, that nothing may remain in them that refers to love and love-affairs and the heathen gods. Rhetoric, which teaches the different kinds and principal parts of discourse, together with the rules belonging to them, is important only for such youths as have not more serious studies to pursue, and should be learned only from the holy fathers. Dialectic, on the contrary, is the queen of arts and sciences. In it reason dwells, and is manifested and developed. It is dialectic alone that can give knowledge and wisdom; it alone shows what and whence we are, and teaches us our destiny; through it we learn to know good and evil. And how necessary is it to a clergyman, in order that he may be able to meet and vanquish heretics! Arithmetic is important on account of the secrets contained in its numbers; the Scriptures also encourage its study, since they speak of numbers and measures. Geometry is necessary, because in Scripture figures of all kinds occur in the building of the ark and Solomon's temple. Music and astronomy are required in connection with divine service, which can not be celebrated with dignity and decency without music, nor on fixed and definite days without astronomy."

B. Cathedral and Parochial Schools

Besides the convent or monastic schools, there were two other classes of schools that owed their origin to the Church during the middle ages. They were the cathedral and the parochial schools. The cathedral schools, though

previously existing to some extent, received their perfected organization through Bishop Chrodegang in the
eighth century. The priests connected with each cathedral church were organized into a monastic brotherhood,
one of whose foremost duties was to establish and conduct schools. These were designed chiefly for the instruction of candidates for the priesthood, but were, at the
same time, accessible to others. The instruction in these
schools was very much the same as in the convent-schools,
embracing the seven liberal arts, but laying a little more
stress on religious subjects.

The parochial schools were established in the separate
parishes under the supervision of the priest. They were
designed to acquaint the youth with the elements of
Christian doctrine, to prepare them for intelligent par-
ticipation in public worship, and especially to introduce
them into church membership. Their function was similar to that of the catechetical schools of the primitive
Church. Reading and writing did not usually form any
part of the course of study. The discipline in these, as
in all the other schools of the middle ages, was rough
and severe, the rod being unsparingly used.

C. Charlemagne

THE HOLY ROMAN EMPIRE.—The Holy Roman Em
pire was the great secular power which throughout the
middle ages stood side by side with the ecclesiastical
power. Charlemagne may be regarded as its founder.
By his numerous conquests, which recall the prowess of
Cæsar, he extended his dominion over a large part of
Europe. In the year 800, as he was kneeling in prayer
before the high altar in St. Peter's at Rome, the pope

unexpectedly placed upon his head the crown of the Cæsars. Though this great secular power in later centuries gave rise to bitter conflicts, it was at first regarded as the ally and defender of the Church. Its office was to guard man's secular interests, as that of the latter was to guard his spiritual interests. "The pope, as vicar in matters spiritual," says Bryce, " is to lead men to eternal life; the emperor, as vicar in matters temporal, must so control them in their dealings with one another that they may be able to pursue undisturbed the spiritual life, and thereby attain the same supreme and common end of everlasting happiness." From the days of Charlemagne the empire exerted more or less influence upon the education of the middle ages.

Labors of Charlemagne.—The labors of Charlemagne for the moral and intellectual elevation of his people were intelligent and fruitful. He sought to multiply educational facilities on a large scale, and he even went so far as to contemplate the organization of a popular school system. The sphere of the parochial schools was enlarged, and the village priests were required to teach not only religion, but also reading, arithmetic, and singing.

Efforts at Reform.—In 787, acting upon the advice of Alcuin, Charlemagne made an effort to reform and improve the schools of the empire. Accordingly he published a capitulary, which says: " We esteem it useful not only that care should be exercised to live orderly and religiously in the bishoprics and monasteries entrusted to our care by the grace of God, but also that all those who by God's help are able to teach should give instruction in the sciences. For although it is better to do than to know, yet it is necessary to know in order to be able to do. . . . Hence, we admonish you not only not to neg-

10

lect the study of the sciences, but also to strive after the
ability to fathom easily and certainly the secrets of holy
Scripture.   But, since there are in the same allegories,
figures, and the like, it is evident that he will best understand them in their true spiritual sense who is well
instructed in the sciences.   Hence, let men be chosen for
such work who possess willingness and ability to learn,
and art to teach."

PALACE SCHOOL.—Charlemagne exhibited a great thirst
for knowledge, and was himself a model of diligence in
study. He invited to his court from all parts of Europe
the most distinguished scholars, of whom Alcuin, of England, the most learned man of his time, is best known.
With these he maintained interesting and intimate relations, presiding at their assemblies and sharing in their
discussions. He established a model school at court, and
sometimes visited it in person to note the progress of the
pupils.   It is related of him that he once placed the
diligent pupils on his right, and the idle ones on his left;
and, when he found that the latter were chiefly sons of
noble parents, he addressed them thus: " Because you are
rich and the sons of noblemen you think that your riches
and birth are enough, and that you have no need of those
studies which would do you so much honor. You think
only of dress, play, and pleasure; but I tell you that I
attach no importance to this nobility and wealth which
bring you consideration; and, if you do not speedily make
up by assiduous study for the time you have lost in
frivolity, never will you obtain anything from Charles."

RESULTS.—The efforts of Charlemagne were not un-
availing.   A general interest and activity in education
were stimulated throughout the empire. A letter of
Theodulf, Bishop of Orleans, gives us an interesting

glimpse into the character of at least some of the schools established at this time. Having received his promotion at the hands of Charles, the bishop was especially active in carrying out the wishes of his sovereign. "Let the priests," he says, "hold schools in the towns and villages, and if any of the faithful wish to entrust their children to them for the learning of letters let them not refuse to receive and teach such children. Moreover, let them teach them from pure affection, remembering that it is written, 'the wise shall shine as the splendor of the firmament,' and 'they that instruct many in righteousness shall shine as the stars forever and forever.' And let them exact no price from the children for their teaching, nor receive anything from them, save what their parents may offer voluntarily and from affection."

D. Secular Education

Two Directions.—In the latter half of the middle ages secular education came into prominence. It assumed two directions: the one was the offspring of chivalry, and may be termed *knightly education;* the other arose from the business necessities of the cities, and may be termed *burgher* or *town education.* These secular tendencies were in part a reaction against the one-sided religious character of the ecclesiastical schools, and in part the natural product of peculiar social conditions. What these conditions were will now be examined.

Classes of Society.—Society during the middle ages may be divided into three classes: ecclesiastics, embracing the clergy and monks; warriors, including the nobles and knights; and producers, comprehending mechanics, tradesmen, and peasants. During a great part of the middle ages the ecclesiastics exerted a strict domination over the other two classes, holding in their hands, as they did, the keys of knowledge and salvation. The pope assumed absolute temporal as well as absolute spiritual dominion. Opposition to the Church was punished with excommunication; sometimes with the interdict which forbade the exercise of every religious function within a given territory; and, in extreme cases, with the crusade, which exposed whole provinces to utter destruction.

EFFECT OF CRUSADES.—With the crusades, during which great multitudes rushed with fanatical zeal to the Holy Land to rescue the sepulcher of our Lord from Mohammedan hands, there began a noteworthy change in the social relations of Europe. The crusades, though at an almost incredible cost of life, contributed largely to the progress of civilization. They enlarged the contracted sphere of human knowledge. Foreign lands, and new customs, sciences, and arts were introduced into the circle of popular thought. The knightly class was brought into a new importance, was largely increased in numbers, and admirably ennobled in its aims. The crusades led to the emancipation of many serfs, and elevated them to the rank of free peasants. They quickened commerce, trade, and manufacture; increased and strengthened the burgher class; and extended the power and influence of the cities. The knightly and burgher classes attained to a feeling of self-consciousness and independence. They emancipated themselves, to some extent at least, from ecclesiastical tutelage, and this naturally led to a change in education.

E. Knightly Education

ITS CONTRAST.—Knightly education stood in the sharpest contrast with that of the Church. It attached importance to what the Church schools neglected and condemned. Physical culture received great attention; polished manners were carefully cultivated; and a love of glory was constantly instilled. Women were held in worshipful regard as the embodiment of honor and virtue. The native tongue was cultivated. Nature was not made to stand in unnatural opposition to spiritual interests, but, on the contrary, inspired the noblest sentiments and purest joys.

THREE PERIODS.—Knightly education was usually divided into three equal periods. For the first seven years the young candidate for knighthood remained in the paternal castle under the care of his mother. After that age he was usually sent to live as a page with some friendly knight, where, in constant attendance upon the chatelaine or her lord, he learned music, chess, and knightly manners. At fourteen he was made squire or attendant, and his physical and military education became more exacting. Everywhere, in the pleasures of the chase, the excitement of tournaments, and the dangers of battle, he was the faithful companion of his master. Having proved himself worthy during a long probationary period, the young squire, at the age of twenty-one, was formally elevated, with solemn and imposing ceremonies, to the knightly order. After a season of fasting and prayer, and the celebration of the Lord's Supper, he took the vow to speak the truth, defend the right, honor womankind, and use his sword against the infidels of the East; and then he received, at the hand of a knight or noble lady, his spurs, gauntlets, and suit of armor.

MUSIC AND POETRY.—Such was the education of the knight. Almost the sole intellectual element entering into it was music and poetry. At one time this was very prominent, and one of the richest literary treasures coming down to us from the middle ages is the large collection of knightly songs comprehended under the term *Minne*, or love-poetry. These songs were employed, during the long nights of winter or the prevalence of stormy weather and deep snows, to relieve the monotony of life within the castle walls. The newspaper, works of fiction, theatrical or literary entertainments, and highly developed music—the great resources of modern life against *ennui* —were then wanting. Apart from tales of adventure and a few rude games, minstrelsy was the only resource left the company of the castle. Accordingly, they were accustomed to gather at night in the principal hall around the great log-fire; and as the men sat by their ale-cups or worked at replenishing their quivers, and the ladies apart stitched their embroidery, some knight, perhaps one just welcomed to friendly shelter, took up the lute, and, with rude accompaniment, poured forth song after song, or related by the hour his rhythmical tales.

F. Burgher Schools

The growth of the cities and the increasing power of the trading and artisan classes have already been noticed. With the growing importance of these two classes there came the conscious need of an education that would have immediate reference to the practical wants of life. Reading, writing, and arithmetic were indispensable. Out of this need arose a class of schools which have borne different names, as town, burgher, or writing schools. In addition to the elementary studies just mentioned, geography, history, and natural science were pursued, in a small way, in connection with the mother-tongue. Latin

also was early introduced. Notwithstanding the fact that
the burgher schools were secular institutions, both in
origin and aim, the clergy as the only authorized teachers
claimed the right to control them. This claim, which
was often resisted by the civil magistrates, frequently
occasioned strife, in which sometimes the one party and
sometimes the other was successful. Where the civil
authorities maintained ascendency, they appointed teachers whose duties were prescribed by a contract. The
principal teachers, who were engaged for one year at a
time, employed and paid their assistants. The salaries
were so small that they barely sufficed to procure the
necessaries of life. The teachers generally led a wandering life, moving from city to city in search of employment. The itinerant teacher, known as bacchant or vag-
rant, was sometimes accompanied by a crowd of pupils
called A B C shooters, whose habits of purloining fowls
and other articles of food did not contribute to their
popularity nor to the elevation of the profession of teaching. As there were no schoolhouses at this period,
instruction was given in churches, municipal buildings,
or other houses rented for the purpose.

G. Female Education

During the middle ages female education, outside of
the knightly order, was generally neglected. Here and
there, in connection with nunneries, a few women attained
distinction by their learning, but these cases were exceptional. Among the knightly class, where women were
held in high honor, great attention was paid to female
culture. Not only were the young women instructed in
the feminine arts of sewing, knitting, embroidery, and

housekeeping, but they also received an intellectual training which, in addition to reading and writing, often included an extended acquaintance with Latin.

PEASANT CLASS.—The peasant class, during all this period, were almost entirely neglected. The only provision made for their instruction was in the parochial schools, which were devoted almost exclusively, as we have seen, to religious instruction. The peasants were indeed wanting in the educational impulse. They failed to see how education would help them in their drudging toil, and hence were not responsive to any effort for their intellectual improvement.

H. Methods and Discipline

The teacher, as a rule, was a stern taskmaster. The principle of authority naturally prevailed in instruction. The teachers read or lectured, dictated or explained, while the pupils listened, wrote, and memorized, in order afterward to reproduce their lessons. There was no encouragement to independent thought or investigation. The discipline was generally severe, and even slight offenses called forth rude chastisement. Unquestioning obedience was exacted from the pupil. A poem of the time expressed the prevailing sentiment and practise:

> Who spares the rod with spirit mild,
> He surely hates and harms his child.
> Stripes and fear are right;
> But who disowns their might,
> And trains his son in tender way,
> Unfits him for life's earnest fray.

I. Brethren of the Common Life

CHARACTER OF THE ORDER.—In the fourteenth century a brotherhood, founded by Gerhard Groot, and known as Hieronymians, or Brethren of the Common Life, devoted themselves to the work of education, with special reference to the poorer classes. Without assuming monastic vows, the members of this brotherhood led a life of purity, and labored with unselfish devotion for the good of others. Establishing a community of goods, they supported themselves by the work of their own hands, especially by the transcribing of the Scriptures and Church fathers. By its pure and self-sacrificing life the brotherhood rapidly grew in popular favor, was extensively patronized, received papal recognition and protection, and soon spread over the northern part of Germany. It maintained its existence till the sixteenth century.

RELIGIOUS EDUCATION.—Special emphasis was laid on religious education. " Spend no time," said the founder, " either on geometry, arithmetic, rhetoric, logic, grammar, poetry, or astrology. All these branches Seneca rejects; how much more, then, should a spiritually-minded Christian pass them by, since they subserve in no respect the life of faith! Of the sciences of the pagans, their ethics may not be so scrupulously avoided, since this was the special field of the wisest of them, as Socrates and Plato. That which does not improve a man, or, at least, does not reclaim him from evil, is positively hurtful. Neither ought we to read pagan books, nor indeed the Holy Scriptures, in order merely to penetrate into the mysteries of Nature by that means." Practically, however, the order departed considerably from this religious narrowness, and devoted itself not simply to the elementary instruction of the people, but also to the higher education.   Though suffusing their instruction with a spirit of genuine piety, the Brethren later became friendly to the revival of learning, and counted among their pupils Erasmus and Luther.

J. Mohammedan Learning

Not only the crusades and the growth of cities, but also the spread of Mohammedanism, contributed to the intellectual elevation of Europe. This militant faith, with its fundamental declaration, " There is but one God, and Mohammed is his prophet," was, in the seventh and eighth centuries, carried by force of arms over large portions of Asia, Africa, and Europe. Empires were established, in which learning kept pace with political power. The caliphs of Cordova and Bagdad became rivals in their patronage of learning, no less than in political power and ostentatious luxury.   The writings of the Greeks, especially those of Aristotle and Euclid, were translated into Arabic from Syriac versions. Flourishing schools were established in all the principal cities, notably at Bagdad and Damascus, in the East, and at Cordova, Salamanca, and Toledo, in the West.   Here grammar, mathematics, astronomy, philosophy, chemistry and medicine were pursued with great ardor and success. The Arabians originated chemistry, discovering alcohol, and nitric and sulphuric acids. They gave algebra and trigonometry their modern forms, applied the pendulum to the reckoning of time, repeated the Greek experiments that ascertained the size of the earth by measuring a degree, and made catalogues of the stars. For a time, they were the intellectual leaders of Europe. Their schools in Spain were largely attended by Christian youth from other European countries, who carried back with them to their homes the Arabian science, and through it stimulated intellectual activity in Christian nations. In the eleventh century, having imparted its intellectual treasures to the Christian world, Arabian learning began to decline, and has since fallen into utter insignificance.

K. Rise of the Universities

FREE ASSOCIATIONS.—The richest fruit of the newly-awakened scientific spirit in Europe was the founding of the universities. They arose independently of both Church and State. In the beginning they consisted of free associations of learned men and aspiring youths, who were held together alone by their mutual interest in science. In this way the University of Bologna had its origin in the twelfth century for the study of law, and the University of Salerno shortly afterward for the study of medicine. Toward the close of the twelfth century the University of Bologna numbered no less than twelve thousand students, most of whom came from distant countries. During this century the cathedral school of Paris was enlarged into a university, in which the study of theology was predominant. This became the most distinguished seat of learning in Europe, and at one time was attended by more than twenty thousand students.

A NEED OF THE TIME.—The universities answered a deep need of the time. Had it been otherwise, neither papal nor royal patronage would have been able to gather in them such multitudes of eager students. The universities afforded an intellectual freedom not enjoyed elsewhere, and hence they multiplied and flourished to a degree that may well put more enlightened times to shame. By the end of the fifteenth century there were nearly eighty universities in different parts of Europe, attended by thousands of students.

SPECIAL PRIVILEGES.—The members of the universities enjoyed substantially the same immunities and privileges that were extended to the clergy. They were exempt from every form of taxation; they were absolved from all military service; and in case of legal processes, they were entitled to special courts. In 1158 Frederick Barbarossa, in the imperial constitution promulgated at the Diet of Roncaglia, says in special reference to the masters and students of Bologna: " We will that the students, and above all the professors of divine and sacred laws, may be able to establish themselves and dwell in entire security in the cities where the study of letters is practised. It is fitting that we should shelter them from all harm. Who would not have compassion on these men who exile themselves through love of learning, who expose themselves to a thousand dangers, and who, far from their kindred and their families, remain defenseless among persons who are sometimes of the vilest?"

PAPAL PATRONAGE.—The universities enjoyed the patronage of the papacy. As the learning of the time was largely devoted to the exposition and defence of theology, the universities were regarded as handmaids of the Church. The spirit of free investigation had not yet reached a point that endangered the authority or power of the hierarchy. In 1331, in the bull founding the University of Cahor, John XXII says: " After having considered how precious is the gift of wisdom and knowledge, and how desirable it is to possess them, since by them the shadows of ignorance are dissipated and the obscurities of error dispelled, because they permit the curious intelligence of mortals to order and dispose their acts in the light of truth, . . . we desire ardently, and with all our heart, that the study of letters should everywhere flourish and be increasingly developed." In 1422 Martin V declared, in founding the University of Dôle, in Burgundy, that " by the study of letters the worship of divine things increases and the Catholic faith is fortified."

ROYAL PATRONAGE.—Kings and princes, in lending their patronage to universities, were animated by the same considerations of utility. They looked upon these schools of higher learning as instruments of renown and civic virtue. As the popes fostered them to make good churchmen, the princes supported them to make good subjects. Not infrequently they became bulwarks of royal power, and in the conflicts of kings with the pope, they sided with the former. When Frederick Barbarossa accorded recognition to the University of Bologna, in 1158, he justified the protection he promised to teachers and students by saying that " their science illuminated the entire world, and that, thanks to it, subjects learned how to live in obedience to God, and to the emperors, who are the ministers of God."

ORGANIZATION.—The universities were thoroughly organized. At the head of each university was the chancellor, who was ordinarily appointed by the pope, and who watched over the general interests of the institution. Next to him in authority was the rector, to whom the deans of the different faculties were responsible for the work done in their departments. The professors were divided into the four faculties of philosophy, theology, medicine, and law, which have since been retained in universities, though the studies in each department have been greatly extended.

For the purpose of better government, the vast throngs of students were divided into different bodies, according to nationality. These different bodies had special buildings called halls and colleges, in which they lodged and boarded under official supervision. The payment of tuition fees was at first a voluntary matter, but late in the thirteenth century a fixed sum was required.

METHOD AND SPIRIT.—The lecture system, either by dictation or oral discourse, was the general method employed in university instruction. There was no real spirit of free, untrammeled inquiry. The principle of authority prevailed in the universities as in the Church. Books, not things, were studied; and from the dictum of the professor there was no appeal. " Men preferred," says the Dictionnaire de Pédagogie, " to keep on repeating, mechanically and laboriously, paraphrases scrutinized a hundred times already; to close their eyes to the realities of the world in order to concentrate, and at the same time to squander, on certain pages of marvellously bad Latin, prodigious efforts of attention." Furthermore, the practise of disputation, which formed an important feature of university life, was greatly abused. It was employed, not in the honest search or determination of truth, but in sharpening the wit and displaying dialectic skill. It became an intellectual fencing match, and was resorted to in season and out of season.

DEGREES.—The principal degrees, which are now used to mark the conclusion of the several courses of study, date from the thirteenth century. In the schools of antiquity we hear nothing of examinations or conferring of degrees. The idea appears to have been borrowed from the trade guilds of the middle ages, which recognized three grades, namely, *apprentice, assistants, or companions* and *masters.* The bachelor's degree, which was conferred after an examination and public disputation, marked the conclusion of a period of severe labor and mental discipline. This degree began with the faculty of philosophy or arts, but was afterwards extended to law, medicine and theology. The degree of *licentiate* followed a special test by way of examination or disputation. The conferring of the mastership and doctorate, which was attended with a good deal of ceremony, prepared the candidate to fill a professor's chair.

UNIVERSITY LIFE.—The university life of the middle ages naturally had its good and its bad side. A sense of equality prevailed among the student body; a strong *esprit de corps,* especially among the students of the same nation, existed, and the relations between teacher and student were intimate and cordial. There was at times an absorbing devotion to study, so that Petrarch was able to exclaim in reference to his school life at Montpellier, " What tranquillity reigned there ! What peace ! " But this ideal condition of things was rather exceptional, and the records of university life in the middle ages are filled with descriptions of riot and tumult. Sometimes the students of different faculties, as those of law and medicine, were hostile to one another; and the bad feeling, which frequently existed between the students and the citizens of the town, sometimes led to disorder and bloodshed. The moral tone was very low, and fighting, gambling, and rowdyism of every sort, were not infrequent. " The students," say the Vienna statutes, " shall not spend more time in drinking, fighting, and guitar-playing, than at physics, logic, and the regular courses of lectures; and they shall not get up public dances in the streets. Quarrelers, wanton persons, drunkards, those that go about serenading at night, or who spend their leisure in following after lewd women; thieves, those that insult citizens, players at dice—having been properly warned and not reforming, besides the ordinary punishment provided by law for those misdemeanors, shall be deprived of their academical privileges and expelled." These prohibitions give us a clear insight into the university life of the time, for it was not worse at Vienna than at Paris and elsewhere.

L. Summary

Education in this period did not have a complete and beautiful development. It was unworthily enslaved to other interests, and both in theory and practise it showed its servile condition. Yet the long, dark period of the middle ages was not without blessings for mankind. It was the winter that gathers strength for the blossoming of spring and the fruit-bearing of summer. The foundations of future progress were laid. The Germanic nations were placed in possession of Christianity and civilization. One-sided tendencies worked themselves out, and have since remained for the instruction of our race. The work of this period was largely negative. If the middle ages have not taught us what to do in education, they have at least showed us a good deal to avoid. And, as the history of our race proves, this negative work has always to be done before humanity makes any signal progress. Heathenism had to exhaust its intellectual strength before the world was ready to accept Christianity.

IV

EDUCATION FROM THE RISE OF PROTESTANTISM TO THE PRESENT TIME

GENERAL SURVEY.—The Protestant movement of the sixteenth century was not an isolated event. There were many concurring circumstances which prepared the way for it, and gave it power in the world. Toward the end of the middle ages there was a remarkable growth of national life and of national feeling. The great inventions and discoveries of the fourteenth and fifteenth centuries exerted a favorable influence upon the intellectual development of Europe. The invention of gunpowder, as soon as it led to the use of firearms, helped to bring about a salutary change in the organization of society. It destroyed the military prestige of the knightly order, brought the lower classes into greater prominence, and contributed to the abolition of serfdom. The discovery of America, and of a sea-passage to the East Indies, enlarged the circle of knowledge. Correct views of the earth supplanted the Ptolemaic system. The commercial activity of the world began to move in new directions, and to assume enlarged proportions. The invention of printing, about the middle of the fifteenth century, supplanted the tedious and costly method of copying books by hand, multiplied the sources of knowledge, and brought them within the reach of a larger circle of readers. All these circumstances, to which must be added the revival of classical learning, were so many levers that cooperated in lifting the world to a higher intellectual plane.

11

1. THE REVIVAL OF LEARNING AND THE HUMANISTS

ORIGIN.—The revival of learning was so intimately related to the Reformation, and to the educational advancement dating from that time, that it calls for consideration in some detail. It had its beginning in Italy. The three great Italian writers of the fourteenth century—Dante, Boccaccio, and Petrarch—may be regarded as its pioneers. Dante was familiar with the Latin classics, and in the Inferno it is Virgil who serves him as guide. Boccaccio was distinguished for his scholarship. He was zealous in collecting books and manuscripts, and is said to have been the first Italian who imported a copy of the Iliad and the Odyssey from Greece. Petrarch was a zealous student of Latin and Greek antiquity. He traveled through Italy, France, Spain, and Germany in search of manuscripts, some of which he copied with his own hand. In 1396, Manuel Chrysoloras, a native Greek, was appointed teacher by the city of Florence, where he introduced the literary treasures of his country through public lectures.

A NEW IMPULSE.—Though there had previously been, as we have just seen, a turning of thought to Roman and Greek antiquity, the movement received a mighty impulse in 1453, when the capture of Constantinople by the Turks drove many Greek scholars to Italy. The way had been prepared for them in the revived interest in Greek learning. They were accordingly welcomed by noble patronage, and under its fostering care became for a time the teachers of Christian Europe. The interest in antiquity deepened into enthusiasm. Libraries were founded and manuscripts collected with great ardor. Several of the popes, without suspecting danger, became generous patrons of ancient learning: Nicholas V founded the celebrated Vatican Library, and collected for it a large number of Greek and Latin manuscripts; and under Leo X Rome became a center of classical scholarship.

EXPANSION OF THE MOVEMENT.—But this new movement was not to be confined to Italy. Eager scholars from England, France, and Germany sat at the feet of Italian masters in order afterward to bear beyond the Alps the precious seed of the new culture. During the reign of Lorenzo de Medici, several Oxford students, among whom were Linacre and Grocyn, visited Florence to complete their studies. Linacre received instruction along with Lorenzo's own children, one of whom afterward became Leo X. Returning to England, they gave a fresh impulse to the study of the Greek language and literature. German scholars, like Peter Luder and Samuel Karoch, introduced the new learning into the German universities. Various cities—Strasburg, Nuremberg, Augsburg, and others—became centers of culture, where literature and art were pursued with engrossing ardor.

DIFFERENT RESULTS.—The revival of learning did not everywhere follow the same lines of development and produce similar results. In Italy classical learning became an end in itself; and hence, while enlarging and refining culture, it tended to paganize its adherents. Ardor for antiquity became intoxication; Athens was reproduced in Christian Rome. Unbelief became so prevalent that the Tenth Lateran Council judged it advisable to reaffirm the doctrine of the immortality of the soul by a special decree.

Among the Teutonic nations, particularly in Germany,

Holland, and England, the revival of learning produced far more salutary results than in Italy. The deep moral earnestness of the Teutonic race preserved it from pagan debasement. After a time the new learning was cultivated with as much zeal north as south of the Alps, but its results were utilized in the interests of a purer Christianity. The Greek and Hebrew Scriptures were studied as well as the Latin and Greek classics. Critical editions of the Old and New Testaments were published by able scholars, and by this means, as many believed, theological dogma was placed on a more assured foundation.

A. Agricola

BIOGRAPHICAL FACTS.—This able scholar, the father of German humanism, was born in 1443 near Groningen, Germany. His real name was Husmann (that is, houseman or husbandman), which, according to a custom of the humanists, he Latinized into Agricola. For a time he was a pupil of Thomas à Kempis; then he passed several years at the University of Louvain; subsequently he studied at Paris, and afterward in Italy, where he attended lectures by the most celebrated literary men of the age. His learning and eloquence gave him a wide reputation; and, upon his return to Germany, several cities and courts vied with one another in the effort to secure his services. At length, upon the solicitation of Dalberg, Bishop of Worms, who was an old and intimate friend, he established himself at Heidelberg. He divided his time between private studies and public lecturing; and, through his labors and influence, he was largely instrumental in transplanting the learning of Italy into his native land. He understood French and Italian, and set great store by his mother-tongue. At the age of forty-one he began the study of Hebrew, in order to be able to read the Old Testament in the original.

OPINION OF SCHOOLS.—Agricola did not have a high opinion of the average school of his time. Having been called to take charge of a school at Antwerp, he wrote: " A school is to be committed to me. That is a difficult and vexatious thing. A school is like a prison, in which there are blows, tears, and groans without end. If there is anything with a contradictory name, it is the school. The Greeks named it *schola*—that is, leisure; the Latins, *ludus literarius*—literary play; but there is nothing further from leisure than the school, nothing harder and more opposed to play. More correctly did it receive from Aristophanes the name *phrontizerion*—that is, place of care."

SELECTING A TEACHER.—Agricola did not accept the school offered him at Antwerp, but in declining gave the authorities there the following advice: " It is necessary to exercise the greatest care in choosing a director for your school. Take neither a theologian nor a so-called rhetorician, who thinks he is able to speak of everything without understanding anything of eloquence. Such people make in school the same figure, according to the Greek proverb, that a dog does in a bath. It is necessary to seek a man resembling Phœnix, the tutor of Achilles; that is, who knows how to teach, to speak, and to act at the same time. If you know such a man, get him at any price; for the matter involves the future of your children, whose tender youth receives with the same susceptibility the impress of good and of bad examples."

EMPTY ELOQUENCE.—He thought little of the eloquence which so many students were striving after and which subsequently became still more prominent in education. " Very many devote themselves," he says, " to those phrase-mongering and empty discussions, which people frequently take for wisdom. They waste the day in refined and tedious disputations, and, to use a fitting expression, in riddles, which in the course of centuries have found no Œdipus to solve them, and will find none. With this sort of learning they torture the ears of their pitiable youths. To such nourishment they drive their students, as it were, by force. Thus they destroy promising talent, and kill the fruit in the bud."

To give fluency and worth to discourse, Agricola recommended the study of the best authors with translations into the mother tongue. "It will be very useful to you," he says in writing to a friend, "to express in the most fitting words of the mother tongue all that you read in the classic authors. For through this exercise you will bring it about that, when you must write or speak anything, you will in meditating the subjects, at once associate the Latin expressions with idioms of the mother tongue. Further, when you wish to express anything in writing, it is to be recommended that you conceive of the matter fully and correctly in the mother tongue, and then express it in pure and appropriate Latin. In this way the exposition will be clear and exhaustive." Grace of style seemed to him a matter of secondary consideration.

METHOD OF STUDY.—As to methods of study, he expressed himself very clearly and forcibly. "Whoever in the acquisition of a science," he says, "wishes to obtain results answerable to his trouble, must especially consider three things. He must clearly and correctly *apprehend, faithfully retain* in memory what he has apprehended, and put himself in a position, by means of what he has learned, to *produce* something of himself. Therefore, the first requisite is careful reading, the second a trustworthy memory, and the third continued practise." In reading he held it necessary to understand the scope as well as the details of books. " Nevertheless, it is not well to spend too much time in clearing up obscurities; one often finds elucidation further on. One day gives light to another."

THE STUDY OF PHILOSOPHY.—Agricola recommended especially the study of philosophy, in which he included ethics and physics. " If you cherish the correct idea," he writes, " that what is noble is to be sought for its own sake, then I advise you to turn to philosophy, that is, to give yourself the trouble to gain a correct knowledge of all subjects and the ability to give fitting expression to what you have learned. Now knowledge, just as the nature of the things that form its object, is twofold. The one department aims at our acts and morals. Upon it rests the whole theory of a righteous and well-ordered life. It detaches from the trunk of philosophy the science of ethics, and deserves very especially our attention. But we need not seek it alone with the philosophers who treat it as a branch of literature, as Aristotle, Cicero, Seneca, and others, but also with the historians, poets, and orators. They by no means teach ethics systematically, but they show—and that is precisely the most effective teaching— through praise of the good, through censure of the bad, and through the presentation of examples, virtue and its opposite, as it were, in a mirror. Through a reading of these authors one should pass on to the Holy Scripture. For according to its precepts, one must order his life, and trust it as an experienced guide in matters of the soul's salvation." The study of natural philosophy seemed to him less important. Though not strictly necessary in the development of a morally good man, it is still favorable to virtue. " For when a genuine interest for scientific investigation has once laid hold of a man, there is no longer room in his soul for common and ignoble pursuits."

B. Reuchlin

BIOGRAPHICAL FACTS.—One of the greatest representatives of the new learning was Reuchlin, who was born at Pforzheim, Germany, in 1455. At the age of eighteen he went to Paris, where he studied under a native Greek. After leaving Paris, he taught Latin and Greek at Basel, and subsequently became a professor at Tübingen. He resided for a time at Heidelberg, and in the interests of Greek scholarship issued several elementary text-books of Greek, which were used in Germany for many years. Melanchthon, the distinguished scholar and reformer, was his nephew and adopted son.

HEBREW STUDIES.—But Reuchlin's studies were not confined to the Latin and Greek classics. He took a profound interest in the Hebrew language, and is justly regarded as the father of Hebrew studies in Germany. In 1498 he was sent on an embassy to Rome, where he employed all his leisure in studying Hebrew under a learned Jew, and in collecting Greek and Hebrew manuscripts. The motive that urged him to prosecute his studies in Hebrew is explained in a letter to Cardinal Hadrian: " I devoted myself to the Hebrew language because I perceived the great value which it would have for religion and true theology. To this end I have always directed my labors, and continue to direct them more than ever. As a true worshiper of our Lord, I have done all for the restoration and glorification of the true Christian Church." On the publication of his Hebrew grammar and lexicon, in 1506, the first work of the kind prepared in Germany, he could exclaim, in the language of Horace: "I have erected a monument more durable than brass." Luther wrote him, in appreciation of his labors: "The Lord has been at work in you, that the light of Holy Scripture might begin to shine in that Germany where for so many years, alas! it was not only stifled but extinct."

A BITTER CONTROVERSY.—In the year 1510 there began in Germany a long and acrimonious controversy about Hebrew literature, in which Reuchlin became a prominent figure. A baptized Jewish rabbi, John Pfefferkorn, with the zeal of a proselyte, appealed to the Emperor Maximilian to have all Jewish books, except the Bible, destroyed. Reuchlin, having been asked to give his opinion, advised the destruction of only such books as were written against Christianity. "The best way," he added, "to convert the Israelites would be to establish two professors of the Hebrew language in each university, who should teach theologians to read the Bible in Hebrew, and thus refute the Jewish doctors." This attitude brought upon Reuchlin a most virulent attack from the Dominican friars of Cologne. The controversy became general. The friends of learning naturally rallied to the support of the great Hebrew scholar; and after a conflict of nine years, the pope, to whom the case had been appealed, decided in Reuchlin's favor.

During this controversy Erasmus wrote to Cardinal Raphael: "In supporting Reuchlin, you will earn the gratitude of every man of letters in Germany. It is to him really that Germany owes such knowledge as it has of Greek and Hebrew. He is a learned, accomplished man, respected by the Emperor, honored among his own people, and blameless in life and character. All Europe is crying shame that so excellent a person should be harassed by a detestable persecution, and all for a matter as absurd as the ass's shadow of the proverb. The princes are at peace again. Why should men of education and knowledge be still stabbing each other with poisoned pens?"

C. Erasmus

BIOGRAPHICAL.—Erasmus, born in Rotterdam in 1467, was perhaps the acutest scholar of his day. In his youth he gave promise of the eminence he afterward attained. His teacher at Deventer, who belonged to the Brethren of the Common Life, once enthusiastically embraced him with these words: "You will one day attain the highest summits of knowledge." In his youth Erasmus was persuaded to become an Augustinian monk; but finding conventual life entirely unfitted to his tastes and character, he was released by the Bishop of Cambray, and sent to the University of Paris. To eke out his meager allowance he took pupils in Greek, the elements of which he had acquired by private study. "I have given up my whole soul to Greek learning," he wrote, "and as soon as I get any money I shall buy Greek books, and then I shall buy some clothes."

At various times he visited England, France, Germany, and Italy, and everywhere his wit, learning, and fame secured him a cordial reception. In 1497 he went to England, where he met Thomas More, then a young man of twenty, heard Colet lecture at Oxford, and admired the learning of Linacre and Grocyn—all, like himself, enthusiastic humanists. "I have found in Oxford," he wrote, "so much polish and learning that now I hardly care about going to Italy at all, save for the sake of having been there. When I listen to my friend Colet, it seems like listening to Plato himself. Who does not wonder at the wide

range of Grocyn's knowledge? What can be more searching, deep, and refined than the judgment of Linacre?
When did nature mold a temper more gentle, endearing,
and happy than the temper of Thomas More?" Later he
became, for a brief period, a lecturer on Greek at the University of Cambridge. Henry VIII, of England, was his
friend and patron; and among his acquaintances were Pope
Julius II and Leo X.

CHIEF WORKS.—Among his best known works is the
Encomium Moriæ, or the Praise of Folly. It is a satire
upon various classes of society. But of still more importance was Erasmus's edition of the Greek New Testament,
accompanied with a Latin translation and notes. "It is my
desire," he said in the preface, "to lead back that cold
dispute about words called theology to its real fountain.
Would to God that this work may bear as much fruit to
Christianity as it has cost me toil and application." This
work, which appeared in 1516, helped to make Europe
acquainted with the Gospel as it was preached by Christ
and his apostles.

PEDAGOGY.—An enthusiastic student of the ancient
classics, the pedagogical views of Erasmus do not differ
materially from those of Plutarch, Quintilian, and Seneca.
What he has written on education appears at times a mere
paraphrase of these ancient educators. Among his educational writings may be mentioned the Adages (1500),
The Order of Studies (1512), The Education of a Christian Prince (1516), and The Institution of Christian Marriage (1526). He dwelt upon the importance of early
domestic training, during which the soil should be prepared
for subsequent instruction. The health of children should
be carefully attended to through proper food and clothing, healthful rooms, and merry companionships. By

means of plays the Greek and Roman alphabets might be learned, and through appropriate training the virtues of reverence and obedience should be developed.

INTELLECTUAL CULTURE.—Formal instruction should not begin before the seventh year. Much care should be exercised in the choice of a teacher, whose efficiency concerned not only the welfare of the child but also the welfare of the state. He reproached parents for taking more pains in the selection of a hostler than in the employment of a teacher for their children. Not only the learning of the teacher, but especially his character should be considered. During the first years of instruction private tutors seemed to Erasmus preferable to large monastic schools. In the latter the danger of moral contamination appeared to him too great, and the labors of the teacher too much divided.

As a genuine humanist, Erasmus insisted that the knowledge of words should precede the knowledge of things. Greek and Latin grammar should be studied together, for these two languages contained almost everything that is worth knowing. The rules of grammar should be few in number and restricted to what is most important; for skill in language is best acquired through conversation and reading. When a sufficient foundation in language had been laid, the pupil should turn to the study of things; and the sources of science Erasmus found in the writings of the ancient Greeks. Especial attention, he urged, should be given to the cultivation of the memory, through which the results of learning are made available. There are three principal aids to memory, namely, a right understanding of the subject, a proper order of thought, and a careful noting of distinctions. He recommended the study of geography, history, and natural science, not for their own sake, but as necessary adjuncts in understanding and explaining the classics.

IMITATION OF CICERO.—Erasmus valued thought more than style, and inveighed against the superficial imitation of Cicero then prevalent. He laughed at the verbal trifling of the grammarians, and the insignificant quibblings of the philosophers. " You are charged," he said to the Ciceronians, " with a very difficult task; for, besides the errors of language that have escaped Cicero, the copyists have sown his works with a multitude of mistakes, and many of the writings attributed to this author are not authentic. Finally, his verses translated from the Greek are worth nothing. And you would imitate all that, the good and the bad, the authentic and the non-authentic! Certainly, your imitation is very superficial; it is unworthy of your master. Your imitation is servile, cold, and dead, without life, without movement, without feeling; it is an apishness in which one discovers none of the virtues that have made the glory of Cicero, such as his happy inspiration, the intelligent disposition of his subjects, the wisdom with which he treats each subject, his large acquaintance with men and affairs, and his ability to move those who hear him. These are what should be imitated in Cicero; and, in order to imitate him, we must, like him, identify ourselves with the age in which we live, that we may be able to adapt our language to it; otherwise, our speech has no longer that seal of reality which animated the discourse of Cicero."

METHOD IN TEACHING.—Erasmus favored a mild discipline; praise and rewards, he said, accomplish more than threats and blows. The business of the teacher was to help his pupils, and not to display his own learning. Too much talk on his part was a hindrance rather than a help. " The teacher," he said, " ought to explain only what is strictly necessary for understanding the author; he ought to resist the temptation of making on every occasion a display of his knowledge. The end of this rule is to concentrate the attention of the pupil upon his author, to bring him into contact with him. Too many digressions break the force of the author, and prevent the pupil from feeling and enjoying that inspiration, so well suited to quicken him who breathes it freely."

RELIGIOUS CULTURE.—Erasmus placed moral and religious culture in the foreground of education. Throughout his writings he advocated a genuine piety of heart as over against theological refinements and religious ceremonialism. " Unless I have a pure heart," he says, " unless I put away envy, hate, pride, avarice, lust, I shall not see God. But a man is not damned because he can not tell whether the Spirit has one principle or two. Has he the fruits of the Spirit? That is the question. Is he patient, kind, good, gentle, modest, temperate, chaste? Inquire if you will, but do not define. True religion is peace, and we can not have peace unless we leave the conscience unshackled on obscure points on which certainty is impossible."

The first religious instruction should teach the child to fear and love God, the omnipresent and omniscient Creator and Upholder of all things; who through his Son has given eternal life to those who believe in him and keep his commandments; who dwells through the Holy Spirit in the hearts of the righteous; and who rewards the good and punishes the wicked. Belief in angels and reverence for the Scriptures should be inculcated. The child should be taught to contemplate the splendor of the heavens, the fulness of the earth, the welling fountains, the flowing rivers, the immeasurable sea, the numberless species of ani-

mals, an to look on all these things as created for the
service of men. The best means of inculcating morality
and religion is example, for children have a special aptitude for imitation.

FEMALE EDUCATION.—Erasmus entertained enlightened
views about female education. He maintained that girls
should have intellectual as well as moral and domestic
training. Though most persons thought it foolish, he
said, intellectual culture was advantageous in maintaining
a noble and chaste spirit. More care should be taken in
the moral training of girls than of boys. The first effort
should be to fill their hearts with holy feelings; the second,
to preserve them from contamination; the third, to guard
them from idleness. As innocence suffers most through
evil example, Erasmus admonished parents against all un-
seemly conduct in the presence of their daughters. Min-
gling in society seemed to him less dangerous for young
women than to be kept in monastic seclusion.

2. THE RELATION OF PROTESTANTISM TO EDUCATION

PREVALENT DISSATISFACTION.—The ecclesiastical revolution of the sixteenth century—that great movement
which divided the Church and established Protestantism
in northern Europe—was not due, as has been sometimes
alleged, to insignificant causes. At the beginning of the
century and for many years previously, there existed, for
various reasons that can not here be examined in detail, a profound dissatisfaction within the Church. The
growing intelligence of the people and the development of
a strong national self-consciousness tended to bring about
a reaction against ecclesiastical authority; meanwhile writ-

ers like Erasmus attacked with bitter sarcasm the schools of the church and the lives of the monks, and undermined the confidence and loyalty of a large part of the laity. The times were thus ripe for the religious revolution which almost simultaneously broke out in Germany, Switzerland, and England and changed the subsequent course of European history and education.

3. THE PROTESTANT LEADERS

A. Luther

BIOGRAPHICAL.—The greatest of these leaders, whether we consider his relation to the Protestant Church or to education, was Martin Luther. He was born of humble parentage at Eisleben, Germany, November 10, 1483. His home training was exceedingly strict in its austere piety. At the age of fourteen he was sent to the school at Magdeburg, conducted by the Brethren of the Common Life. A year later he passed to Eisenach, where, in a school conducted by the learned humanist, John Trebonius, his secondary training was completed. In 1501 he entered the University of Erfurt, which, unlike many other universities of the day, had welcomed the study of the Latin and Greek classics. After taking the Master's degree in 1505, he entered the Augustinian convent of mendicant friars at Erfurt, where he passed through a profound religious experience. In 1507 he was ordained to the priesthood, and a year later was called to the newly founded University of Wittenberg, where he lectured first on Aristotle and then on the Scriptures. In 1511 he made a journey to Rome on some mission connected with the Augustinian order. On the 31st of October, 1517, in opposition to John Tetzel, who was distributing indulgences throughout Germany,

Luther nailed his famous Ninety-five Theses to the door
of the Castle Church at Wittenberg. This event, which
led to the subsequent conflict with the papacy, is commonly regarded as the beginning of the Protestant movement.

INTEREST IN EDUCATION.—The necessities of Protestantism gave Luther an intense interest in education.
Apart from frequent discussions of the subject in other
writings, he prepared two treatises which exhibit great
breadth of view and a marvelous energy of expression. The
first of these is a Letter to the Mayors and Aldermen of the
Cities of Germany in Behalf of Christian Schools, which
was written in 1524, and the second a Sermon on the Duty
of Sending Children to School, which was prepared in 1530.
These treatises touch on nearly every important phase of
education, and are admirable in their statement of principles and suggestion of methods. The commendation
of Dittes is not unmerited. " If we survey the pedagogy
of Luther in all its extent," he says, " and imagine it fully
realized in practise, what a splendid picture the schools
and education of the sixteenth century would present! We
should have courses of study, text-books, teachers, methods,
principles, and modes of discipline, schools and school
regulations, that could serve as models for our own age.
But, alas! Luther, like all great men, was little understood by his age and adherents; and what was understood
was inadequately esteemed, and what was esteemed was
only imperfectly realized."

METHOD OF INSTRUCTION.—Luther's practical insight
led him to discourage ungentle methods of instruction.
His attitude toward children was one of tenderness and
sympathy. As a means of fixing truth in the childish
mind, he recommended simplicity and repetition. In pre-

12

senting a truth or principle, the child should not be confused by a needless variety of expression. There should be no undue haste in teaching. "Allow ample time for the lessons," he says in reference to his catechism. " For it is not necessary that you should, on the same occasion, proceed from the beginning to the end of the several parts." Naturally Luther insisted on thoroughness; and the practical duties of religion were to pass from the memory into conduct. The Seventh Commandment, for example, he would have enforced with the utmost earnestness upon those who might be inclined to theft or dishonesty.

END OF EDUCATION.—With Luther education was not an end in itself, but a means to more effective service in Church and State. If people or rulers neglect the education of the young, they inflict an injury on the cause of Christ and on the weal of the commonwealth; they advance the cause of Satan, and bring down upon themselves the curse of heaven. This is the fundamental thought that underlies all Luther's writings on education. " The common man," he says, " does not think that he is under obligation to God and the world to send his son to school. Every one thinks that he is free to bring up his son as he pleases, no matter what becomes of God's word and command. Yea, even our rulers act as if they were exempt from the divine command. No one thinks that God has earnestly willed and commanded that children be brought up to his praise and work—a thing that can not be done without schools. On the contrary, every one hastens with his children after worldly gain, as if God and Christianity needed no pastors and preachers, and the State no chancellors, councilors, and scribes."

In his letter to the mayors of the German cities, Luther

says: " But even if there were no soul, and we had not the least need of schools and the languages for the sake of the Scriptures and of God, this one reason should suffice to cause the establishment of the very best schools everywhere, both for boys and girls, namely, that the world needs accomplished men, and women also, for maintaining its outward temporal prosperity, so that the men may be capable of properly governing the country and people, and the women of superintending the house, children, and servants. Now, such men must come of boys, and such women of girls; therefore, the object must be rightly to instruct and educate boys and girls for these purposes."

CIVIL GOVERNMENT.—As already indicated, Luther placed great emphasis on the importance and sanctity of the State. In his Sermon on the Duty of Sending Children to School, he says: " Civil government is a beautiful and divine ordinance, an excellent gift of God, who ordained it, and who wishes to have it maintained as indispensable to human welfare; without it men could not live together in society, but would devour one another like the irrational animals. . . . It is the function and honor of civil government to make men out of wild animals, and to restrain them from degenerating into brutes. It protects every one in family, so that the members may not be wronged; it protects every one in body, house, lands, cattle, property, so that they may not be attacked, injured, or stolen." `

COMPULSORY EDUCATION.—It is not strange that Luther, holding the views just presented, should advocate compulsory education. He maintained that the sovereign had a right to compel towns and villages to maintain schools, and likewise to require parents to send their children. In his Sermon on the Duty of Sending Children to

School, he says: " I maintain that the civil authorities are under obligation to compel the people to send their children to school, especially such as are promising. For our rulers are certainly bound to maintain the spiritual and secular offices and callings, so that there may always be preachers, jurists, pastors, scribes, physicians, schoolmasters, and the like; for these can not be dispensed with. If the government can compel such citizens as are fit for military service to bear spear and rifle, to mount ramparts and perform other martial duties in time of war, how much more has it a right to compel the people to send their children to school, because in this case we are warring with the devil, whose object it is secretly to exhaust our cities and principalities of their strong men, to destroy the kernel and leave a shell of ignorant and helpless people, whom he can sport and juggle with at pleasure. That is starving out a city or country, destroying it without a struggle, and without its knowledge."

DOMESTIC TRAINING.—Luther cherished a beautiful ideal of domestic life. Marriage should be honored as a divine institution—the source of the sweetest earthly pleasures. The family occupies a fundamental relation to both civil and divine government, since it has the training of the future citizen and servant of God. Children are to be regarded as a precious gift of God, and their training should be conducted in wisdom and love. The parents should in all things set an example of upright living; and as long as the children are under parental control, they should be held to respect, love, and obedience. " A principality," Luther said, " is a collection of districts and duchies, a kingdom a collection of principalities, an empire a collection of kingdoms. These are all composed of separate families. Where now father and mother govern badly, and let children have their own way, there can neither city, town, village, district, principality, kingdom, nor empire be well and peacefully governed. For the son will become a father, judge, mayor, prince, king, emperor, preacher, schoolmaster; if he has been badly brought up, the subjects will become like their master, the members like their head."

Again he says: " But this is another sad evil, that all live on as though God gave us children for our pleasure or amusement, and servants that we should employ them like a cow or donkey, only for work, or as though all we had to do with our subjects were only to gratify our wantonness, without any concern on our part as to what they learn or how they live; and no one is willing to see that this is the command of the supreme Majesty, who will most strictly call us to an account and punish us for it, nor that there is no great need to be intensely anxious about the young. For if we wish to have proper and excellent persons both for civil and ecclesiastical government, we must spare no diligence, time, or cost in teaching and educating our children, that they may serve God and the world, and we must not think only how we may amass money and possessions for them. . . . Let every one know, therefore, that above all things it is his d- .y (for otherwise he will lose the divine favor) to _.ing up his children in the fear and knowledge of God; and if they have talents, to have them instructed and trained in a liberal education, that men may be able to have their aid in government and in whatever is necessary."

RELIGIOUS TRAINING.—Luther had a profoundly religious nature. He looked upon Christianity not only as the highest interest of life, but as the basis of all worthy living. It was natural, therefore, that he should emphasize religious instruction, and make the Scriptures prominent in schools of every grade. "In schools of all kinds," he said, "the chief and most common lesson should be the Scriptures, and for young boys the Gospel; and would to God each town had also a girls' school, in which girls might be taught the Gospel for an hour daily, either in German or Latin! . . . But where the Holy Scriptures are not the rule, I advise no one to send his child." To promote this knowledge of the Scriptures, Luther translated the Bible into German, which was seized upon with such avidity that in a few years nearly half a million copies were in circulation. It became a mighty influence, not only in unifying the German language, but in uplifting the German people.

SUBJECTS OF STUDY.—Besides the Bible and the catechism, Luther's scheme of studies embraced the mother tongue, the ancient languages, rhetoric and logic, history, natural science, music, and gymnastics. In determining a course of study, he was guided by considerations of practical utility. In the study of language he distinguished between the knowledge of words and the knowledge of things. "Knowledge," he said, "is of two kinds—one of words, and the other of things. Whoever has no knowledge of the things will not be helped by a knowledge of the words. It is an old proverb that 'one can not speak well of what one does not understand.' Of this truth our age has furnished many examples. For many learned and eloquent men have uttered foolish and ridiculous things in speaking of what they did not understand. But whoever thoroughly understands a matter will speak wisely and reach the heart, though he may be wanting in eloquence and readiness of speech."

STUDY OF LANGUAGES.—Luther was loyal to his native language. He introduced it into public worship, and encouraged the establishment of primary schools in which it was employed. Through his sermons, books, hymns, and especially his translation of the Bible, he gave the German language a literary form, and laid the basis of its cultivation and development. A few years after his death, John Clajus published a German grammar, in which Luther's writings were taken as the standard.

At the same time Luther set great store by the ancient languages, not indeed for their superiority as a mental gymnastic, but for their utility in the service of the Church and State. In his Letter to the Mayors of Germany he discusses the subject at great length. " In the same measure," he says, " that the Gospel is dear to us, should we zealously cherish the languages. For God had a purpose in giving the Scriptures only in two languages, the Old Testament in the Hebrew, and the New Testament in the Greek. What God did not despise, but chose before all others for his Word, we should likewise esteem above all others. . . .

" And let this be kept in mind, that we shall not preserve the Gospel without the languages. The languages are the scabbard in which the Word of God is sheathed. They are the casket in which this jewel is enshrined; the cask in which this wine is kept; the chamber in which this food is stored. And, to borrow a figure from the Gospel itself, they are the baskets in which this bread, and fish, and fragments are preserved. If through neglect we lose the languages (which may God forbid), we shall not only lose the Gospel, but it will finally come to pass that we shall lose also the ability to speak and write either Latin or German."

STUDY OF NATURE.—Luther's attitude to nature is full of interest. He was brought up in schools in which, according to the methods of the middle ages, nature was studied, not by observing the earth, air, and skies, but by perusing the works of Aristotle and Pliny. It was the reign of words, not of things. Luther's great sympathetic heart was open to the beauty of the world about him. " We are at the dawn of a new era," he said, " for we are beginning to recover the knowledge of the external world that we had lost through the fall of Adam. We now observe creatures properly, and not as formerly under the papacy. By the grace of God we already recognize in the most delicate flower the wonders of divine goodness and omnipotence. See that force display itself in the stone of a peach. It is very hard, and the germ it encloses is very tender, but when the moment has come the stone must open to let out the young plant that God calls into life. Erasmus passes by all that, takes no account of it, and looks upon external objects as cows look upon a new gate."

MUSIC AND GYMNASTICS.—Luther's fondness for music was remarkable. He desired the young to be diligently exercised in vocal and instrumental music, and insisted on musical attainments as an indispensable qualification in the teacher. In the schools that were established under Luther and his coadjutors, music formed a part of the regular course of study. It was honored not only as a useful adjunct in public worship, but also as a beneficent influence upon character and life. Luther regarded gymnastic exercises as salutary both for the body and the soul. " It was well considered and arranged by the ancients," he says, " that the people should practise gymnastics, in order that they might not fall into reveling, unchastity, gluttony, intemperance, and gaming. Therefore these two exercises and pastimes please me best, namely, music and gymnastics, of which the first drives away all care and melancholy from the heart, and the latter produces elasticity of the body and preserves the health."

ESTABLISHMENT OF LIBRARIES.—For the preservation and encouragement of learning, Luther favored the founding of public libraries. He devoted to this subject the concluding pages of his Letter to the Mayors of Germany, and his recommendations abound in practical wisdom. "No cost nor pains," he urges, "should be spared to procure good libraries in suitable buildings, especially in the large cities, which are able to afford it. For if a knowledge of the Gospel and of every kind of learning is to be preserved, it must be embodied in books, as the prophets and apostles did. This should be done, not only that our spiritual and civil leaders may have something to read and study, but also that good books may not be lost, and that the arts and languages may be preserved. . . .

"In the first place, a library should contain the Holy Scriptures in Latin, Greek, Hebrew, German, and other languages. Then the best and most ancient commentators in Greek, Hebrew, and Latin. Secondly, such books as are useful in acquiring the languages, as the poets and orators, without considering whether they are heathen or Christian, Greek or Latin. For it is from such works that grammar must be learned. Thirdly, books treating of all the arts and sciences. Lastly, books on jurisprudence and medicine, though here discrimination is necessary."

ESTIMATE OF TEACHERS.—Luther set a high estimate upon the office of teaching. "Where would preachers, lawyers, and physicians come from," he asks, "if the liberal arts were not taught? From this source must they all come. This I say, no one can ever sufficiently remunerate the industrious and pious teacher who faithfully educates children, as the heathen Aristotle has said. And yet people shamefully despise this calling among us, as if it were nothing, and at the same time they pretend to be Christians! If I were obliged to leave off preaching and other duties, there is no office I would rather have than that of school-teacher; for I know that this work is with preaching the most useful, greatest, and best: and I do not know which of the two is to be preferred. For it is difficult to make old dogs docile and old rogues pious, yet that is what the ministry works at, and must work at, in great part, in vain; but young trees, although some may break, are more easily bent and trained. Therefore, let it be one of the highest virtues on earth faithfully to educate the children of others who neglect it themselves."

CONCLUSION.—In his pedagogical writings Luther had in mind three classes of schools, which form a comprehensive system of education: (1) Schools for the common people, in which they might be fitted for the various nonprofessional callings of life; (2) Latin schools, to which he gave most prominence as the agencies of secondary instruction; and (3) the universities, which he desired to see reformed. His efforts in behalf of education were far-reaching. All Protestant Germany was aroused by his appeals. In 1525 he was commissioned by the Duke of Mansfeld to establish two schools in his native town, Eisleben, one for primary and the other for secondary instruction. Both in the course of study, and in the methods of instruction, these schools became models after which many others were fashioned. As a direct and comprehensive result of Luther's educational endeavors, the forms of Church government adopted by the various Protestant cities and states contained provisions for the establishment and management of schools. In a few years the Protestant portion of Germany was supplied with schools. They were still defective in almost every particular; but, at the same time, they were greatly superior to any that had preceded them. Though no complete system of popular instruction was established, the foundation for it was laid. To this great result Luther contributed more than any other man of his time; and this fact makes him the leading educational reformer of the sixteenth century.

B. Melanchthon

BIOGRAPHICAL.—Philip Melanchthon, who has been called the *Preceptor Germaniæ*, was born at Bretten in 1497. He received his early education from a faithful schoolmaster, who held his young pupil rigidly to grammar and punished him for mistakes with a rod. His precocity and thirst for knowledge were remarkable, and Reuchlin one day playfully brought him a doctor's hat. Melanchthon took his bachelor's degree at the University of Heidelberg at the age of fifteen. He then went to the University of Tübingen, first as a student and then as a lecturer, where he became a warm advocate of classical learning. It was here that his career as an author began; for, as early as 1516, he published an edition of Terence. A little later he prepared a Greek grammar, in which he announced " that he intended, in conjunction with a number of his friends, to edit the works of Aristotle in the original." In 1518 he accepted a call to the University of Wittenberg as professor of Greek, where he became the friend and co-laborer of Luther until the latter's death in 1546. With the possible exception of Erasmus, Melanchthon was the greatest scholar of his time.

INTEREST IN LEARNING.—During his whole life Melanchthon was a student of remarkable industry. He often arose as early as two or three o'clock in the morning to pursue his studies, and many of his works were written between that hour and dawn. The twenty-eight folio volumes of the Corpus Reformatorum that contain his works exhibit the results of his prodigious activity. Literature was his passion, and it was against his will that he was drawn into theological controversy. He earnestly desired the diffusion of learning. " I apply myself solely to one thing," he says, " the defense of letters. By our example we must excite youth to the admiration of learning, and induce them to love it for its own sake, and not for the advantage that may be derived from it. The destruction of learning brings with it ruin of everything that is good —religion, morals, and all things human and divine. The better a man is, the greater his ardor in the preservation of learning; for he knows that of all plagues ignorance is the most pernicious."

AS TEACHER.—Melanchthon exerted an influence upon the educational progress of Germany in various ways. First of all, he was an able teacher, whose instruction was largely attended. Two thousand students, from all parts of Europe, thronged his lecture-room at Wittenberg, and bore away the precious seed both of the gospel and of ancient learning. His personal relations with students were peculiarly cordial. He welcomed them to his home, and gave them individual encouragement and aid. " I can truthfully affirm," he says, " that I love all the students with a fatherly affection, and feel the greatest solicitude for their welfare."

For the benefit of the students who came to the University of Wittenberg without adequate preparation, he opened a private school in which, along with history, geography, and mathematics, the ancient languages were given special prominence. Many of the leading educators of Protestant Germany, among whom may be mentioned Camerarius, Michael Neander, and Trotzendorf, were once his students.

AUTHOR OF TEXT-BOOKS.—Melanchthon exerted a still wider influence upon education through his text-books. At the age of twenty-one, he published a Greek grammar which was used in the schools of Germany for a hundred years. His Latin grammar, in more than fifty editions, was used in all the schools of Saxony down to the beginning of the eighteenth century. He wrote also text-books on rhetoric, dialectic, ethics, and physics, and edited nearly the whole circle of ancient classics studied in the secondary schools and universities. All these works were written in a clear, scientific form, and most of them long held their place in the schools of the time. His Loci Communes, which appeared in 1521, has the distinction of being the first work on dogmatic theology produced in the Protestant Church.

SECONDARY SCHOOLS AND UNIVERSITIES.—The advice and help of Melanchthon, as an able teacher and distinguished scholar, were sought far and wide in relation to schools. We still have the correspondence between him and fifty-six cities, in which his assistance is asked in founding and conducting Latin schools and gymnasia. In many cases he wrote the basis of organization, laid out the courses of study, and nominated the principal instructors. The gymnasial course of instruction recommended by Melanchthon, which included Latin, Greek, Hebrew, rhetoric, logic, mathematics, and cosmology, remained essentially unchanged in Germany till the beginning of the nineteenth century. His influence in university instruction was scarcely less extended. He prepared the statutes by which the faculties of the University of Wittenberg were reorganized. The University of Königsberg, which was founded in 1544, and the University of Jena, which was founded in 1548, were organized according to directions given by Melanchthon. His plans were adopted also in the reorganization of the Universities of Tübingen, Leipzig, and Heidelberg. The influence thus exerted by Melanchthon on the secondary and higher education of Germany is beyond all estimate.

PEDAGOGICAL VIEWS.—Though Melanchthon was preeminently a humanist, he substantially agreed with Luther in his pedagogical views, and worked in harmony with the great reformer in the preparation of forms of Church government for various cities and principalities, in which provision was made for the establishment and maintenance of schools. In the Saxony School Plan, which he drew up in 1528, he directs that parents be admonished to send their children to school both for the sake of the Church and of the civil government. This, it will be remembered, was the fundamental view of Luther. " Preachers should admonish the people," Melanchthon says, " to send their children to school, in order that people may be brought up who are able to teach in the Church and to rule in the State. For some think that it is enough for a preacher to be able to read German. But such a belief is a hurtful delusion. For whoever is to teach others must have large experience and especial skill, which are to be obtained only by study from youth up. . . . And such competent people are needed, not alone for the Church, but also for the civil government, which God wishes to have maintained."

EVILS TO BE CORRECTED.—In the Saxony School Plan, Melanchthon points out certain evils in the schools, and at the same time indicates the means by which they are to be corrected. The teachers of the time were accustomed to make an ostentatious display of their learning, and to burden the children with too great a multiplicity of studies—evils which, unfortunately, it may be observed, were not confined to the schools of the sixteenth century. Melanchthon says: " There are now many mistakes in the schools. In order that the young may be properly instructed, we have drawn up the present form. In the first place, teachers should instruct the children only in Latin, and not in German or Greek, as some have hitherto done, who burden the poor children with a multiplicity of subjects, which is not only not profitable, but even hurtful. It is evident that such schoolmasters seek not the welfare of the children in teaching so many languages, but their own reputation. In the second place, they should not burden the children with many books, but in every way avoid a multiplication of studies. In the third place, it is necessary that the children be divided into three grades."

THE LATIN SCHOOL.—Melanchthon gives minute directions for the instruction of each grade. These instructions are of the greater interest because they lie at the basis of the humanistic or classical instruction which came to prevail not only in Germany, but also in England and America. It is almost exclusively a literary training, the basis of which is Latin grammar and Latin literature. Other subjects of study are entirely subordinate.

The first grade embraces primary pupils. " They shall first learn to read the primer, in which are found the alphabet, the Lord's Prayer, the Creed, and other prayers. When this has been learned, they shall take up Latin grammar and Cato, the former to read, and the latter to translate. . . . At the same time the children must learn to write, being required to show their copy-books daily to the teacher. In order to enlarge their Latin vocabulary, a list of words shall be given them every evening. The children shall be kept at music, and sing with the others."

For the second grade Melanchthon gives still more numerous directions, which are in substance as follows: After an exercise in music for the whole school, the teacher explains to the second grade the fables of Æsop. When these have been mastered with their declensions and constructions, the teacher proceeds to Terence, which the pupils are required to learn by heart. " Yet the teacher must see to it that the children are not overburdened." Then follow such fables of Plautus as are suitable. The morning hours are always to be devoted to grammar, including etymology, syntax, and prosody. " And the grammar shall always be gone over again and again, until it is firmly fixed in the minds of the children. For when this is not done, all learning is lost and in vain."

" In cases where such labor is a vexation to the teacher, as often happens, he shall be dismissed, and the authorities shall seek another, who will keep the children at their tasks. For no greater harm can be done the arts than to fail to exercise the young in grammar. One day each week, Saturday or Wednesday, shall be set apart for religious instruction. For some learn nothing at all from the Holy Scriptures, and others nothing at all but the Holy Scriptures, neither of which is to be tolerated. For it is necessary to teach the children the beginning of a Christian and godly life. Yet there are many reasons why other books are to be placed before them. The teacher shall hear the whole grade, one after another, repeat the Lord's Prayer, the Creed, and the Ten Commandments. Afterward he shall explain them in a simple and proper manner, so that the children may thoroughly understand the fear of God, faith, and good works, which are necessary to an upright life. He shall not accustom the children to make sport of monks or of others. He shall require them to learn a few easy Psalms, in which are contained the principles of a holy life."

" When the children have thoroughly learned the Latin grammar, the brightest among them may be selected to form the third grade." Musical instruction is continued. Virgil is studied, and afterward Ovid's Metamorphoses taken up. In the evening the Offices or Letters of Cicero are read. The pupil is trained in writing verse. Rhetoric and logic take the place of grammar. In the second and third grades written exercises, such as letters or verses, are required once a week. The boys are required to speak Latin, and the teacher himself, as far as possible, speaks nothing but Latin to them, in order that they may be accustomed and stimulated to the exercise.

C. Other Leaders

A few words must suffice for the other leading reformers. Calvin and Zwingli both appreciated the importance of learning, and contributed directly to its advancement.

CALVIN.—The ecclesiastical polity that Calvin established in Geneva in 1541 did not overlook the interests of education. A few years later he reorganized the Latin

13

school there, and impressed upon it a rigorous type of discipline and piety. In summer the recitations began at six in the morning; in winter at seven. The students were required to attend divine worship once every school-day, and thrice on Sunday. The Lord's Prayer and the Creed were in the course of study, and all the students were taught to sing and intone the Psalms. As in the gymnasia of Germany, the ancient languages, as an aid to biblical exercises, occupied a large part of the seven years' course. Calvin himself was one of the teachers, and it is said that his auditors daily numbered a thousand. In discussing a suitable head for the institution, he said: " Let the principal, being a man of at least average knowledge, be especially of a debonair spirit, and not rude or severe in his manner, in order that he may give a good example to the children in all his life, and that' he may thus bear so much more gently the labor of his office."

ZWINGLI.—As early as 1524, the same year in which Luther made his appeal to the authorities of the German cities, Zwingli published a little work entitled, How to Educate the Young in Good Manners and Christian Discipline. It is divided into three parts: (1) Instruction in the things that belong to God; (2) in the things that pertain to self;·and (3) in the things that concern our fellow men.

As with the other Protestant leaders, religious instruction is made prominent. " Although it is not in human power," he says, " to bring the heart of man to believe in God, even with an eloquence greater than that of Pericles; and, although our heavenly Father alone, who draws us to himself, can accomplish that work, yet faith, as Paul teaches, comes by hearing, namely, the hearing of the Word of God. Therefore, we must seek to instil faith in youth by the clearest and commonest words from the mouth of God, at the same time praying that He who alone begets faith would enlighten him whom we instruct. It also seems to me not discordant with the teaching of Christ, if we lead the young through visible things to the knowledge of God, placing before their eyes the beauties of the whole world, and showing them under the mutations of Nature the immutable Being who holds the manifold world in such admirable order. Then we may lead them to see that it is not possible for Him, who has so wisely and beautifully ordered all things, to neglect the work of his hands, since even among men we blame the father who does not watch over and provide for his household."

Under the second division, Zwingli advocated a study of Hebrew and Greek as an aid to the clear and assured apprehension of Scripture truth. Latin was to be studied for its general utility. Yet these linguistic attainments should not be associated with pride, but with a sincere and unpretentious love of truth. Christ was held up as the prototype of every virtue, upon which life should be formed. Zwingli encouraged the study of mathematics and gymnastics, and urged especially the learning of a trade, by which, in case of necessity, a livelihood might be earned.

In regard to the duties of social life, he emphasized the truth that men are born to live, not for themselves alone, but also for the welfare of others. To this end they should cultivate the virtues of righteousness, truth, fidelity, faith, and steadfastness, by which they will be most useful to the Church, to society, and to the State. Parents should be held in reverence. " He is no true Christian," Zwingli says, " who only knows how to talk about God, but does not endeavor to do noble things."

4. ABSTRACT THEOLOGICAL EDUCATION
(1550–1700)

THREE TENDENCIES.—After the rise of Protestantism various influences, often in conflict with one another, control the course of events. During the period extending from the middle of the sixteenth to the beginning of the eighteenth century, three leading tendencies are apparent in education. These may be characterized as the theological, the humanistic, and the practical. As the theological tendency, however, maintained an ascendency over the others in the schools, it is allowed to give name to the period. The humanistic tendency, which was most marked in secondary schools, was an echo from the revival of learning. The practical or realistic tendency was a reaction against the sterile learning cultivated by ecclesiasticism and humanism.

THEOLOGICAL ACTIVITY.—The period under discussion was one of extraordinary theological activity. A large share of the intellectual strength of the age was turned to theology. Every phase of religious truth, particularly in its doctrinal and speculative aspects, was brought under investigation. Theology was elevated into a science, and doctrinal systems were developed with logical precision, and extended even to trifling subtleties.

But this great effort to reduce the whole body of religious truth to an infallible logical statement was attended with unfortunate results. Theologians became bigoted and intolerant. In their efforts to give Christian doctrine a scientific form, they lost its spirit. Losing its earlier freedom and life, Protestantism degenerated in large measure

into what has been called " dead orthodoxy." The intellectual apprehension of elaborate creeds was made the basis
of Christian fellowship. Christian life counted for little,
and the Protestant world broke up into opposing fac-
tions. Says Kurtz, who is disposed to apologize for this
period as far as possible: " Like medieval scholasticism,
in its concern for logic theology almost lost vitality.
Orthodoxy degenerated into orthodoxism; *externally*, not
only discerning essential diversities, but disregarding the
broad basis of a common faith, and running into odious
and unrestrained controversy; *internally*, holding to the
form of pure doctrine, but neglecting cordially to embrace
it, and to live consistently with it."

STUDIES AND DISCIPLINE.—The schools, which stand
in close relation to religion, were naturally influenced in
a large measure by the theological tendencies of the age.
Theological interests imposed upon the schools a narrow
range of subjects, a mechanical method of instruction, and
a cruel discipline. The principle of authority, exacting a
blind submission of the pupil, prevailed in the schools of
every grade. The young were regarded, not as tender plants
to be carefully nurtured and developed, but as untamed
animals to be repressed and broken. " Education," says
Dittes, " in the form that it had assumed in the sixteenth
century, could not furnish a complete human culture. In
the higher institutions, and even in the wretched town
schools, Latin was the Moloch to which countless minds
fell an offering in return for the blessing granted to a
few. A dead knowledge of words took the place of a living
knowledge of things. Latin school-books supplanted the
book of Nature, the book of life, the book of mankind.
And in the popular schools youthful minds were tortured
over the spelling-book and catechism. The method of

teaching was almost everywhere, in the primary as well as in the higher schools, a mechanical and compulsory drill in unintelligible formulas; the pupils were obliged to learn, but they were not educated to see and hear, to think and prove, and were not led to a true independence and personal perfection; the teachers found their function in teaching the prescribed text, not in harmoniously developing the young human being according to the laws of Nature—a process, moreover, that lay under the ban of ecclesiastical orthodoxy. The discipline answered to the content and spirit of the instruction; it was harsh, and even barbarous; the principle was to tame the pupils, not to educate them. They were to hold themselves motionless, that the school exercises might not be disturbed; what took place in their minds, and how their several characters were constituted, the school pedants did not understand and appreciate."

MULTIPLICATION OF SCHOOLS.—This is the darker side of the theological or ecclesiastical influence. In other particulars it was favorable to education. In Protestant countries it led to a multiplication of schools of every grade; and in Catholic countries, the Jesuits in particular displayed an extraordinary activity in secondary and higher education. The country or village schools were connected with the local church, and were usually taught by the sexton or some other subordinate officer. In addition to the catechism and singing the course of instruction included reading, writing, and arithmetic.

With the town schools it was somewhat better. The range of instruction was of a higher order; the theological influence was felt in a less degree; the needs of practical life were better kept in view. But these schools were still very far from being models. They did not emancipate themselves from the mechanical methods and cruel discipline then in vogue, and the teachers, as a rule, were unfit for their vocation. They were usually people who for some reason had been unsuccessful in other pursuits. They were poorly paid, and but little respected. In the school ordinances of the time they are admonished to refrain from cruel discipline, and to maintain, both in and out of school, a becoming deportment.

EDUCATION OF PRINCES.—The education of princes was usually in the hands of special instructors. As the princes of Europe exerted great influence in ecclesiastical affairs, especial care was exercised in their religious culture. Whether Catholic, Lutheran, or Reformed, they were thoroughly drilled in the distinctive doctrines of their respective branches of the Church. The daily routine of George III of Saxony, who was born in 1647, may be taken as a type of princely education. At seven o'clock in the morning he arose with a brief prayer. While he was being dressed, the attendants sang a hymn; then with the court he went to morning prayers; afterward he retired to his apartment for private worship, or on days of preaching to the church. Then followed two hours of study, which began with a brief prayer for divine assistance and concluded with a psalm of thanksgiving. The hour from ten to eleven was devoted to recreation. After dinner several hours were devoted again to study, including instruction in dancing. From five to six recreation and supper; at eight, prayer with the whole court, after which the prince withdrew to his apartment, and after private worship, retired promptly at nine o'clock.

SCHOOLS FOR GIRLS.—The numerous school orders adopted in Protestant Germany made provision for the education of girls. In every community separate schools, presided over by well-approved female teachers, were to be maintained at public cost. The range of studies was narrow, but these schools laid the foundation for better things. The school order of Braunschweig, promulgated in 1548, may be taken as an example. It required that in all towns and villages girls' schools should be established, in which reading and writing, the singing of hymns, and Luther's catechism should be taught. The pupils were to read stories from the German Bible at home, and at school repeat the substance of them from memory. The school day embraced two hours in the forenoon and two hours in the afternoon. Before leaving the school each day, the girls were required to sing a psalm or hymn, in order that they might learn singing with delight and without effort. An honorable matron was to be chosen as teacher, who loved God's Word and was fond of reading in the Bible and other good books. She was to be paid out of the common treasury from twenty to thirty florins a year; and in case the towns were able to afford it, she was to have an assistant with a salary of twenty florins a year.

LATIN SCHOOLS.—In the Latin schools, or gymnasia, humanism asserted itself by the side of theology. As indicated by the name, Latin formed the chief subject of study. These schools, some of which became famous, were founded in large numbers in the sixteenth century, and some of them, especially in England, have continued to the present day. In Germany, Camerarius established a flourishing school at Nuremberg (1526), Trotzendorf at Goldberg (1531), Sturm at Strasburg (1538), and Neander at Ilfeld (1543). These distinguished school directors were all more or less influenced by Melanchthon, with whom they had maintained cordial relations as pupils or friends. Academic gymnasia, which occupied a middle ground between the Latin schools and universities and were provided especially for such students as were too young to enter upon the freedom and dangers of university life, were founded at Danzig, Hamburg, Bremen, Zürich, and elsewhere. In England the great public schools of Shrewsbury (1551), Westminster (1560), Rugby (1567), Merchant Taylors' (1561), and Harrow (1571), were established. As Sturm represented most completely the humanistic tendency of his age, it is worth while to consider his educational work in some detail.

A. John Sturm

BIOGRAPHICAL.—John Sturm was born at Schleiden, Prussia, in 1507; he died at Strasburg in 1589. After teaching at Louvain and Paris, he was appointed rector of the gymnasium at Strasburg, over which he presided for forty years. He boasted of his institution that it reproduced the best periods of Athens and Rome; and, in fact, he succeeded in giving to his adopted city the name of New Athens. In religion he was a Calvinist, and he is justly regarded as the greatest educator that the Reformed Church produced during this period. More than any one else, perhaps, he gave shape to the secondary classical instruction of Europe and America for the next two hundred and fifty years.

AIM OF EDUCATION.—Sturm had a definite idea of what he was to accomplish in his work at Strasburg. His ideal of education was that of Protestantism in general, namely, an intelligent Christian manhood. " A wise and persuasive piety," he said, " should be the aim of our studies. But, were all pious, then the student should be distinguished from him who is unlettered, by scientific culture and eloquence. Hence, knowledge, and purity and elegance of diction, should become the aim of scholarship, and toward its attainments both teachers and pupils should sedulously bend their every effort."

For attaining this culture the chief instrumentality was Latin. It constituted, as we shall see, the backbone of the course of study, and its use was enjoined upon both teachers and pupils. The teachers were to use German only in explanations; and the students were forbidden to speak German even on their way to or from school. It was permitted, however, to vary Latin with Greek! The supreme aim of Sturm was to Latinize his students. "Cicero," he said, "was but twenty years old when he delivered his speeches in behalf of P. Quintius and Sextus Roscius; but in these latter days where is the man, of fourscore even, who could bequeath to the world such masterpieces of eloquence? And yet, there are books enough, and there is intellect enough. What, then, do we need further? I reply, the Latin language, and a correct method of teaching. Both these we must have, before we can arrive at the summit of eloquence."

METHOD AND DISCIPLINE.—In his Classic Letters, Sturm clearly sets forth his ideas of method and discipline. Step by step, with a careful cultivation of the memory, the student is to mount from the alphabet to the mastery of elegant discourse. Nothing is to be forgotten. "To keep what has been acquired," he says, "is no less an art than the first acquisition of it." The students are not to be tasked beyond their powers. The structure of language as revealed in grammar and rhetoric is made prominent from beginning to end. The students are to be drilled in the use of dialectic or logic. Throughout the gymnasium course the discipline is to be sufficiently strict. "In these classes," says Sturm, "the boys must be kept under the discipline of the rod, nor should they learn according to their own choice, but after the good pleasure of the teacher."

The gymnasium at Strasburg owed its reputation in no small degree to the unity of method and purpose that Sturm knew how to give it. He was a model rector. He advised his teachers as to the best methods of doing their work, and cheered them on in their tasks. He reminded them that all were working in a common cause, and that their labors were mutually complementary. Their work of the upper classes could not be done successfully, unless a good foundation had been previously laid; and the work of the lower classes would be largely in vain, unless it was completed in the subsequent courses. All the teachers were to follow the same method, and thus make the gymnasium a well-ordered machine for turning out classically trained scholars.

POPULARITY OF THE SCHOOL.—In a few years Sturm's school became famous, and attracted students from all parts of Europe. "The man was," to quote the words of Raumer, "of one piece, a whole man—a man of character, in whom strength of will was admirably united with force and tact in execution. Hence, it is not to be wondered at that Sturm found recognition among his contemporaries, and enjoyed their highest confidence. In 1578 the Strasburg school numbered several thousand pupils, among them about two hundred of noble birth, twenty-four counts and barons, and three princes. Not simply from Germany, but from the most different countries, from Portugal and Poland, Denmark, France, and England, youths were sent to Sturm. But his pedagogical activity was not limited to the Strasburg Gymnasium; in wide circles he exerted by counsel and example, and through his pupils, a very great influence as a second *Preceptor Germaniæ*."

COURSE OF STUDY.—The course of study at the Strasburg Gymnasium was divided into ten classes. As this institution became a model for many other classical schools, it is well to present briefly the work of each class. We thus gain a clear insight into the Latin schools of this period, and are prepared to appreciate both their excellence and their defects:

Tenth Class.—The alphabet, reading, writing. Latin declensions and conjugations. The German or Latin catechism.

Ninth Class.—Latin declensions and conjugations continued. Memorizing of Latin words used in common life. Irregularities of formation were introduced.

Eighth Class.—Continuation of words in common use. The parts of speech. Declension and conjugation in connection with sentences. Composition of Latin phrases. Some letters of Cicero were read and explained. Toward the close of the year, exercises in style.

Seventh Class.—Latin syntax, with a few rules and examples from Cicero. Rules to be constantly applied in reading Cicero's letters. Exercises in composition. On Sunday, translation of German catechism into classic Latin, in which, however, such terms as *Trinitas, sacramentum*, and *baptismus* might be employed.

Sixth Class.—Review. Translation of Cicero's letters into German. Translation of Latin poetry. On Saturday and Sunday, translation of catechism, and reading of some letters of Jerome. Greek begun.

Fifth Class.—Study of words designating things unknown to the pupils. Versification. Mythology. Cicero, and Virgil's Eclogues. Greek vocabulary. Exercises in style and Latin versification. Translation of oratorical extracts into German, and afterward back into Latin. On Saturday and Sunday, one of Paul's epistles.

Fourth Class.—Well acquainted with Latin and Greek grammar, the pupils were required to read a great deal, to learn by heart, and to explain. The sixth oration against Verres was read, because it contains almost all kinds of narration. Epistles of Horace. Greek grammar continued, with reading. Exercises in style. Reviews. Reading and paraphrasing some of Paul's epistles.

Third Class.—Reviews. Rhetoric. Oration *pro Cluentio.* Select orations of Demosthenes. The Iliad or Odyssey. Paul's epistles. Exercises in style. Translation of oratorical extracts from Greek into Latin, and from Latin into Greek. Composition of poetry and letters. Representation of the comedies of Plautus and Terence in the four higher classes. All the plays of these authors to be acted.

Second Class.—The pupils explained, under the direction of the teacher, the Greek orators and poets. Peculiarities of oratorical and poetical language. Remarkable passages copied. Dialectic and rhetoric studied in connection with orations of Cicero and Demosthenes. Exercises in style. Oratorical composition and declamation. Memorizing and recitation of the Epistle to the Romans. Representation of the comedies of Terence and Plautus, and some drama of Aristophanes; Euripides, and Sophocles.

First Class.—Dialectic and rhetoric continued. Virgil, Horace, Homer. Translation of Thucydides and Sallust. Weekly dramatic entertainments. All written composition to be artistic. Reading and explanation of Paul's epistles.

CRITICISM.—This course has the merit of being well fitted together, and of harmoniously tending to the desired end. It is carefully graded throughout, each class furnishing a definite preparation for the succeeding one. Yet it has obvious and serious defects. It is too narrow in its scope. An unjustifiable prominence is given to Latin and Greek, while many other important studies are wholly neglected. History, mathematics, natural science, and the mother-tongue are ignored. A great gap is left between the gymnasium and life—a gap that could not be filled even by the university. In aiming to reproduce Greece and Rome in the midst of modern Christian civilization, Sturm's scheme involves a vast anachronism.

" And what a strange mistake," exclaims Paroz, " to wish to confine the scientific culture of a nation in the forms of a foreign language ! In order to succeed, it would have been necessary at the start to overcome the resistance of a young, vigorous, popular, national language. But such a result was neither possible nor desirable. The future belonged to the mother-tongue ; and true modern culture, the culture suited to modern needs and to the genius of the people, was not found in the Latin gymnasia of the sixteenth and seventeenth centuries—it lay germinally in the religious work of the period ; that is, in the translation of the Bible, in hymns, sermons, and catechisms, and in those poor popular schools in which the mother-tongue was spoken. We are astonished to-day that Sturm did not make the German language a branch of instruction, and that he even despised French and German, although he somewhere acknowledges that Luther and Philippe de Comines have written as well as the most celebrated of the ancients."

B. The Universities

ECCLESIASTICAL RELATIONS.—The universities were affected most, perhaps, by the theological influences of the period. These institutions were established in considerable numbers for the promulgation of particular types of theology. The universities established between 1550 and 1700, with their ecclesiastical relations, are as follows: Strasburg, Lutheran, 1621; Geneva, Reformed, 1558; Jena, Lutheran, 1557; Dillingen, Catholic, 1554; Helmstädt, Lutheran, 1576; Altorf, Lutheran, 1575; Herborn, Reformed, 1654; Grätz, Catholic, 1586; Paderborn, Catholic, 1592; Giessen, Lutheran, 1607; Rinteln, Lutheran, 1619; Salzburg, Catholic, 1622; Münster, Catholic, 1631; Osnabrück, Catholic, 1632; Bamberg, Catholic, 1648; Duisburg, Reformed, 1655; Kiel, Lutheran, 1665; Innsbruck, Catholic, 1670; Halle, Lutheran, 1694. Of these, Helmstädt, Altorf, Rinteln, and Duisburg were subsequently dissolved.

COURSES OF STUDY.—No important changes were made in the organization of the universities. The course of instruction, which continued in the hands of the four faculties of philosophy, theology, law, and medicine, remained narrow. History and the modern tongues were entirely neglected; mathematics received but little attention; physics, astronomy, and natural history—the only natural sciences recognized—were taught out of Aristotle, Ptolemy, and Pliny, and medicine out of Hippocrates and Galen. Even Greek was accorded only an inferior position. In the universities, as in the gymnasia, Latin was the chief subject of study. "Thus was the circle of studies," says Raumer, "at the schools as at the unversities extremely restricted, as compared with the range of subjects in our time. It is clear, as I have repeatedly remarked, that all the time and strength of the youth were forcibly concentrated upon the learning and exercising of Latin. Grammar was studied for years in order to learn to speak and write Latin correctly; dialectic, in order to use it logically; and rhetoric, in order to handle it oratorically.

Facility was sought by means of debate, declamation, and representations of Terence. The classics were read in order to collect words and phrases from them for speaking and writing, without particular concern for the thought."

STATE OF MORALS.—The state of morals at the universities of the sixteenth and seventeenth centuries was very low. Idleness, drunkenness, disorder, and licentiousness prevailed in an unparalleled degree. The practise of hazing was universal, and new students were subjected to shocking indignities. The following graphic description, contained in a rescript of Duke Albrecht of Saxony to the University of Jena in 1624, would apply equally well to any other university of the time: "Customs before unheard of," he says, "inexcusable, unreasonable, and wholly barbarian, have come into existence. When any person, either of high or low rank, goes to any of our universities for the sake of pursuing his studies, he is called by the insulting names of pennal, fox, tape-worm, and the like, and treated as such; and insulted, abused, derided, and hooted at, until, against his will, and to the great injury and damage of himself and his parents, he has prepared, given, and paid for a stately and expensive entertainment. And at this there happen, without any fear of God or man, innumerable disorders and excesses, blasphemies, breaking up of stoves, doors, and windows, throwing about of books and drinking-vessels, looseness of words and actions, and in eating and drinking, dangerous wounds, and other ill deeds; shames, scandals, and all manner of vicious and godless actions, even sometimes extending to murder or fatal injuries. And these doings are frequently not confined to one such feast, but are continued for days together at meals, at lectures, privately and publicly, even in the public streets, by all manner of misdemeanors in sitting, standing, or going, such as outrageous howls, breaking into houses and windows, and the like; so that by such immoral, wild, and vicious courses, not only do our universities perceptibly lose in good reputation, but many parents in distant places either determine not to send their children at all to this university— founded with such great expense by our honored ancestors, now resting in peace with God, and thus far maintained by ourselves—or to take them away again."

The custom of hazing was broken up in Germany about 1660, after which time the moral condition of the universities showed a marked improvement.

C. The Jesuits

HISTORICAL.—Within the Roman Catholic Church education was promoted chiefly by the Jesuits. This order, established by Ignatius Loyola in 1534, found its special mission in combating the Reformation. As the most effective means of arresting the progress of Protestantism, it aimed at controlling education, particularly among the wealthy and the noble. The organization was, perhaps, the most compact that has ever existed. Only men of marked ability were admitted to it, and on entering they gave up their personality in complete consecration to the interests of the order. The will of the general was supreme, and from his headquarters in Rome he directed the movements of the society with absolute precision and certainty. At length the order excited opposition by its ambitious schemes and increasing power, and after banishment from nearly every country in Europe, it was finally abolished by Pope Clement XIV in 1773. Though restored by Pope

14

Pius VII in 1814, and possessed of its earlier spirit, it has not since been so powerful.

EDUCATIONAL ACTIVITY.—From the time of its organization, the Society of Jesus, permeated with the fanatical zeal of its founder, worked with indomitable energy. More than any other agency it stayed the progress of the Reformation, and even won back territory already conquered by Protestantism. Although employing the pulpit and the confessional, it worked chiefly through its schools, of which it established and controlled large numbers. Secondary and higher education in all Catholic countries gradually passed into its hands. Its schools were praised and patronized even by Protestants. "Take example by the schools of the Jesuits," said Bacon, "for better do not exist. When I look at the diligence and activity of the Jesuits, both in imparting knowledge and in molding the heart, I bethink me of the exclamation of Agesilaus concerning Pharnabazus: 'Since thou art so noble, I would thou wert on our side.'" In 1710 the order had no fewer than six hundred and twelve colleges, one hundred and fifty-seven normal schools, twenty-four universities, and two hundred missions. Many of these institutions had a large patronage. In 1675 the College of Clermont, for example, numbered three thousand students.

CONSTITUTIONES AND RATIO STUDIORUM.—The educational system of the Jesuits is set forth in detail in the Constitutiones, which was drawn up probably by Loyola himself in 1559, and in the Ratio Studiorum, which, after fifteen years of painstaking labor, was published by Aquaviva in 1599. Though the Jesuit system of education has since undergone slight modifications to accommodate it better to the needs of the times, it has remained loyal to the spirit of these documents.

In the Jesuit schools there was a lower and higher course of instruction. The lower course, which corresponds closely to that of Sturm, occupied six years. The principal stress was laid on Latin, though Greek also was taught.

1. Rudiments of Latin grammar.
2. Middle grammar class.
3. Latin syntax.
4. The humanities.
5. Rhetoric (two years).

The higher course of instruction usually extended through six years. Two years were devoted to philosophy, logic, ethics, and mathematics. Aristotle furnished the leading text-books. Four years were given to theology, including Holy Scripture, Hebrew, and the writings of the scholastics.

NEGLECT OF PRIMARY EDUCATION.—It is a remarkable fact that the Jesuits have never given themselves to primary instruction. All their efforts have been expended on secondary and higher education. This neglect of primary schools is to be explained, not by a scarcity of teachers, but by the Jesuit distrust of popular education. The interest of the Jesuits in education does not spring from a deep love of humanity, but from a self-denying devotion to their order and to the Roman Catholic Church, in whose interests they can use it as a tremendous power. Accordingly we read in the Constitutiones: " None of those employed in the domestic service of the Society ought to know how to read and write, or if they already know, ought to learn further. No instruction shall be imparted to them except with the consent of the General of the order, for it is enough for them to serve Jesus Christ our Master in all simplicity and humility."

DISTINGUISHING FEATURES.—The chief distinguishing features of the Jesuit system of education may be pointed out as follows:

1. It is characterized by a conservative spirit dominated by the principle of authority. In the schools of the Jesuits only well-established views or doctrines were to be presented; and all efforts at independent investigation and independent thought were systematically and assiduously discouraged. "In every department," says the Constitutiones, "let our teachers follow the safer and more approved doctrine and the authors that teach it." Accordingly Thomas Aquinas, the scholastic theologian of the thirteenth century, was taken as the standard of theology, and Aristotle, the Athenian philosopher, as the standard in logic, natural philosophy, and metaphysics.

2. Only the disciplinary side of education was regarded. The course of training, both in its subjects and in its methods, was that of mental gymnastics. "The gymnasia will remain," said General Beckx, "what they are by nature, a gymnastic for the intellect, which consists far less in the assimilation of real matter, in the acquisition of different knowledges, than in a culture of pure form." Hence, the acquisition of knowledge through wide reading and a comprehensive course of study was systematically discouraged.

3. The basis of Jesuit education was the ancient languages, especially the Latin. From the beginning stress was laid upon grammar; then upon translations from the classics; afterward upon Latin exercises in prose and verse; and lastly, upon public disputations in Latin. Latin was the language of the classroom and the ordinary means of communication among the students. And to the

attainment of elegance and fluency in its use, the mother-tongue, modern languages, and history were ruthlessly sacrificed. "All use of the mother-tongue," says the Ratio Studiorum, "should be forbidden. Those who make use of it ought to bear a mark of humiliation, to which a light punishment also should be added, unless the pupil succeed the same day in throwing the double load upon a comrade whom he has detected, in school or upon the street, committing the same fault."

4. The cultivation of the memory occupied a prominent place in the Jesuit system from the first lesson in the grammar to the last lectures in philosophy. In addition to the rules of grammar, the young student had to memorize the catechism and selected passages from Cicero. In the higher classes there were frequent declamations. Throughout the course reviews were made at the close of each week, month, and term. In this way the mind of the student was stored with considerable information that was ready for use at any moment.

5. Large use was made of disputation. Subjects of discussion were assigned very frequently, and the students were required to debate them in the presence of the professor and the school. The discussions, which were always in Latin, were conducted in strict logical form. This intellectual pugilism, which aimed at victory rather than at truth, was thought to be of special utility in sharpening the intellect and in cultivating eloquence of speech. It made ready and skilful debaters of Jesuit students.

6. The Jesuits made much of emulation, and in their eager desire to promote it they adopted means that could not fail to excite jealousy and envy. "He who knows how to excite emulation," says the Ratio Studiorum, "has found the most powerful auxiliary in his teaching. Let

the teacher, then, highly appreciate this valuable aid, and let him study to make the wisest use of it. Emulation awakens and develops all the powers of man. In order to maintain emulation, it will be necessary that each pupil have a rival to control his conduct and criticize him; also magistrates, questors, censors, and decurions should be appointed among the students. Nothing will be held more honorable than to outstrip a fellow student, and nothing more dishonorable than to be outstripped. Prizes will be distributed to the best pupils with the greatest possible solemnity. Out of school the place of honor will everywhere be given to the most distinguished pupils."

7. The supreme end of education was salvation. To the Jesuit mind this meant not only the building up of character, but especially a training in the faith and practise of the Roman Catholic Church. "Because the purpose of our Society," says the Constitutiones, "in acquiring knowledge is, with the gracious help of God, to promote our own salvation and that of others, this in general and particular must be the criterion, according to which our students must take up and pursue definite departments of learning." Not only was Christian doctrine taught by means of the catechism, lectures, and private conversations, but a formal piety was likewise exacted. The students were required daily to attend mass, and at regular intervals to go to confession. Prayer was encouraged at frequent intervals, and a high moral tone was required both in the schoolroom and on the playground.

8. The studies were few in number, and carefully adjusted to the pupil's ability. In all cases short lessons and thorough work was the rule. To gain influence with the higher classes, from which they desired to draw their chief patronage, the Jesuits cultivated elegant manners,

and encouraged physical training by means of gymnastics. A strict watch, which often assumed the form of hateful espionage, was kept over the pupil. Corporal punishment, resorted to only in extreme cases, was administered, not by a member of the order, but by a corrector kept for that purpose. The Ratio Studiorum explains this precaution. " Pupils," it says, " that in view of their age or exterior appear weak, insignificant, and perhaps contemptible, will soon be youths and men, who may attain to position, fortune, or power, so that it is possible we may be obliged to seek their favor, or to depend upon their will; this is why it is important to consider well the manner of treating and punishing them."

CONCLUSION.—It only remains to sum up in a word the results of this investigation. The Jesuit system of education, based not upon a study of man, but upon the interests of the order, was necessarily narrow. It sought showy results with which to dazzle the world. A well-rounded development was nothing. The principle of authority, suppressing all freedom and independence of thought, prevailed from beginning to end. Religious pride and intolerance were fostered. While our baser feelings were highly stimulated, the nobler side of our nature was wholly neglected. Love of country, fidelity to friends, nobleness of character, enthusiasm for beautiful ideals, were insidiously suppressed. For the rest, we adopt the language of Quick: " The Jesuits did not aim at developing *all* the faculties of their pupils, but merely the receptive and reproductive faculties. When the young man had acquired a thorough mastery of the Latin language for all purposes; when he was well versed in the theological and philosophical opinions of his preceptors; when he was skilful in dispute, and could make a brilliant display from the resources of a well-stored memory, he had reached the highest points to which the Jesuits sought to lead him. Originality and independence of mind, love of truth for its own sake, the power of reflecting, and of forming correct judgments, were not merely neglected, they were suppressed in the Jesuits' system. But in what they attempted they were eminently successful, and their success went a long way toward securing their popularity."

5. REACTION AGAINST ABSTRACT THEOLOGICAL EDUCATION

PHILOSOPHY AND SCIENCE.—Hitherto we have considered the darker aspects of the seventeenth century, but there is a brighter side which is now to claim our attention. By the side of narrow theological and humanistic tendencies, there was developed a liberal progressive spirit, in which lay the hope of the future. It freed itself from traditional opinions, and pushed its investigations everywhere in search of new truth. In England Bacon set forth his inductive method, by which he gave an immense impulse to the study of Nature; in France Descartes laid a solid foundation for intellectual science; and in Germany Leibnitz "quickly reached the bound and farthest limit of human wisdom, to overleap that line and push onward into regions hitherto unexplored, and dwell among yet undiscovered truths." Great progress was made in the natural sciences. Galileo invented the telescope, and discovered the moons of Jupiter. Newton discovered the law of gravitation, and explained the theory of colors. Harvey found out the circulation of the blood. Torricelli invented the barometer, Guericke the air-pump, Napier logarithms. Pascal ascertained that the air has weight, and Roemer measured the velocity of light. Kepler announced the laws of planetary motion. Louis XIV established the French Academy of Sciences, and Charles II the Royal Society of England.

PROGRESS IN LITERATURE.—The progress in literature was no less marked. Upon two European nations the golden age of letters shed its luster. In England, Bacon, Shakespeare, and Milton wrote; in France, Corneille, Molière, and Racine. "No other country," says Macaulay, "could produce a tragic poet equal to Racine, a comic poet equal to Molière, a trifler so agreeable as La Fontaine, a rhetorician so skilful as Bossuet. Besides these, who were easily first, there were Pascal, whose Provincial Letters created a standard for French prose; Fénelon, whose Telemachus still retains its wonderful popularity; Boileau, who has been styled the Horace of France; Madame de Sévigné, whose graceful letters are models of epistolary style; and Massillon, who pronounced over the grave of Louis XIV a eulogy ending with the sublime words, ' God alone is great! ' "

INTELLECTUAL EMANCIPATION.—All over Europe the human mind, gradually coming to a sense of its native dignity and power, was emancipating itself from traditional and ecclesiastical authority. Reason was asserting its rights. In the presence of this independent and investigating spirit, the imperfections of the existing education —its one-sidedness, its narrow and unpractical course of study, its unworthy aims, its mechanical methods and cruel discipline—could not escape attention. Prophetic voices were raised against it, its leading defects were noted, and many of the principles and methods now employed in our best schools were given to the world. Says Karl Schmidt: " Books, words, had been the subjects of instruction during the period of abstract theological education. The knowledge of things was wanting. Instead of the things themselves, words about the things were taught— and these, taken from the books of the ' ancients ' about stars, the forces of Nature, stones, plants, animals—astronomy without observations, anatomy without dissection of the human body, physics without experiments, etc. Then appeared in the most different countries of Europe an intellectual league of men who made it their work to turn away from dead words to living nature, and from mechanical to organic instruction. They were indeed only preachers in the wilderness, but they were the pioneers of a new age." These now come before us.

A. Montaigne

BIOGRAPHICAL.—Montaigne, a celebrated writer of France, was born in 1533. Great care was taken with his education. At an early age he was entrusted to a German tutor who did not understand French, and who employed Latin in communicating with his pupil. As a result, he was able at the age of six years to speak Latin. At thirteen he completed his studies at the College of Guienne, at Bordeaux, and subsequently studied law. At twenty he was elected a member of the Parliament of Bordeaux, and was afterward chosen mayor of the city. But possessed of ample means, and having no political ambition, he withdrew to his estate to live in philosophic retirement.

ESSAYS.—It was here that he produced his celebrated Essays—discussions of all sorts of subjects caught up apparently by chance. In these essays, which are written in an easy colloquial style and abound in unpretentious wisdom, Montaigne repeatedly touches on education. The

fullest statement of his views is found in the essay entitled, On the Education of Children, which was addressed
to his friend, the Countess de Gurzon. Montaigne was a
man of keen penetration and strong practical sense. He
points out with singular clearness and force many of the
defects in the education of his day, and his views, often
far in advance of his time, exhibit a strong reactionary
tendency. He grasped the true idea of education. " It is
not a soul," he says, " it is not a body that we are training, but a man, and we ought not to divide him."

HUMANISTIC EDUCATION.—At the College of Guienne
he had observed the methods and results of the prevailing
education. He condemned the neglect of the mother-
tongue, found fault with the amount of time devoted to
the ancient languages, and expressed dissatisfaction with
the unsubstantial character of the student's acquirements
at the end of his course. " Fine speaking," he says, " is a
very good and commendable quality, but not so excellent
or so necessary as some would make it; and I am scandal-
ized that our whole life should be spent in nothing else. I
would first understand my own language, and that of my
neighbor with whom most of my business and conversation
lies. No doubt Greek and Latin are very great ornaments,
and of very great use; but we may buy them too dear."
" Do but observe him," he says again, " when he comes
back from school, after fifteen or sixteen years that he
has been there, there is nothing so awkward and maladroit,
so unfit for company or employment; and all that you
shall find he has got is, that his Latin and Greek have only
made him a greater and more conceited coxcomb than
when he went from home. He should bring his soul replete
with good literature, and he brings it only swelled and
puffed up with vain and empty shreds and snatches of

learning and has really nothing more in him than he had before."

POURING-IN PROCESS.—Montaigne inveighs against the authoritative pouring-in process then in vogue. It appears better to him to arouse the student's interest, and to call into play a cooperative activity. " It is the custom of schoolmasters," he says, " to be eternally thundering in their pupils' ears as if they were pouring into a funnel, while the pupils' business is only to repeat what their masters have said. Now, I would have a tutor correct this error, and that at the very first; he should, according to the capacity he has to deal with, put it to the test, permitting his pupil himself to taste and relish things, and of himself to choose and discern them, the tutor sometimes opening the way to him, and sometimes making him break the ice himself; that is, I would not have the tutor alone to invent and speak, but that he should also hear his pupils speak."

KNOWLEDGE AND CHARACTER.—Montaigne did not regard the cramming of the memory with information as the most important part of education. The development of a sound judgment and upright character appeared to him of greater value than filling the head with knowledge. There should not be such an overcrowding in study as to prevent a healthful assimilation of what was learned. " Too much learning stifles the soul," he said, " just as plants are stifled by too much moisture, and lamps by too much oil. Our pedants plunder knowledge from books and carry it on the tip of their lips, just as birds carry seeds to feed their young. The care and expense our parents are at in our education point at nothing but to furnish our heads with knowledge; but not a word of judgment or virtue. We toil and labor only to stuff the memory, but leave the conscience and understanding unfurnished and void."

DISCIPLINE.—Montaigne did not approve of the harsh, tyrannical discipline that prevailed in his day. His own early training at home had been tempered with kindness, and he had thus learned by experience that gentle leading in the paths of learning is better than unsympathetic and cruel driving. " Education," he said, " ought to be carried on with a severe sweetness quite contrary to the practise of our pedants, who, instead of tempting and alluring children to letters by apt and gentle ways, do in truth present nothing before them but rods and ferules, horror and cruelty. Away with this violence! away with this compulsion! than which I certainly believe nothing more dulls and degenerates a well-descended nature. If you would have him apprehend shame and chastisement, do not harden him to them."

NATURE AND HISTORY.—Montaigne wished to have learning transmuted into wisdom. Education he regarded not as an end in itself, but as a means to attain a broad outlook and a sound judgment in life. Association with men, observation of nature, and a perusal of history all tend, as he argued, to rid us of provincialism, and to make us, like Socrates, citizens of the world. History seemed to him to have an especial value in enabling us to form correct estimates of ourselves and of society about us. The mistakes of others, as revealed in history, put us on our guard against error, and their vices fortify us in the opposite virtues. " This great world," he says, " is the mirror wherein we are to behold ourselves, to be able to know ourselves as we ought to do. In short, I would have this to be the book my young gentleman should study with the most attention; for so many humors, so many sects, so many judgments, opinions, laws, and customs, teach us to judge right of our own, and inform our understandings to discover their imperfection and natural infirmity, which is no trivial speculation. So many mutations of states and kingdoms, and so many turns and revolutions of public fortune, will make us wise enough to make no great wonder of our own. So many great names, so many famous victories and conquests drowned and swallowed in oblivion, render our hopes ridiculous of eternizing our names by the taking of half a score of light-horse, or a paltry turret, which only derives its memory from its ruin. The pride and arrogance of so many foreign pomps and ceremonies, the tumorous majesty of so many courts and grandeurs, accustom and fortify our sight without astonishment to behold and endure the luster of our own. So many millions of men buried before us, encourage us not to fear to go seek so good company in the other world."

B. Bacon

BIOGRAPHICAL.—Francis Bacon, who has done more, perhaps, for the advancement of knowledge than any other man of his time, was born in London in 1561. He was of delicate constitution, but endowed with remarkable intellectual power. Queen Elizabeth, delighted with his youthful precocity, playfully called him her young Lord Keeper. He was educated at the University of Cambridge, and in 1590 entered Parliament as member from Middlesex. After the accession of James I, in 1603, Bacon rose rapidly in position and honor, until in 1618 he was made Lord High Chancellor, the summit of his ambition and political elevation. He was greater in intellect than in character, and in

1621 he was convicted on his own confession of accepting bribes. He died in disgrace and repentance in 1626.

NOVUM ORGANUM.—The Novum Organum, part of a vast unfinished work, was published in 1620, and contains the principles of the Baconian or inductive philosophy. The characteristic features of this philosophy are investigation, experiment, and verification. It urges men to quit barren, transcendental speculation for fruit-bearing research in nature. It has been potent in turning modern thought into new channels, and has contributed largely to the scientific and natural progress of the present. To quote the words of Lewes, " Bacon was modern in culture, in object, and in method; " and this statement holds true, not only of philosophy, but also of education.

ADVANCEMENT OF LEARNING.—Bacon's first great philosophical work, published in 1605, was the Advancement of Learning. It was the aim of this work to take a complete survey of the field of knowledge, for the purpose of indicating what departments of learning had received due attention, and what subjects yet needed cultivation. To use his own words: " I have made, as it were, a small globe of the intellectual world, as truly and faithfully as I could discover; with a note and description of those parts which seem to me not constantly occupate, or not well converted by the labor of man." In this work, as in the Novum Organum and elsewhere, he was led to treat of various aspects of education.

NARROW SCHOLARSHIP.—Already at the university his keen penetration detected the faults belonging to the higher education of the time. He found himself, to use his own language, " amid men of sharp and strong wits, and abundance of leisure, and small variety of reading, their wits being shut up in the cells of a few authors, chiefly Aristotle, their dictator, as their persons were shut up in the cells of monasteries and colleges; and who, knowing little history, either of nature or time, did, out of no great quantity of matter, and infinite agitation of wit, spin cobwebs of learning, admirable for the fineness of thread and work, but of no substance or profit."

SPECULATIVE LEARNING.—Bacon found fault with *a priori* or speculative philosophy, which seeks to deduce all truth from the inner resources of the mind. It was this philosophy that had been regnant in the universities of the latter part of the middle ages. Instead of extolling the native powers of the mind, and of relying upon its innate powers, Bacon urged a careful investigation of nature as the only sure way of arriving at truth. "The wit and mind of man," he says, "if it work upon matter, which is the contemplation of the creatures of God, worketh according to the stuff, and is limited thereby; but, if it work upon itself, as the spider worketh his web, then it is endless, and brings forth indeed cobwebs of learning, admirable for the fineness of thread and work, but of no substance or profit."

THE PRINCIPLE OF AUTHORITY.—With his vigorous, independent intellect, it was but natural that Bacon should condemn the principle of authority in education. He complained of the systematic efforts made in the universities to discourage and prevent independent investigation and judgment. "In the universities," he says, "all things are found opposite to the advancement of the sciences; for the readings and exercises are here so managed that it can not easily come into any one's mind to think of things out of the common road: or if, here and there, one should venture to use a liberty of judging, he can only impose the task upon himself without obtaining assistance from his fellows; and, if he could dispense with this, he will still find his industry and resolution a great hindrance to his fortune. For the studies of men in such places are confined, and pinned down to the writings of certain authors; from which, if any man happens to differ, he is presently reprehended as a disturber and innovator."

OPINION OF THE ANCIENTS.—Bacon was, perhaps, the first great modern author to rebel against the thraldom of the ancients. He maintained that since their day the field of knowledge has been broadened; and that, therefore, instead of sitting at the feet of Aristotle, Plato, and the rest, we should draw upon the resources of modern knowledge. This attitude of mind, far better justified to-day than in Bacon's time, is rapidly changing the character of education. "The opinion," he says in the Novum Organum, "which men cherish of antiquity is altogether idle, and scarcely accords with the term. For the old and increasing years of the world should in reality be considered antiquity, and this is rather the character of our own times than of the less advanced age of the world in those of the ancients. For the latter, with respect to ourselves, are ancient and elder; with respect to the world, modern and younger. And, as we expect a greater knowledge of human affairs and more mature judgment from an old man than from a youth, on account of his experience, and the variety and number of things he has seen, heard, and meditated upon, so we have reason to expect much greater things of our own age (if it knew but its strength and would essay and exert it) than from antiquity, since the world has grown older, and its stock has been increased and accumulated with an infinite number of experiments and observations. We must also take into our consideration that many objects in nature fit to throw light upon

15

philosophy have been exposed to our view and discovered by means of long voyages and travels, in which our times have abounded. It would, indeed, be dishonorable to mankind if the regions of the material globe, the earth, the sea, and stars, should be so prodigiously developed and illustrated in our age, and yet the boundaries of the intellectual globe should be confined to the narrow discoveries of the ancients."

HUMANISTIC LEARNING.—While not indifferent to the graces of style, Bacon criticized the excessive humanistic tendency of his time. He distinguished between form and substance; and to his practical judgment no elegance of style could make up for lack or feebleness of matter. He regarded the humanistic devotion to style rather than to truth as tending to bring learning into discredit. "How is it possible," he asks, "but this should have an operation to discredit learning, even with vulgar capacities, when they see learned men's works like the first letter of a patent or limned book, which, though it hath large flourishes, yet it is but a letter? It seems to me that Pygmalion's frenzy is a good emblem or portraiture of this vanity, for words are but the images of matter; and, except they have life of reason and invention, to fall in love with them is all one as to fall in love with a picture."[1]

THE PURPOSE OF LEARNING.—Bacon assigned a high end to learning. This end should be, not pleasure or lucre, but a due development and use of our faculties in the service of mankind. "Men have entered into a desire of learning and knowledge," he says, "sometimes upon a natural curiosity and inquisitive appetite, sometimes to entertain their minds with variety and delight, sometimes for orna-

---

[1] Pygmalion, a sculptor of the island of Cyprus, cherished a settled aversion to women, but fell in love with an ivory statue that he had made.

ment and reputation, and sometimes to enable them to victory of wit and contradiction—and, most times, for lucre and profession; and seldom sincerely to give a true account of their gift of reason, *to the benefit and use of man:* as if there were sought in knowledge a couch, whereupon to rest a searching and restless spirit, or a terrace for a wandering and variable mind to walk up and down with a fair prospect; or a tower of state, for a proud mind to raise itself upon; or a fort or commanding ground, for strife and contention; or a shop, for profit or sale; and not a rich storehouse, *for the glory of the Creator and the relief of man's estate.*"

A BROAD FOUNDATION.—Bacon insisted on a liberal culture as the basis of a professional career. A broad foundation should precede the work of specialization. The hurried completion of a liberal course of study with the view of entering as early as possible upon professional work seemed to him a cause of the small progress of learning in his day. A liberal culture should be sought with serious purpose. " If men judge," he says, " that learning should be referred to action, they judge well; but in this they fall into the error described in the ancient fable, in which the other parts of the body did suppose the stomach had been idle, because it neither performed the office of motion, as the limbs do, nor of sense, as the head doth; but yet, notwithstanding, it is the stomach that digesteth and distributeth to all the rest: so, if any man think philosophy and universality to be idle studies, he doth not consider that all professions are from thence served and supplied. And this I take to be a great cause that hath hindered the progression of learning, because these fundamental knowledges have been studied but in passage. For, if you will have a tree bear more fruit than it hath used to do, it is not anything you can do to the boughs, but it is the stirring of the earth and putting new mold about the roots that must work it."

LEARNING AND RELIGION.—Bacon held that learning is conducive to religion. Though a little learning might incline a man to unbelief, profound attainments would bring him back to the recognition of a great first cause. " It is an assured truth," he says, " and a conclusion of experience, that a little or superficial knowledge of philosophy may incline the mind of man to atheism, but a further proceeding therein doth bring the mind back again to religion; for, in the entrance of philosophy, when the second causes, which are next unto the senses, do offer themselves unto the mind of man, if it dwell and stay there, it may induce some oblivion of the highest cause; but when a man passeth on farther, and seeth the dependence of causes and the works of Providence, then, according to the allegory of the poets, he will easily believe that the highest link of Nature's chain must needs be tied to the foot of Jupiter's chair."

RAUMER'S ESTIMATE.—These extracts, which might be indefinitely extended, show that a strong voice had been raised against the theologico-humanistic education of the seventeenth century. His modern spirit, with his masterful penetration, gives Bacon a prominent place in the line of educational reformers. " This significance," says Raumer, " Bacon receives as the first to say to the learned men who lived and toiled in the languages and writings of antiquity, and who were mostly only echoes of the old Greeks and Romans, yea, who knew nothing better than to be such: ' There is also a present; only open your eyes to recognize its splendor. Turn away from the shallow springs of traditional natural science, and draw from the unfathomable and ever freshly flowing fountain of creation. Live in Nature with active senses; ponder it in your thoughts, and learn to comprehend it, for thus you will be able also to control it. Power increases with knowledge.' "

C. Milton

BIOGRAPHICAL.—John Milton, the author of Paradise Lost, was born in London in 1608. He studied at home under a private tutor. He showed extraordinary aptness in learning; and when in 1624 he was sent to Cambridge, he was master of several languages, and had read extensively in philosophy and literature. After a long residence at the university, he retired to Horton in Buckinghamshire, where he devoted five more years to diligent study. He read all the Greek and Latin writers of the classic period, and then feasted " with avidity and delight on Dante and Petrarch." To use his own expression, he was letting his wings grow. It would carry us beyond our limits to follow the career of Milton through the troublous times of the Commonwealth, and the dangers and sufferings of the Restoration; to speak of his embittered controversies and domestic trials; and to portray him, old and blind, in the elaboration of his sublime poem, the cherished thought of a lifetime. Through it all he showed himself a man of unblemished character, of undaunted courage, and of intellectual vigor unequaled in his day.

DEVOTION TO LEARNING.—Milton's devotion to learning was quite unusual. In order to get at his books he rose at the earliest dawn, and to keep his mind clear he was abstemious in diet and regular in exercise. In one of his controversial tracts, replying to certain calumniations, he depicted his manner of life, which possesses the greater interest as showing his earnestness in education. "Those morning haunts," he says, "are where they should be— at home; not sleeping or concocting the surfeits of an irregular feast, but up and stirring in winter, often ere the sound of any bell awakens men to labor or devotion; in summer, as oft with the bird that first rouses, or not much tardier, to read good authors, or cause them to be read, till the attention be weary, or the memory have its full fraught. Then, with useful and generous labors, preserving the body's health and hardiness, to render lightsome, clear, and not lumpish obedience to the mind, to the cause of religion and our country's liberty, when it shall require firm hearts in sound bodies, to stand and cover their stations, rather than see the ruin of our Protestantism, and the enforcement of a slavish life."

TRACTATE ON EDUCATION.—Milton was not without practical experience as a teacher. In 1643 he opened a private school in London, in which, as his nephew Philips states, he received "the sons of some gentlemen that were his friends." Furthermore, he was not indifferent to the educational movements of his times, and he appears to have been familiar with the reformatory efforts of Ratich and Comenius. As a thoughtful student and educator, he gradually developed in his mind an ideal of what education should be in its methods and course of study. At the request of Samuel Hartlib, who was a disciple of Comenius and an apostle of educational reform, Milton consented to put in writing the opinions he had previously expressed to his friend in conversation. The result was the well-known Tractate on Education, which presents, to use the author's own language, "that voluntary idea, which hath long in silence presented itself to me, of a better education, in extent and comprehension far more large, and yet of time far shorter and of attainment far more certain, than hath been yet in practise."

NATURE AND END OF EDUCATION.—Milton thought of education both in its objective and its subjective relations. On the one hand, the purpose of education is to fit us for the duties of practical life. Accordingly, in a famous definition, Milton says: "I call a complete and generous education that which fits a man to perform justly, skilfully, and magnanimously all the offices both private and public, of peace and war." On the other hand, education should aim at developing the individual in virtue and knowledge. Hence he says: "The end of learning is to repair the ruins of our first parents by regaining to know God aright, and out of that knowledge to love him, to imitate him, to be like him, as we may the nearest by possessing our souls of true virtue, which being united to the heavenly grace of faith, makes up the highest perfection. But because our understanding can not in this body found itself but on sensible things, nor arrive so clearly to the knowledge of God and things invisible, as by orderly conning over the visible and inferior creature, the same method is necessarily to be followed in all discreet teaching."

THE STUDY OF LANGUAGES.—Milton took a larger view of language study than was common in his day. As he viewed the matter, the various languages were to be studied, not to gain mental discipline or a Ciceronian elegance of style, but to get possession of their stores of useful knowledge. Mere linguistic attainments seemed to him of small value. Accordingly, in an interesting and emphatic passage, he says: "And seeing every nation affords not experience and tradition enough for all kinds of learning, therefore we are chiefly taught the languages of those

people who have at any time been most industrious after
wisdom; so that language is but the instrument conveying
to us things useful to be known. And though a linguist
should pride himself to have all the tongues that Babel
cleft the world into, yet if he have not studied the solid
things in them, as well as the words and lexicons, he were
nothing so much to be esteemed a learned man as any
yeoman or tradesman competently wise in his mother-
dialect only."

ADAPTATION OF STUDIES.—Milton wished to shorten
the time devoted to grammar, and to adapt all studies to
the capacities of the pupils. To require verses and orations,
for example, of immature students, and to introduce them
suddenly to the abstractions of logic and metaphysics,
seemed to him unreasonable in itself and harmful in its
results. He complained that the years of youth were mis-
spent at the schools and universities " either in learning
mere words, or such things chiefly as were better unlearned."
" We do amiss," he says, " to spend seven or eight years
merely in scraping together so much miserable Latin and
Greek as might be learned otherwise easily and delight-
fully in one year. And that which casts our proficiency
therein so much behind is our time lost partly in too oft
idle vacancies given both to schools and universities; partly
in a preposterous exaction, forcing the empty wits of children to compose themes, verses, and orations, which are
the acts of ripest judgment, and the final work of a head
filled by long reading and observing with elegant maxims
and copious invention. These are not matters to be wrung
from poor striplings, like blood out of the nose, or the
plucking of untimely fruit; besides all the ill habit which
they get of wretched barbarizing against the Latin and
Greek idiom, with their untutored Anglicisms, odious to

be read, yet not to be avoided without a well-continued and judicious conversing among pure authors, digested, which they scarce taste."

MORAL CULTURE.—With a noble character himself, and with lofty conceptions of human duty, Milton naturally made moral culture prominent in education. Accordingly, after acquainting students in a short time with the principal rules of grammar, he would take up some easy and delightful book on education, such as Plutarch or Plato, for the sake of its moral lessons. But in attaining Milton's exalted ideal of personal and civic virtue, the skill and character of the teacher were held of prime importance; for he was not only to impart moral instruction, on every suitable occasion, but constantly to lead them on by a beautiful example. "The main skill and groundwork," says Milton, "will be to temper them such lectures and explanations upon every opportunity, as may lead and draw them in willing obedience, inflamed with a study of learning, and the admiration of virtue; stirred up with high hopes of living to be brave men, and worthy patriots, dear to God, and famous to all ages, that they may despise and scorn all their childish and ill-taught qualities, to delight in manly and liberal exercises; which he who hath the art and proper eloquence to catch them with, what with mild and effectual persuasions, and what with the intimation of some fear, if need be, but chiefly by his own example, might in a short space gain them to an incredible diligence and courage; infusing into their young hearts such an ingenuous and noble ardor, as would not fail to make many of them renowned and matchless men."

GYMNASTIC TRAINING.—Milton recognized the one-sidedness both of Spartan and of Athenian education, and proposed to unite in his system their distinctive and praiseworthy elements.   Hence he advocated gymnastic training; and inasmuch as the Tractate was published during the Civil War, when Cromwell's Ironsides were achieving their famous victories, he emphasized martial training in particular.   " The exercise which I commend first," he says, " is the exact use of their weapon, to guard and to strike safely with edge or point; this will keep them healthy, nimble, strong, and well in breath; is also the likeliest means to make them grow large and tall, and to inspire them with a gallant and fearless courage, which being tempered with seasonable lectures and precepts to them of true fortitude and patience, will turn into a native and heroic valor, and make them hate the cowardice of doing wrong.   They must be also practised in all the locks and gripes of wrestling, wherein Englishmen were wont to excel, as need may often be in fight to tug or grapple, and to close."

COURSE OF STUDY.—Apart from travel, which Milton commended as a useful means of acquiring practical knowledge, his course of study is somewhat startling in its magnitude.   He wished to emulate the schools of Pythagoras, Plato, and Aristotle.   There was to be, first of all, a thorough grounding in the ancient languages and the usual classics.   In addition, the students should be " led through all the moral works of Plato, Xenophon, Cicero, Plutarch, Lucretius, and those Locrian remnants," besides David, Solomon, and the New Testament.   " Having passed the principles of arithmetic, geometry, astronomy and geography, with a general compact of physics, they may descend in mathematics to the instrumental science of trigonometry, and from thence to fortification, architecture, engineering, or navigation."   After the study of politics, the students " are to dive into the grounds of law, and legal justice; delivered first, and with best warrant, by Moses; and as far as human prudence can be trusted, in those extolled remains of Grecian lawgivers, Lycurgus, Solon, Zaleucus, Charondas, and thence to all the Roman edicts and tables, with their Justinian; and so down to the Saxon and common laws of England, and the statutes. Sundays also, and every evening, may be now understandingly spent in the highest matters of theology, and Church history, ancient and modern: and ere this time the Hebrew tongue at a set hour might have been gained, that the Scriptures may be now read in their own original; whereto it would be no impossibility to add the Chaldee, and the Syrian dialect." "They may have easily learned at any odd hour the Italian tongue." Milton was not unconscious of the magnitude of his scheme of studies, and he concludes his Tractate with the remark, " I believe that this is not a bow for every man to shoot in that counts himself a teacher, but will require sinews almost equal to those which Homer gave Ulysses."

D. Ratich

A PRACTICAL EDUCATOR.—Ratich was not, like Montaigne, Bacon, and Milton, simply an enlightened critic; he was also a practical educator, who sought to remedy existing evils by the actual introduction of reforms. Though he erred in the application of his principles, and his efforts resulted in failure, yet he has the honor of having made substantial contributions to the permanent stock of pedagogic truth. He laid the foundations well, but failed in rearing the superstructure.

BIOGRAPHICAL.—Wolfgang Ratich, or Ratke, was born at Wilster, in Holstein, 1571. He received his classical training at the Hamburg Gymnasium, and afterward studied theology and philosophy at the University of Rostock. Compelled to give up his purpose of becoming a preacher on account of some impediment of speech, he devoted himself to the study of Hebrew, Arabic, and mathematics. He spent eight years at Amsterdam, where he elaborated his educational views, and offered his method to Prince Maurice, of Orange. The prince wished to restrict him to the teaching of Latin, but, unwilling to accept this condition, the enthusiastic reformer carried his secret to Basel and Strasburg, as well as to several courts, in search of a patron.

EDUCATIONAL CLAIMS.—In 1612 he addressed a memorial to the Electoral Diet, at Frankfort, in which he promised, with divine help, to show: (1) how young and old might acquire, in a short time, Hebrew, Greek, Latin, and other languages; (2) how a school, not only in High German, but also in other languages, might be established, in which all the arts and sciences might be taught; (3) how in the whole country a uniform language, government, and religion might be easily introduced and peaceably maintained. At the same time he attacked the current education, and insisted that the young should learn to read, write, and speak their mother-tongue correctly, before beginning the study of other languages.

The pretensions of this memorial were by no means modest, but it attracted so much attention that a commission of learned men was appointed to investigate Ratich's claims. His views were reported on favorably. Helvicus, a celebrated German scholar of the time, expressed himself in strong terms. " We are," he says, in his report, " in bondage to Latin. The Greeks and Saracens would never have done so much for posterity if they had spent their youth in acquiring a foreign tongue. We must study our own language, and then the sciences. Ratich has discovered the art of teaching according to nature. By this method languages will be quickly learned, so that we shall have time for science; and science will be learned even better still, as the natural system suits best with science, which is the study of Nature."

SCHOOL AT KOTHEN.—Finally, after repeated failures, Ratich succeeded in getting Prince Ludwig, of Anhalt-Köthen, interested in his scheme, and in 1619 received at the hands of the prince every facility for opening a model school; in return for which he made extravagant promises. A printing-house, provided with type in six different languages, was opened for the publication of text-books; and a number of teachers were set apart to receive a special drill in the new methods. It was given out that Hebrew, Greek, and Latin would be learned in less than half the time required in other parts of Germany, and besides with much less trouble.

The inhabitants of Köthen responded readily to the appeal for pupils, and a school was opened with two hundred and thirty-one boys and two hundred and two girls. It was divided into six grades. In the three lowest only the mother-tongue was to be used; in the fourth Latin was taken up, and in the sixth Greek. Besides languages, arithmetic, singing, and religion were taught. The teacher of the lowest grade was to be an affable man, who, as stated in the plan, should " form the speech of these young pupils by daily prayer, short biblical proverbs, and easy conversations; and correct by constant practise the faults acquired out of school."

METHOD OF TEACHING.—In teaching the mother-tongue, Ratich began with the letters of the alphabet, which he regarded as the simplest element of grammar. As he drew each letter slowly on the blackboard, he directed attention to its form and name; and, in order to deepen the impression, he compared its shape with other objects (as *o* with a ring), and required the pupil to make it himself. The next step was in forming syllables and words, which were likewise to be written and pronounced. The transition to reading was made without delay, and in a novel manner. The teacher took some easy and interesting book like Genesis, and read it through before the class, going over each chapter twice, and requiring the pupils to follow with eye and finger. Then, turning again to the beginning, he read over the first chapter; after which the pupils were permitted to read, each one pronouncing four lines. Reading having been learned in this way, the study of grammar was begun. The teacher first read and explained some section of the grammar, for example, that treating of nouns; then the pupils read the same one or more times; after which they took up the book previously used in reading, and with the aid of the teacher pointed out the substantives. In this way all the principles of grammar were exemplified.

In Latin, as in the mother-tongue, grammar followed reading. Terence was the favorite author for beginners. A translation of some one of his plays was first placed in the pupil's hands. "The master then," to use Quick's convenient condensation of the tedious German account, " translated the play to them, each half-hour's work twice over. At the next reading the master translated the first half-hour, and the boys translated the same piece the second. Having thus got through the play, they began again, and only the boys translated. After this there was a course of grammar, which was applied to the Terence, as the grammar of the mother-tongue had been to Genesis.

Finally, the pupils were put through a course of exercises, in which they had to turn into Latin sentences imitated from the Terence, and differing from the original only in the number or person used."

COMPLETE FAILURE.—The school at Köthen did not have the success that these methods would seem to assure; on the contrary, it turned out a complete failure. Several external causes concurred in bringing this about. Ratich displeased his patrons, who were all Calvinistic, by his uncompromising Lutheranism; he offended his colleagues and supporters by his arrogance, and he provoked unfriendly criticism. His school was soon in disorder. And, having fallen into a quarrel with the prince, he was thrown into prison, from which he obtained his release only upon signing a declaration that " he had claimed and promised more than he knew or could bring to pass." Ratich endeavored for many years to establish his system elsewhere; but, during the commotions of the Thirty Years' War, he was able to accomplish but little.

EDUCATIONAL PRINCIPLES.—His theories, however, are not to be judged by his failure as a teacher. Many of his educational principles are excellent; and, though he failed in the attempt to apply them, they have survived, and enter into the education of the present. His chief educational maxims are the following:

1. Everything after the order or course of nature. All teaching that is forced, violent, or contrary to nature, is harmful.

2. Teach only one thing at a time. There is nothing that hinders the understanding more than the attempt to learn many things at once.

3. Often repeat the same thing. It thus sinks deeply into the understanding.

4. Everything first in the mother-tongue. The pupil's attention is thus fixed only upon what he has to learn, and not upon the medium through which he learns it.

5. Everything without compulsion. Compulsion is against nature, and also renders studies hateful to the young.

6. Nothing should be learned by rote. This is hurtful to the understanding.

7. There should be uniformity in all things, in methods of teaching, as well as in the form of text-books.

8. First the thing itself, then the manner of the thing. Rules without matter confuse the understanding.

9. Teach everything by experiment and analysis. Nothing should be received on mere authority; the reason and evidence should be examined and apprehended.

SUMMARY.—These principles, though liable to abuse, are a valuable contribution to pedagogy. They show the pedagogical insight of Ratich, and establish his claim to an honorable place among educational reformers. The nature of his work has been thus summed up by Paroz: "Ratich, as we have just seen, is dissatisfied with the past, and commences in Germany the reaction against the defective system of study inaugurated and perfected by men like Luther, Trotzendorf, Sturm, and the Jesuits—a system whose base, middle, and summit was Latin, a servile imitation of Cicero. His attempts were unskilful, and his principles commonly exaggerated. It is not astonishing, therefore, that he succumbed in an undertaking above his strength, and when he had the age against him, instead of for him, as the men whom I have just named. Nevertheless, he has brought out, like Montaigne, a truth which no force will henceforth be able to overthrow, namely, that the old methods—if we may so call an empirical instruction based on memory and imitation—are defective, and that it has become necessary to reform our instruction by methods based on nature, and by the adoption of new subjects, such, for example, as the mother-tongue."

E. Comenius

BIOGRAPHICAL.—The most celebrated educational reformer of the seventeenth century was John Amos Comenius. He was born in Moravia, March 28, 1592. His family belonged to that body of Protestants known as Moravian Brethren. Though few in number, this body has always been distinguished for simplicity of faith, earnest piety, and missionary zeal. These characteristics were early developed in Comenius, and they imparted to his long life of labor and trial peculiar beauty.

As with many other illustrious men, little is known of his early years. When quite young he lost his parents, and was brought up under the care of guardians. He received the limited instruction in reading, writing, arithmetic, and the catechism imparted in the primary schools of the time. It was not till the age of sixteen that he began the study of Latin, then the staple of learning. " Yet, by the goodness of God," he says, " that taste bred such a thirst in me that I ceased not from that time, by all means and endeavors, to labor for the repairing of my lost years."

Comenius completed his studies at the College of Herborn and the University of Heidelberg. In 1616 he was ordained to the ministry in the Moravian Church, and was placed over the congregation in Fulneck. Along with his pastoral duties, he had charge of a recently established school, and began to consider more fully the subject of education. Here he married, and for two or three years he

16

led an active and happy life—the only period of tranquillity he was ever to enjoy in his native country. The Thirty Years' War broke out, and made troublous times. In 1621 Fulneck was taken by the Spaniards, and Comenius lost all his property. Instigated by the Jesuits, the Austrian Government proscribed the evangelical pastors, and forced them to fly. Comenius took refuge for a time in his native mountains, but, as the persecution waxed hotter, he fled to Lissa, in Poland. On crossing the border, he devoutly knelt and prayed God that the truth might not be quenched in his native land.

THE GREAT DIDACTIC.—At Lissa he found employment in the Moravian Gymnasium, of which he seems to have become rector. He applied himself with new ardor to his educational studies. He acquainted himself with the best educational writings of the age, perusing among others the works of Ratich and Bacon. He was greatly impressed by them. " Yet," he says, " observing here and there some defects and gaps, as it were, I could not restrain myself from attempting something that might rest upon an immovable foundation, and which, if it could be found out, should not be subject to any ruin. Therefore, after many workings and tossings of my thoughts, by reducing everything to the immovable law of Nature, I lighted upon my Didactica Magna, which shows the art of readily and solidly teaching all men all things."

In this work, which was not published for several years, Comenius made a comprehensive and profound study of education, and announced those principles which were destined to transform the schools of all Christian lands. Though it attracted but little attention at the time of its publication, it is a monumental work in the field of pedagogy. Its scope and aims can not be given better than by quoting its full title: The Great Didactic, setting forth the whole art of teaching all things to all men; or a certain inducement to found such schools in all parishes, towns, and villages of every Christian kingdom, that the entire youth of both sexes, none being excepted, shall quickly, pleasantly, and thoroughly become learned in the sciences, pure in morals, trained to piety, and in this manner instructed in all things necessary for the present and for the future life, in which, with respect to everything that is suggested, its fundamental principles are set forth from the essential nature of the matter, its truth is proved by examples from the several mechanical arts, its order is clearly set forth in years, months, days, and hours, and, finally, an easy and sure method is shown, by which it can be pleasantly brought into existence."

IDEA OF DEVELOPMENT.—Comenius was the first educator to grasp clearly the idea of individual development. He conceived of education, not as something added from without, but as an unfolding of the faculties from within. He thought of education as a development of the whole man.   The means to bring about this result was not a cramming of the memory, but the acquisition of knowledge through individual research and observation.   The key to method was to be found in the processes of nature.   The following passage shows the firm foundation on which Comenius reared his system: " The right instruction of youth," he says, " does not consist in cramming them with a mass of words, phrases, sentences, and opinions collected from the authors, but in unfolding the understanding that many little streams may flow therefrom as from a living fountain.   Hitherto the schools have not labored that the children might unfold like the young tree from the impulse of its own roots, but have been contented when they covered themselves with foreign branches. Thus they have taught the youth, after the manner of Æsop's crow, to adorn themselves with strange feathers. Why shall we not, instead of dead books, open the living book of Nature? Not the shadows of things, but the things themselves, which make an impression on the senses and the imagination, are to be brought before youth. By actual observation, not by a verbal description of things, must instruction begin. From such observation develops a certain knowledge. Men must be led as far as possible to draw their wisdom not from books, but from a consideration of heaven and earth, oaks and beeches; that is, they must know and examine things themselves, and not simply be contented with the observations and testimony of others." This brief extract contains the two fundamental truths upon which all correct education must rest.

UNIVERSAL EDUCATION.—It is likewise to the credit of Comenius that he firmly grasped the idea of popular education and advocated it as a means of improving society. It would exalt the general plane of thought, efficiency, and life. He felt the worth of the individual more deeply than any of his predecessors since the days of Paul; and instead of an education intended almost exclusively for the ruling classes in Church and State, he wished to make provision for all persons as a right in keeping with the dignity of their nature and vocation in the world. "If any ask," he says, "what will be the result if artisans, rustics, porters, and even women become lettered, I answer: if this universal instruction of youth be brought about by the proper means, none of these will lack the material for thinking, choosing, following, and doing good things. All will know how the actions and endeavors of life should be regulated, within what limits we must progress, and how each man can protect his own position. Not only this, but all will regale themselves, even in the midst of their work and toil, by meditation on the words and works of God, and, by the constant reading of the Bible and other good books, will avoid idleness, which is so dangerous to flesh and blood."

EDUCATION OF WOMAN.—He uttered a brave, strong word in behalf of woman's education, and with his accustomed insight, placed it on an immovable foundation. He rose above the orientalism that had weighed for centuries upon the female sex, and proclaimed the fact that woman, no less than man, is a child of God, and that she is endowed with equal penetration and capacity for knowledge. " Nor can any sufficient reason be given," he says, " why the weaker sex (to give a word of advice on this point in particular) should be altogether excluded from the pursuits of knowledge whether in Latin or in their mother-tongue. They also are formed in the image of God, and share in his grace and in the kingdom of the world to come. They are endowed with equal sharpness of mind and capacity of knowledge (often with more than the opposite sex), and they are able to attain the highest positions, since they have often been called by God himself to rule over nations, to give sound advice to kings and princes, to the study of medicine and of other things which benefit the human race, even to the office of prophesying and of inveighing against priests and bishops. Why, therefore, should we admit them to the alphabet, and afterward drive them away from books? Do we fear their folly? The more we occupy their thoughts, so much the less will the folly that arises from emptiness of mind find a place."

GATE OF TONGUES.—After preparing his Great Didactic, from which the preceding extracts are taken, Comenius set about reforming the methods of teaching Latin. It was, perhaps, a fortunate circumstance that he entered, as we have seen, upon the study of Latin so late in his youth. He was better able to judge of the methods and discipline to which he had to conform. He complained that the schools of his time "are the terror of boys and the slaughter-houses of minds—places where a hatred of literature and books is contracted, where ten or more years are spent in learning what might be acquired in one, where what ought to be poured in gently is violently forced in and beaten in, where what ought to be put clearly and perspicuously is presented in a confused and intricate way, as if it were a collection of puzzles—places where minds are fed on words." It seemed to him that so much time was spent on words that the student could never learn about things, and that life was thus consumed in preparing for life. To remedy these evils he prepared his Gate of Tongues Unlocked (Janua Linguarum Reserata), the character of which may be judged from the following brief extract: "My fundamental principle—an irrefragable law of didactics—is that the understanding and the tongue should advance in parallel lines always. The human being tends to utter what he apprehends. If he does not apprehend the word he uses, he is a parrot; if he apprehends without words, he is a dumb statue. Accordingly, under one hundred heads, I have classified the whole universe of things in a manner suited to the capacity of boys, and I have given the corresponding language. I have selected from lexicons the words that had to be introduced, and I include eight thousand vocables in one thousand sentences, which are at first simple, and thereafter gradually become complex."

As this passage shows, the Gate of Tongues possessed

several great merits. It was suited to the pupil's capacity; it carried him along by easy gradations; and, above all, it taught him things in connection with words. Its success was instantaneous and immense. It was translated into Greek, Bohemian, Polish, German, Swedish, Belgian, English, French, Spanish, Italian, Hungarian, Turkish, Arabic, and one of the languages of India.

PANSOPHIC SCHEME.—Comenius long gave affectionate thought and zealous labor to a pansophic scheme which he fancied for many years was to constitute his principal life-work. This scheme, suggested to him by Bacon, was the publication of a work that would embrace and fully exhibit the whole circle of knowledge. As the execution of this plan was obviously beyond the powers of any one man, his practical mind suggested the establishment of an institution in which all departments of learning should be represented by the ablest scholars, and from which this encyclopedia of knowledge was to proceed. It was in relation to this pansophic scheme that Comenius was invited by the English Parliament to London in 1641. Though his plans were favorably received, they were brought to naught by the commotion preceding the outbreak of the Civil War. Afterward he was invited to Sweden, where Oxenstiern, "that eagle of the North," closely questioned him about his pansophic and didactic principles for several days.

LATEST METHOD.—The pansophic plans of Comenius were not encouraged by Oxenstiern; and, as a result of this conference, he was induced to prepare a work in which his principles should be carefully wrought out in reference to teaching languages. For this purpose, he took up his residence at Elbing, in Prussia, where he was supported by De Geer, a wealthy and intelligent Dutchman. Here, after four years of labor, he produced his Latest Method with Languages (Methodus Linguarum Novissima). In this work he points out three evils in the current teaching of Latin: (1) that words are taught without being understood; (2) that boys are introduced at once into the intricacies of grammar; and (3) that they are required to make impossible leaps, being forced prematurely into works above their comprehension. In this connection, he laid down the important principles that words and things should be learned together; that theory should not be dissevered from practise, and that study should advance by easy gradations.

WORLD ILLUSTRATED.—No sooner had Comenius accomplished the work assigned him by his Swedish advisers, than he received a call to reform the schools of Transylvania, in Hungary. Accordingly, he went, in 1650, to the town of Patak, where he established a model school. This he designed, under the patronage of wealthy friends, to develop into a pansophic institution; but it appears that he never organized more than the lower classes.

He remained at Patak four years, which were characterized by surprising literary activity. During this short period he produced no less than fifteen different works, among them his World Illustrated (Orbis Pictus), the most famous of all his writings. This work contained, as stated in the title-page, "the pictures and names of all the principal things in the world, and of all the principal occupations of man." It admirably applied the principle that words and things should be learned together. It contained not only a simple treatment of things in general, but also pictures to illustrate the subject of each lesson. The philosophic basis of the work is presented by Comenius in the following extract: "The foundation of all learning consists in representing clearly to the senses sensible objects, so that they can be apprehended easily. I maintain that this is the basis of all other actions, inasmuch as we could neither act nor speak wisely unless we comprehended clearly what we wished to say or do. For it is certain that there is nothing in the understanding which has not been previously in the sense; and consequently, to exercise the senses carefully in discriminating the differences of natural objects, is to lay the foundation of all wisdom, all eloquence, and all good and prudent action." The World Illustrated had an enormous circulation, and remained for a long time the most popular text-book in Europe.

LAST YEARS.—In 1654 Comenius returned to his former home at Lissa. Here one more misfortune awaited him before the close of his eventful career. When that town was plundered by the Poles, in 1656, Comenius lost his house, books, and, above all, his manuscripts, which embodied the labors of many years. " This loss," he said, " I shall cease to lament only when I cease to breathe." After several months' wandering in Germany, he was offered an asylum in Amsterdam by Laurence de Geer, the son of his former patron. Here, in comparative ease, he spent the remaining years of his life, devoting himself to teaching as a means of support, and to the promulgation and defense of his educational views. Through the liberality of friends, he was enabled to publish a complete edition of his works. His last days were somewhat embittered by envious attacks upon his character and methods, but in all his trials he exhibited a meek, forbearing Christian spirit. He died in 1671, at the advanced age of eighty years.

SCHOOL SYSTEM.—The school system proposed by Comenius is not unworthy of mention. It embraced four grades of schools. The first was the domestic school, in which the child was to learn the use of its senses, acquire its native language, and gain a rudimentary knowledge of things in general. The next was the vernacular, or popular school. This the child attended from the age of six to twelve, and studied reading, writing, arithmetic, singing, the catechism, history, and geography. Then followed the Latin school, in which the young student devoted six years to grammar, physics, mathematics, ethics, logic, and rhetoric. Lastly, the university, as the home of all branches of learning, formed the natural completion of the system. This is substantially the system in use at the present day.

PRINCIPLES OF PEDAGOGY.—The most lucid and comprehensive statement of the pedagogical principles of Comenius is found in his Great Didactic. In successive chapters he lays down fundamental principles, from which, after due exposition and defense, he draws practical inferences. The universal requirements of teaching and learning are given as follows:

" 1. Nature observes a suitable time.

" 2. Nature prepares the material before she begins to give it form.

" 3. Nature chooses a fit subject to act upon, or first submits one to a suitable treatment in order to make it fit.

" 4. Nature is not confused in its operations, but in its forward progress advances distinctly from one point to another.

" 5. In all the operations of nature the development is from within.

" 6. Nature, in its formative processes, begins with the universal and ends with the particular.

" 7. Nature makes no leaps, but proceeds step by step.

" 8. If nature commence anything, it does not leave off until the operation is completed.

" 9. Nature carefully avoids obstacles and things likely to cause hurt."

From these general principles Comenius deduces such practical inferences as the following: (1) " All the subjects that are to be learned should be so arranged as to suit the age of the students ; " (2) that the knowledge of things should precede their expression in language, and that examples should come before rules; (3) that all studies should be carefully graduated.

The principles of facility in teaching are stated as follows:

" 1. Nature begins with a careful selection of materials.

" 2. Nature prepares its material so that it actually strives to attain the form.

" 3. Nature develops everything from beginnings which, though insignificant in appearance, possess great potential strength.

" 4. Nature advances from what is easy to what is more difficult.

" 5. Nature does not overburden herself, but is content with a little.

" 6. Nature does not hurry, but advances slowly.

" 7. Nature compels nothing to advance that is not driven forward by its own mature strength.

" 8. Nature assists its operations in every possible manner.

" 9. Nothing is provided by nature of which the practical application is not soon evident.

" 10. Nature is uniform in all its operations."

From these general principles Comenius deduces such practical rules as these :• (1) the method of instruction should lighten the drudgery of learning; (2) each rule should be expressed in the shortest and clearest words; (3) all explanations should be given in the language that the pupils understand; (4) the student should not be confused with many studies at one time; (5) everything should be arranged to suit the capacity of the pupil; (6) nothing should be learned by heart that has not been thoroughly grasped by the understanding; (7) nothing should be set for pupils to do until its nature has been thoroughly explained to them, and rules of procedure have been given; (8) only those things should be taught whose utility can be easily demonstrated.

CONCLUSION.—If space allowed, these wise practical maxims might be indefinitely extended. But we close this sketch with the words of a judicious writer on educational history. "Comenius," says Raumer, "is a grand and venerable figure of sorrow. Wandering, persecuted, and homeless, during the terrible and desolating Thirty Years' War, he yet never despaired, but with enduring truth, and strong in faith, he labored unweariedly to prepare youth by a better education for a better future. Suspended from the ministry, as he himself tells us, and an exile, he had become an apostle to the Christian youth; and certainly he labored for them with a zeal and love worthy of the chief of the apostles."

F. Locke

BIOGRAPHICAL.—John Locke was born at Wrington, near Bristol, in 1632. His father served as captain in the Parliamentary army during the Civil War. After receiving a preparatory training at Westminster School, he proceeded to Oxford, where he took his bachelor's degree in 1655.

He was endowed with a penetrating and practical mind, and, like Bacon at Cambridge, he early found fault with Oxford on account of its extreme conservative tendencies. After taking his degree, Locke studied medicine, not with the view of becoming a practitioner, but of improving his feeble health.   He spent a year at the Court of Berlin as secretary to the English envoy, Sir William Swan.   On his return to England he made the acquaintance of the Earl of Shaftesbury, of whose son he subsequently became tutor.   In 1689 he published his great philosophical work, An Essay Concerning Human Understanding, which was designed to establish the limitations and capabilities of the human mind.   It had a wide circulation not only in England, but also in France and Germany; and everywhere it exerted an immense influence upon philosophic thought.

THOUGHTS CONCERNING EDUCATION.—In 1693 Locke published a treatise entitled Some Thoughts Concerning Education.   This work, which touches upon nearly every phase of education with strong, practical sense, has since remained an educational classic.   It was translated into French, and to some extent molded the opinions of Rousseau.   The medical knowledge of Locke naturally gave him an interest in physical culture.   And, having filled several public offices, he attached more importance to the practical side of education than to mere learning.   His treatise begins with these words, which present his conception of the end of education: " A sound mind in a sound body is a short but full description of a happy state in this world; he that has these two has little more to wish for, and he that wants either of them will be but little the better for anything else."

LEARNING AND CHARACTER.—Locke did not set much store by mere bookish learning.   A noble manhood, well equipped for the duties of practical life, appeared to him far more important than any amount of training in Latin and Greek. "Reading, writing, and learning," he says, "I allow to be necessary, but yet not the chief business. I imagine you would think him a very foolish fellow that should not value a virtuous or a wise man infinitely before a scholar. Not but that I think learning a great help to both, in well-disposed minds; but yet it must be confessed, also, that in others not so disposed it helps them only to be the more foolish, or worse men. I say this, that, when you consider of the breeding of your son, and are looking out for a schoolmaster, or a tutor, you would not have (as is usual) Latin and logic only in your thoughts. Learning must be had, but in the second place, as subservient only to greater qualities. Seek out somebody that may know how discreetly to frame his manners; place him in hands, where you may, as much as possible, secure his innocence, cherish and nurse up the good, and gently correct and weed out any bad inclinations, and settle in him good habits. This is the main point; and, this being provided for, learning may be had into the bargain."

PHYSICAL TRAINING.—Locke attached great importance to the care of the body, and devoted the first part of his book to a consideration of the hygienic laws to be observed. Though erring, perhaps, in his directions for hardening the body, the wisdom of his rules will be generally recognized. He concludes his observations with these remarks: "And thus I have done with what concerns the body and health, which reduces itself to these few and easily observable rules: Plenty of open air, exercise, and sleep; plain diet, no wine or strong drink, and very little or no physic; not too warm and strait clothing; especially the head and feet kept cold, and the feet often used to cold water and exposed to wet."

CHILD STUDY.—He maintained that the disposition and native capacity of pupils should be studied as an antecedent to wise discipline and instruction.   Children are to be considered, not as insensible objects to be dealt with in a blind, mechanical way, but as living creatures to be carefully nurtured and developed.   Education can not impart a new set of endowments; it can only strengthen those that already exist.   " He therefore that is about children," says Locke, " should well study their natures and aptitudes, and see, by often trials, what turn they easily take, and what becomes them; observe what their native stock is, how it may be improved, and what it is fit for; he should consider what they want, whether they be capable of having it wrought into them by industry, and incorporated there by practise; and whether it be worth while to endeavor it.   For, in many cases, all that we can do, or should aim at, is to make the best of what Nature has given, to prevent the vices and faults to which such a constitution is most inclined, and give it all the advantages it is capable of. Every one's natural genius should be carried as far as it could, but, to attempt the putting another upon him, will be but labor in vain; and, what is so plastered on, will at best sit but untowardly, and have always hanging to it the ungracefulness of constraint and affectation."

KNOWLEDGE OF THINGS.—With Milton, Comenius, and other educational reformers of the time, Locke held that the exercises imposed upon pupils should be wisely adjusted to their powers and attainments.   He condemned the practise then in vogue of requiring verses and essays on abstract subjects—tasks that were necessarily beyond the pupil's capabilities.   The study of language should be combined with an acquisition of substantial knowledge. "The learning of Latin," he says, "being nothing but the learning of words, a very unpleasant business both to young and old, join as much other knowledge with it as you can, beginning still with that which lies most obvious to the senses—such as is the knowledge of minerals, plants, and animals, and particularly timber and fruit trees, their parts and ways of propagation, wherein a great deal may be taught a child, which will not be useless to the man; but, more especially, geography, astronomy, and anatomy. But, whatever you are teaching him, have a care still that you do not clog him with too much at once; or make anything his business but downright virtue, or reprove him for anything but vice, or some apparent tendency to it."

THE STUDY OF NATURE.—Locke thought that the importance of a knowledge of Latin was badly overrated. Though regarding it as indispensable to the wealthy English gentleman, he strongly disapproved of forcing Latin upon children who would find no use for it in subsequent life. In such cases he regarded directly practical studies as of far more value. "Latin I look upon as absolutely necessary to a gentleman," he says; "and indeed custom, which prevails over everything, has made it so much a part of education that even those children are whipped to it, and made spend many hours of their precious time uneasily in Latin, who, after they are once gone from school, are never to have more to do with it as long as they live. Can there be anything more ridiculous than that a father should waste his own money, and his son's time, in setting him to learn the Roman language, when, at the same time, he designs him for a trade, wherein he, having no use of Latin, fails not to forget that little which he brought from school, and which it is ten to one he abhors for the ill-usage it procured him? Could it be believed, unless we had everywhere among us examples of it, that a child should be forced to learn the rudiments of a language, which he is never to use in the course of life that he is designed to, and neglect all the while the writing a good hand, and casting accounts, which are of great advantage in all conditions of life, and to most trades indispensably necessary?"

ORDER OF LANGUAGES.—In regard to the order of language study, Locke took a position, the wisdom of which, though amply justified on pedagogical grounds, has not yet been fully recognized. He held that French should precede the study of Latin, as being nearer the English idiom and as forming a natural bridge to the more difficult Roman tongue. But the mother-tongue, of all languages, has the highest claims upon us, and therefore should be most diligently cultivated. It required nearly two hundred years for our higher institutions of learning to recognize this truth and to adjust their courses of study to it. " This I think will be agreed to," says Locke, "that if a gentleman is to study any language, it ought to be that of his own country, that he may understand the language which he has constant use of with the utmost accuracy." And again, " Since it is English that an English gentleman will have constant use of, that is the language he should chiefly cultivate, and wherein most care should be taken to polish and perfect his style."

KNOWLEDGE VALUES.—Locke discussed the relative value of different kinds of knowledge—a subject much discussed in more recent years. Since the field of knowledge is so broad, the capacity of the human mind so limited, and the duration of life so brief, he held that some sort of selection is necessary. The least valuable kinds

17

of knowledge are consciously and deliberately to be sacrificed to what is most valuable. First of all he would discard "all that maze of words and phrases which have been invented and employed only to instruct and amuse people in the art of disputing, and which will be found, perhaps, when looked into, to have little or no meaning." He would not have too laborious an inquiry into what other men have thought, for "truth needs no recommendation, and error is not mended by it." A polished style in foreign languages, together with a critical knowledge of insignificant foreign authors, seemed to Locke not worth the labor spent in acquiring them. He would not extend the study of antiquity to insignificant matters, such as the exact dimensions of the Colossus. He would likewise neglect "nice questions and remote, useless speculations, as where the earthly paradise was, or what fruit it was that was forbidden, where Lazarus's soul was while he lay dead, etc." All these subjects he would not absolutely forbid, but "they are not to be made our chief aim, nor first business, and are always to be handled with some caution."

Locke groups the kinds of knowledge that he esteems of most worth under three heads, in the order of their relative importance. He places morality and religion first, because they assure our highest welfare, not only in this life, but in the life to come. Under the second head he places the knowledge that will help us in a wise conduct of life, and thus secure the largest amount of happiness for ourselves and of usefulness to others. And thirdly he maintains that every one should learn a manual trade, by which he may be able to earn his bread. It is under this third head, the least important of all, that Locke includes the study of letters. To quote his words on these points:

"1. Heaven being our great business and interest, the

knowledge which may direct us thither is certainly so too, so that this is without peradventure the study that ought to take the first and chiefest place in our thoughts.

" 2. The next thing to happiness in the other world is a quiet prosperous passage through this, which requires a discreet conduct and management of ourselves, in the several occurrences of our lives. The study of prudence then seems to me to deserve the second place in our thoughts and studies. A man may be, perhaps, a good man (who lives in truth and sincerity of heart toward God), with a small portion of prudence, but he will never be very happy in himself nor useful to others without it. These two are every man's business.

" 3. If those who are left by their predecessors with a plentiful fortune are excused from having a particular calling, in order to their subsistence in this life, it is yet certain that, by the law of God, they are under an obligation of doing something; which, having been judiciously treated by an able pen, I shall not meddle with, but pass to those who have made letters their business; and in these I think it is incumbent to make the proper business of their calling the third place in their study."

SUMMARY.—If space permitted, it would be interesting and profitable to extend these quotations further, for Locke's treatise abounds in wise and suggestive thought. But we conclude this sketch with the following excellent summary from Quick: " Locke's aim was to give a boy a robust mind in a robust body. His body was to endure hardness, his reason was to teach him self-denial. But this result was to be brought about by leading, not driving him. He was to be trained, not for the university, but for the world. Good principles, good manners, and discretion, were to be cared for first of all; intelligence and intellectual activity next; and actual knowledge last of all. His spirits were to be kept up by kind treatment, and learning was never to be a drudgery. With regard to the subjects of instruction, those branches of knowledge which concerned things were to take precedence of those which consist of abstract ideas. The prevalent drill in the grammar of the classical languages was to be abandoned, the mother-tongue was to be carefully studied, and other languages acquired either by conversation or by the use of translations. In everything the part the pupil was to play in life was steadily to be kept in view; and the ideal which Locke proposed was not the finished scholar, but the finished gentleman."

G. Jansenism

RELIGIOUS REACTION.—The reaction hitherto considered against abstract theological and humanistic education was chiefly philosophical and realistic. We pass now to the consideration of another reaction that had its basis in religion, and was common to both the Catholic and the Protestant Church, though it assumed a different form in each. Europe had just passed through the misfortunes and sorrows of the Thirty Years' War, and men were in a condition to realize the insufficiency of a religion that consisted in outward forms and mere intellectual assent to doctrinal systems. The need of a religion of the heart and life was felt.

NATURE OF JANSENISM.—This movement in the Roman Catholic Church was named after its originator, Jansenius, a bishop in the Netherlands. He was an ecclesiastic and educator of wide influence. He sharply distinguished between philosophy and theology, holding that the former is based on logical thinking and the latter on authority and memory. In a spirit of ascetic piety he opposed the excessive study of pagan philosophy, and showed himself particularly inimical to Aristotle. He was a profound student of Augustine, and his work on that ecclesiastical father, which was published posthumously in 1640, became the occasion of a prolonged and bitter controversy. His views gained many adherents, especially among men of station and ability, who labored in a self-denying way for the improvement of society. They displayed a remarkable interest and independence in education, and their achievements, both in theory and practice, are worthy of note. Among those who distinguished themselves as educators may be mentioned Nicole, a teacher of philosophy, who published in 1670 a series of general reflections on education entitled The Education of a Prince, Lancelot, a teacher of grammar, who wrote a book on Methods of Language Study, and Arnauld, a great theologian, who, besides a General Grammar, composed the Regulation of Studies in the Humanities.

PORT ROYAL.—In France Jansenism had several distinguished adherents, among whom were Pascal and Fénelon. The center of the movement in that country was Port Royal, an ancient convent, a few miles from Paris, where a number of pious and learned men devoted themselves to study, teaching, and the practise of piety. They gave much attention to the instruction of youth, and by the use of wise methods they achieved excellent results. They prepared neat and excellent text-books on grammar, philosophy, and other branches of knowledge; they translated many of the classic authors; they produced a large number of devotional and practical works, in which they exhibited a pure, chaste, and agreeable style. In connection with their primary schools, they invented and employed the phonic system of spelling. The study of language began with the mother-tongue, and not, as had hitherto been the case in France, with Latin.

SAINT-CYRAN.—Saint-Cyran best represents the spirit of Port Royal. With him education had a religious purpose. He looked upon man as debased by original sin; and the innocence which has been restored by the grace of baptism should be preserved, he maintained, by education. This should fortify the soul against the wiles of the devil. " It is always necessary," he says, " to pray for souls, and always to be on guard as in a beleaguered city. The devil makes his circuit outside; he early attacks the baptized; he comes to reconnoiter the place; if the Holy Spirit does not fill it, he will fill it." Consequently there is no more noble service, and none more useful to the State, than to instruct the young and form them to virtue.

TUTORIAL SYSTEM.—The entire system of Port Royal depends on the fundamental view just presented. Accordingly, the tutorial system of instruction is preferred both to the large public school, where too many temptations are to be met with, and to family training, where the children are too much isolated. " Five or six children being together," says Coustel, " they can divert themselves, and enjoy the gaiety that is suitable to their age—a thing necessary for those that study. . . . On the other hand, a single instructor is sufficient for five or six children, while it would be impossible to drill them as they need if there were a larger number and different lessons. Finally one avoids the corrupting influence which a too great number of pupils brings."

SELECTION OF TEACHERS.—Like the Jesuits, the Port-Royalists wished to have as complete control of their pupils as possible. Great care was taken to preserve a wholesome moral influence in the school. Whenever the influence of a pupil was felt to be injurious, he was inexorably dismissed. Understanding the force of example upon the young, the Port-Royalists selected only teachers of upright religious character. "As it is almost impossible," they said, "that children who are still under the dominion of sense, should not do what they see others do, the effort was made to teach them still more by example than by precept." The pupils were guarded in every way from seeing what might be injurious to modesty of demeanor or purity of thought. Expurgated editions of the ancient classics were used. The theatre was denounced; and travel as a means of culture was discouraged, because it only showed "the devil dressed in various modes."

METHOD AND DISCIPLINE.—In contrast with the Jesuits, the Port-Royalists banished emulation from their schools, for they held that it sharpened the intellect at the expense of character. The sole ambition which they cultivated in the minds of their pupils was a desire to approach more nearly the ideal of a Christian manhood. Their discipline was mild, the rod being called into requisition only when all other means of correction had failed. The teachers were instructed to be a little indulgent to their pupils, and to take notice of only grave misdemeanors. "Speak little," said Saint-Cyran, "bear much, and pray more." Words of moral instruction were to be delivered, not in set discourses, but on occasions when the circumstances would make the pupils receptive. The teachers were to be men of prayer. "Those who plant and those who water," to the mind of Saint-Cyran, "were nothing; it is God alone who, possessing all the power, produces all the effect. It was therefore of him that all progress should be sought. The teacher is only the instrument of a success, of which God is truly the author."

FORMATION OF JUDGMENT.—The education of Port Royal was first of all a religious education. At the same time, it provided a general training, through which the student might be better able to discern his duty. The Port-Royalists cared little for a showy culture, but much for solid attainments. They emphasized especially the development of a sound judgment. " To form the judgment," says Nicole, " is to impart to the mind a love and discernment of truth; it is to render it delicate in discovering false reasonings; it is to learn not to be put off with obscure words and principles, and not to be satisfied till the foundations are reached; it is to render it subtle in seizing the point in complicated questions and to discern what is irrelevant; it is to fill it with principles of truth which will be helpful in finding it in all things, and especially in those of which it has need."

PROGRESSIVE CHARACTER.—Unlike the Jesuits, Port Royal was progressive. It looked to the future rather than to the past. One of its maxims was: " Follow reason rather than routine." It introduced improvements in educational methods, among which a larger use of the mother-tongue is to be noted. Contrary to general usage at that time, the Port-Royalists used a Latin grammar written in French; and Lancelot, its author, defends his innovation in the following manner: " Since common sense itself teaches us that it is always necessary to begin with things that are easiest, and that what we know already ought to serve us as a light to clear up what we do not know, it is evident that we ought to make use of our native tongue as a means to enter into the languages that are foreign and unknown to us. To set forth the first elements of a language which we wish to teach, in the terms of that language, is that not supposing that the pupil already knows what we wish to teach him?"

NEW METHOD IN LATIN.—The Port-Royalists evolved a new method of teaching Latin. Attaching importance to substance rather than to show, they first placed in the hands of pupils a translation of the Latin author to be read. When the pupil by repeated reading had made himself familiar with the thought and character of the book, the original was placed in his hands. The similarity of language and the differences of idiom were thus easily and pleasantly learned. It was then that the writing of exercises was begun, in which fidelity to thought was esteemed more than literalness of rendering. "It is sufficient," said Guyot, "if I make Cicero think nothing but what he has thought; but it is not necessary that I make him speak as he has spoken, that is to say, that I make him speak Latin in French words; it is necessary that those who shall read me be able, thanks to the translation, to enter into his sense, although ignorance of the language bar their entrance to it."

A GLIMPSE OF THE SCHOOLS.—An old French writer gives us an interesting description of the studies and methods of the Port Royal schools. "Up to the age of twelve," he says, "the pupils were occupied with the elements of sacred history, geography, and arithmetic, under the form of amusements, in a manner to develop their intelligence without wearying it. At twelve years the regular course of study began. The hours of study and recitation were fixed, but not in an absolute way. If study sometimes intrenched upon recreation, recreation also had its turn, for circumstances were taken into account. In winter, when the weather permitted, the teacher gave his lesson while taking a walk with his pupils. Sometimes they left him to climb a hill or run in the plain, but they came back to listen to him. In summer the class met under the shade of trees by the side of brooks. The teacher explained Virgil and Homer; he commented upon Cicero, Aristotle, Plato, and the fathers of the Church. The example of the teachers, their conversation and familiar instruction, all that the pupil saw, all that he heard, inspired him with a love for the beautiful and the good."

SUMMARY.—We are now prepared to form some idea of the Port Royal education, and to see its direct opposition to the Jesuit system. It ranges the teachers of Port Royal by the side of the illustrious educational reformers considered in the preceding section. It simplified studies, and made them pleasant to the pupil; it gave a worthy prominence to the mother-tongue; it developed the understanding along with the memory; it imparted substantial knowledge in connection with words; it developed the faculties, paid attention to the body, and watched over the formation of character. The Port Royal system, and especially the text-books, provoked the antagonism of the Jesuits, whose ascendency in education it tended to undermine. Finally, after a period of embittered conflict, the schools of Port Royal were suppressed. The loss to the country was unmistakable. "If France," says Paroz, "had developed the pedagogical work commenced by Port Royal, it would be further advanced by almost two centuries."

There were two distinguished educators of France, who held more or less fully the educational views of Port Royal, of whom it is now necesssary to speak. They were Fénelon and Rollin.

H. Fénelon

BIOGRAPHICAL.—This celebrated author and teacher was born in the province of Périgord in 1651. From an early age he was remarkable for his industry, for his amiable disposition, and for his thirst for knowledge. Up to the age of twelve his education was conducted at home; he was then sent to Cahors, and two years later to Paris, where his course of instruction was completed. Destined to the clerical office by his family, and inclined toward it by natural gifts and disposition, he entered the theological seminary of Saint-Sulpice, and won general esteem by his application, ability, and exemplary character. He was ordained priest at the age of twenty-four, and was shortly afterward placed over an institution in Paris designed for the instruction of young women who had renounced the Protestant faith. In 1689 he was appointed tutor to the young Duke of Burgundy, grandson of Louis XIV, and discharged his duties with rare wisdom and success. In 1695 he was appointed Archbishop of Cambray. He led a life of great simplicity, and divided his time between the administration of affairs and the personal instruction of his flock. The later years of his life were rendered unhappy by theological controversies, by the displeasure of the king, and by the loss of his dearest friends. He died in 1715, " like a saint and poet, listening to the sweetest and sublimest hymns, which carried at the same time his imagination and his soul to heaven."

EDUCATION OF GIRLS.—While head of the institution of New Catholics in Paris, Fénelon wrote his Education of Girls. This admirable treatise presents advanced views in regard to female education, and abounds in pedagogical principles of great wisdom, drawn from a profound acquaintance with child-nature. The education of girls, he maintained, should begin in infancy. This early age, which is sometimes abandoned to indiscreet and profligate women, is that in which the deepest impressions are made, and which has consequently a strong influence on all subsequent life. This early education should have reference to the body, the mind, and the character. The health should be cared for; the faculties should not be prematurely developed; the passions should not be inflamed, and patience and self-denial should be inculcated and practised.

WOMAN'S INFERIORITY.—Fénelon shared in the general belief of his time in the intellectual inferiority of woman. Consequently he would exclude her from politics, the law, the ministry, and other vocations that appeared to him distinctively masculine. "But what follows," he asks, "from the natural weakness of women? The weaker they are, the more it is important to strengthen them. Have they not duties to perform, duties that constitute the foundation of all human life? Is it not women that ruin and that sustain households, that regulate all the details of domestic matters, and that consequently decide what concerns most nearly the whole human race? In this way they have the principal part in the good or bad morals of almost the whole world. A judicious, diligent, and pious woman is the soul of a household; she establishes order in it for temporal prosperity and salvation. Even men, who have all public authority, are not able by their deliberations to establish any effective measure for good, unless the women aid them in having it executed."

NECESSITY OF WOMAN'S EDUCATION.—Fénelon regarded the education of woman a necessity. It was not merely a help, as we have just seen, in the duties that naturally fall to her, but it operated as a safeguard in relation to mind and character. Without a liberal education, the minds of young women are apt to turn to empty and dangerous subjects. "Ignorant and idle girls," he says, "always have a wandering imagination. Those possessing ability sometimes become affected, and read all the books that can nourish their vanity; they become excessively fond of romances, comedies, and extravagant adventures, with which unworthy love is commingled. They render their minds visionary, in accustoming themselves to the magnificent language of the heroes of romances; they thus disqualify themselves even for society; for all those beautiful, ethereal sentiments, those generous affections, all those adventures invented by the novelist in order to give pleasure, have no relation with the true motives which are operative in the world, and which decide affairs, nor with the failures which we experience in every undertaking."

METHOD AND STUDIES.—Instruction should be made pleasant; and instead of imposing tasks by harsh authority, the teacher should explain the purpose of each study. "By all means let the child play," says Fénelon; "let wisdom be forced upon him only at intervals, and with a laughing face; beware of tiring him with injudicious exactions." The fondness of children for history should not be unimproved. Instructive narratives should be presented, particularly those of the Bible; for the latter, apart from historical knowledge, have a moral and religious value. The moral and religious instruction should be watched over with special care, and the faults and weaknesses to which girls are liable should be guarded against. The education of woman should have regard to domestic relations, for whose manifold duties and responsibilities a high degree of wisdom is necessary. Girls should be instructed in reading, writing, and arithmetic; in keeping accounts; in the leading principles of justice and government; and, after these fundamental studies, history, language, literature, music, and painting might be taught, yet in such a manner as to preserve pupils from all moral injury."

RELIGIOUS TRAINING.—Fénelon was a man of deep spirituality. He sympathized with Madame Guyon in her quietism; and it was his writings on this subject that brought him into conflict with Bossuet, and led to his censure by the pope. With his deep religious nature, it was natural for him to place much emphasis on religious training; but the piety he commended was not one of monastic austerity. Writing to a lady of rank about the education of her daughter, he says: " Do not frighten her from piety by a useless severity; leave her a worthy freedom and an innocent joy; accustom her to enjoy herself in every way short of sin, and to find her pleasure apart from debasing amusements. Choose companions for her who will not spoil her, and recreations at such hours as will not give her a distaste for the serious occupations of the rest of the day. Try to make her delight in God; do not suffer that she think of him only as a mighty and inexorable judge, who constantly watches us in order to reprove and restrain us on every occasion; make her see how kind he is, how he suits himself to our needs, and has pity for our weaknesses; familiarize her with him as with a tender and compassionate father."

TELEMACHUS.—As tutor of the young Duke of Burgundy, Fénelon wrote several works for his instruction. His Fables and Dialogues of the Dead impart many useful lessons in a delightful and novel form. In the latter book there appear the shades of distinguished men of antiquity, who discuss all kinds of moral, political, and philosophical questions. Plato and Aristotle, for example, discuss philosophy, and Demosthenes and Cicero, eloquence. These dialogues are brief, pointed, and delightful. But the principal work written for the young Duke was Telemachus, which describes the adventures of the young Ithacan in search of his father Ulysses. In its general plan it resembles the Odyssey, to which it is scarcely inferior in interest. As will be readily understood, the plan of the book allows Fénelon to impart to his pupil a large amount of historical, political, and moral instruction. Indirectly the author did not hesitate to give Louis XIV himself a lesson or two, which " the grand monarch " was disposed to resent.

METHOD AS TUTOR.—The young Duke of Burgundy was endowed with fine natural abilities, but possessed of an inordinate pride and furious temper. This disposition rendered Fénelon's task exceedingly difficult, but the result was a tribute to his wisdom and character. The young prince grew up to be affable, considerate, and self-controlled. The following incident shows the wisdom with which Fénelon knew how to deal with his pupil. In a fit of anger occasioned by a gentle reproof, the young duke once said to him: " I know who I am, and who you are! " Fénelon made no reply; but on the following day, in a tranquil but serious tone, he said to his pupil: " You recall, no doubt, the words you spoke to me yesterday. My duty obliges me to reply to you that you know neither who you are nor who I am. If you think yourself above me, you are mistaken; your birth did not depend upon you and gives you no merit, and I have more prudence and knowledge than you. What you know you have learned from me, and I am above you by reason of the authority which the king and your father have given me over you. It was in obedience to them that I have undertaken the difficult and, as it seems, ungrateful task of being your teacher; but, since you appear to think that I ought to feel particularly fortunate in discharging this duty, I wish to go with you at once to the king and request him to relieve me of my duties and to give you another instructor."

This declaration filled the young prince with alarm, and, bursting into tears, he exclaimed: "I am sorry for what happened yesterday. If you speak to the king, I shall forfeit his friendship. If you leave me, what will be thought of me? Forgive me, and I promise that you will have no ground of complaint in the future."

CONCLUSION.—Fénelon was at once a great writer and a great educator. His Telemachus belongs to the classic literature of France. His treatise on the Education of Girls, with its flowing style and pedagogical insight, was a notable contribution to the educational literature of the seventeenth century. " We have to-day," says Paroz, " educational works that are more complete and systematic, but this one will live because of its excellent spirit and beautiful style. In all ages and in every land it will be read with pleasure and profit. Of all the Catholic clergy who have engaged in educational work, Fénelon has perhaps approached nearest to the rational principles which form the basis of modern pedagogy. The order of Nature has a place in his theology, and he knows how to reconcile the needs of temporal life with the spirit of Christianity. This characteristic will always assign him a high rank among educators."

I. Rollin

BIOGRAPHICAL.—Rollin, widely known a generation ago in this country by his Ancient History, was born at Paris in 1661. He was the son of a poor but honest cutler, who intended his son to follow the same vocation. He was rescued from this humble state by a Benedictine friar, who discovered young Rollin's abilities, and had him entered at the Collège du Plessis. Having that ardent desire for knowledge, so often accompanying genius, he made rapid progress, and early established a well-founded reputation. He was especially proficient in literary studies. " Go to Rollin," said his professor of rhetoric, when applied to for any prose or poetic composition; " he will do it better than I can." Rollin studied theology three years at the Sorbonne, the most celebrated of the Catholic seminaries of France.

In 1688 he was elevated to the chair of Eloquence in the Royal College of France, and filled the position with zeal and success. He encouraged the study of the French language and literature, and revived an interest in the ancient tongues, particularly in Greek. In 1694 he was appointed rector of the University of Paris, and signalized his brief tenure of two years by the introduction of some salutary reforms. In 1699 he was made principal of the College of Beauvais, and so great had his reputation now become that he soon filled its deserted halls with students. But his life was not to run on smoothly. His adherence to Jansenism, which has already been explained, brought upon him the unrelenting persecution of the Jesuits, and he was forced to give up his position in 1712.

TREATISE ON STUDIES.—Rollin's Treatise on Studies,

18

which was published in 1726, is the most elaborate work on pedagogy produced in the seventeenth and eighteenth centuries. It might properly be called The Principles, Subjects, and Methods of Education. The full title of the work, which consists of four volumes, will best give an idea of its nature: The Method of Teaching and Studying the Belles-Lettres, or an Introduction to Languages, Poetry, Rhetoric, History, Moral Philosophy, Physics, etc., with Reflections on Taste, and Instructions with Regard to the Eloquence of the Pulpit, the Bar, and the Stage; the whole Illustrated with Passages from the most famous Poets and Orators, Ancient and Modern, with Critical Remarks on Them. It is a treasure-house of learning and pedagogical wisdom, which may be studied with profit by teachers to-day. Rollin was perfectly familiar with the pedagogical writings of the ancients, and the names of Plato, Aristotle, Plutarch, Seneca, Quintilian, and others are of frequent occurrence on his pages. Of modern writers, to whom he expresses obligation, are Fénelon and Locke. With Rollin scholarship took the place of originality.

THE END OF EDUCATION.—His large experience and thorough familiarity with the ancients imparted, as a rule, an instructive and comprehensive breadth to his views. He conceived of education as having a threefold purpose, namely, science, morals, and religion. To his mind the most important element was character. His views are set forth in the following extract: " The end which teachers should have in view," he says, " is not simply to teach their pupils Latin and Greek; to show them how to write exercises, verses, and amplifications; to load their memory with historic facts and dates; to construct syllogisms in due form; and to trace on paper certain lines and figures. This knowledge, I do not deny, is useful and valuable, but as a means and not as an end. . . . The purpose of teachers, in the long course of study, is to accustom their pupils to serious work; to make them esteem and love the sciences; to show them how to make progress; to make them feel the use and value of knowledge—and in this way prepare them for the different pursuits to which Providence may call them. The purpose of teachers, still more than that, is to form the mind and heart of their pupils; to protect their innocence; to inspire them with principles of honor and probity; to have them form good habits; to correct and suppress in them, by gentle means, the bad inclinations that may be observed."

CHARACTER OF THE TEACHER.—Rollin laid great stress on the religious side of education. Its supreme aim is the formation of Christian character. This fact imparts at once a solemn responsibility and an infinite dignity to the office of teaching. What should be the qualifications of the teacher over and above the requisite scholarship? Rollin answers: " When a teacher has asked and received from Jesus Christ, for the management of others and for his own salvation, the spirit of wisdom and knowledge, the spirit of counsel and strength, the spirit of learning and piety, and, above all, the spirit of fear of the Lord, there is nothing further to be said to him; this spirit is an internal teacher that dictates and instructs in everything, and that on every occasion will show him his duties and give him wisdom to perform them. A great indication that one has received it is when he feels an ardent zeal for the salvation of children; when he is touched by their dangers; when he is sensible to their faults; when he experiences something of the tenderness and solicitude that Paul felt for the Galatians."

PUBLIC SCHOOLS.—Rollin discusses at considerable length the comparative merits of education in public schools and by private instruction. He reviews the arguments on both sides, and quotes Quintilian at length. But he does not venture to decide the question, and leaves it for parents to follow the course which in the light of the facts may seem best to them. "As the dangers are very great to youth on all sides," he says, "it is the duty of parents to examine well before God what course they ought to take, equitably to weigh the advantages and disadvantages which occur on both sides, to be determined in so important a deliberation only by the motives of religion, and above all to make such a choice of masters and schools, in case they follow that course, as may, if not entirely dissipate, at least diminish their just apprehensions."

THE MOTHER-TONGUE.—Rollin made a plea for the study of French, and gave particular directions as to method. He would have the French people bestow upon their language the same attention that the ancient Romans bestowed upon Latin. The mother-tongue should have the first place in the study of languages. As the fundamental principles of grammar are substantially the same, a knowledge of French would be helpful to the student in acquiring Latin and Greek. "As the elements of speech," he says, "are in some degree the same in all languages, it is natural to begin the instruction of youth with the rules of the French grammar, the principles of which will serve also for the Latin and Greek, and will appear far less difficult and discouraging, as there will be little more to do than to make them range in a certain order such things as they already know, though somewhat confusedly."

EDUCATION OF WOMAN.—Rollin devotes a long chapter

to the education of girls, in which he frequently borrows from Fénelon. He fails to rise above the limitations of his time, and would, as a rule, restrict a girl's education to reading, writing, arithmetic, and history. She should study Latin only in exceptional cases. Rollin recognized the intellectual ability of girls: " A difference of sex," he said, " does not in itself create a disparity in understandings." But inasmuch as her sphere is the household, woman does not need, he held, a knowledge of the languages and the sciences. To quote his words, women " were never designed by Providence to instruct nations, to govern kingdoms, to make war, to administer justice, to plead causes, or to practise physic. Their empire extends no farther than over the house, and is confined to functions not less useful but less laborious than those of men; and more suitable to the softness of their character, the delicacy of their constitutions and their natural inclination. Hence the emphasis of a girl's education should be placed on her knowledge of domestic affairs. Among other things her mother ought to teach her (1) to adjust her expenses to her income; (2) not to buy on credit; (3) to pay her servants promptly; (4) to audit accounts; and (5) to set apart something for the poor.

SCHOOL MANAGEMENT.—Rollin discusses at considerable length the best methods of interesting and controlling pupils. His most important points have been summarized as follows:

" 1. The first duty of the teacher is to study well the genius and character of children. To wish to place them on the same level, and to subject them to a single rule, is to force nature.

" 2. In education the highest skill consists in knowing how to unite, by a wise temperament, a force that restrains children without repelling them, and a gentleness that wins without enervating them.

" 3. The short and common method of correcting children is with the rod; but this remedy sometimes becomes a more dangerous evil than those which one seeks to cure, if it is employed without reason and moderation.

" 4. The only vice, it seems to me, that deserves severe treatment is obstinacy in evil, but an obstinacy voluntary, determined, and well defined.

" 5. The teacher ought never to punish in anger, especially if the fault which he punishes concerns him personally, such as a want of respect or some offensive speech.

" 6. Cuffs, blows, and other like treatment, are absolutely forbidden to teachers. They ought to punish only to correct, and passion does not correct.

" 7. It is a quite common fault to make use of reprimands for the slightest faults which are almost inevitable to children. This breaks the force of reprimands, and renders them fruitless.

" 8. We should avoid exciting the spite of children by the harshness of our language, their anger by exaggeration, their pride by marks of contempt.

" 9. It is necessary always to show children a substantial and agreeable end which may hold them to work, and never pretend to force them by a direct and absolute authority.

" 10. We should run the risk of discouraging children if we never praised them when they do well. Although praises are to be feared because of vanity, it is necessary to make use of them to encourage children, without cultivating that vice.

" 11. Rewards are not to be neglected for children, and although they are not, any more than praise, the principal motive to make them act, yet both may become useful to virtue, and a strong incentive to its practice.

" 12. It is a great good fortune for young people to find masters whose life is a continual lesson; whose actions do not belie their teaching; who practise what they preach, and shun what they censure; and who are admired more for their conduct than for their instruction."

J. Francke

PIETISM.—Pietism is a term of reproach fixed upon a worthy movement in the Protestant Church in the direction of a consistent Christian life. This movement was opposed to the formality and inconsistency characteristic of the period of " dead orthodoxy." It was begun by Philip Jacob Spener, a man of fine natural abilities, large attainments, and deep spirituality. As leading pastor at Frankfort-on-the-Main, he began, in 1670, to hold meetings at his house for the promotion of biblical knowledge and the cultivation of evangelical piety. He continued his reformatory efforts at Dresden as chief court-preacher, and afterward at Berlin as provost of the Church of St. Nicholas. " A return from scholastic theology to the Holy Scriptures as the living source of all saving knowledge," says Kurtz; " a conversion of the outward orthodox confession into an inner living theology of the heart, and a demonstration thereof in true piety of life—these were the ways and means by which he proposed to effect the desired reform." The Pietistic movement gave rise to a prolonged controversy, whose general influence, in spite of much bitterness and persecution, was favorable to Christian life in the Church.

BIOGRAPHICAL.—Pietism was brought into relation with

education chiefly by August Hermann Francke, who as a successful and consecrated Christian teacher exerted a wide influence. He was born at Lübeck, on the Baltic, in 1663. He received his preparatory training at the Gymnasium of Gotha, after which he attended the universities of Erfurt and Kiel, studying metaphysics, natural science, history, languages, and theology. After leaving the universities he spent a year and a half at Gotha, during which time he read the Hebrew Bible through seven times. In 1684 he went to Leipsic, where his lectures on the Old and New Testaments, differing widely from the cold, logical processes of the universities, attracted considerable attention. He sympathized with Spener's views, and joined the Pietistic reform. In 1687 he went to Hamburg, where he established a primary school that brought him valuable experience and determined the direction of his life. "Upon the establishment of this school," he says, "I learned how destructive the usual school management is, and how exceedingly difficult the discipline of children; and this reflection made me desire that God would make me worthy to do something for the improvement of schools and instruction."

WORK AT HALLE.—In 1691 the University of Halle was founded, and the following year, through the influence of Spener, Francke was appointed Professor of Greek and Oriental Languages, and at the same time pastor of a suburban church. Here in Halle he accomplished a great work, which stands in educational history almost without a parallel. The beginning was very humble. The poor were accustomed to assemble on Thursday before the parsonage to receive alms. The thought occurred to Francke that the occasion might be improved for religious instruction. He invited the crowd of young and old into his house, and along with bread he administered spiritual food. He learned the condition of the poorer classes, and his heart was touched by their ignorance and need. He deprived himself of comforts to administer to their necessities. He solicited aid from his friends, and hung up a poor-box to receive contributions. One day he found in it the sum of seven florins, the gift of a benevolent woman. With the joy of faith he exclaimed: "That is a splendid capital, with which I must accomplish something useful; I will begin a school for the poor!" Books were immediately bought, and a needy student of the university engaged to teach the children two hours a day. The undertaking prospered; the parsonage soon became too small; more commodious quarters had to be engaged. With increasing wants came enlarged contributions, and Francke continued to develop his work till it assumed at length immense proportions. At the time of his death, in 1727, it comprised the following institutions:

1. The *Pedagogium*, having eighty-two students. This school was designed for the higher classes, and provided instruction in religion, Latin, Greek, Hebrew, French, German, arithmetic, geography, history, chronology, geometry, astronomy, music, botany, anatomy, and the essential principles of medicine. In order to render instruction as practicable as possible, the school was equipped with a museum of natural history, a chemical laboratory, apparatus for experiments in physics, and a botanical garden. All this marked a departure in the secondary education of the time, and places Francke among the educational reformers.

2. The Latin School of the Orphan House, with three inspectors, thirty-two teachers, four hundred students, and ten servants.

3. The German Burgher School, with four inspectors, one hundred and six teachers, and seventeen hundred and twenty-eight pupils of both sexes. This held the rank of a good primary school.

4. The Orphan House, with one hundred boys, thirty-four girls, and ten overseers.

5. The Free Table, with six hundred and fifteen indigent scholars.

6. The Drug Store and Book Store, with fifty-three dependents.

7. The Institution for Women, with twenty-nine inmates.

The whole number of teachers, pupils, and dependents in the several institutions under Francke's direction amounted to four thousand two hundred and seventy-three.

OTHER ACTIVITIES.—Besides the direction of all these institutions, a work sufficient to overwhelm an ordinary man, Francke was active in other ways. His pastoral duties were faithfully performed; he founded a printing-office that sent forth before the close of the eighteenth century a million and a half of Bibles and a million copies of the New Testament; under the patronage of the King of Denmark, Frederick IV, he established a mission in India that continued over a hundred years. Through the teachers and ministers sent forth from his institutions, he reached all parts of Europe. Count Zinzendorf, the founder of the Moravian Brethren, was one of his pupils. As professor in the University of Halle, he was instrumental in effecting useful changes in the courses of study and in elevating the moral tone of the body of students. He constantly sought their conversion and spiritual development. Theology became a matter of the heart as well as of the head. "A grain of living faith," Francke says, "is worth more than a pound of historic knowledge; and a drop of love, than an ocean of science."

SPIRIT AND AIMS.—The spirit that animated Francke in his vast enterprises is well worthy of our consideration. A profound personal piety lay at the basis of all his work. He founded his institutions with a firm reliance upon God, and depended upon prayer to bring him the necessary help. He regarded piety as the most essential thing in education. He emphasized the truth that education should have reference to the student's subsequent vocation; he increased the number of utilitarian studies, and laid the foundation of modern practical education. True wisdom was the aim of his endeavors. "And true wisdom," he said, "is nothing else than the eye in man, by which he sees what is for the best and guards himself from harm. Such wisdom concerns not only scholars but all men, no matter what may be their station; wherefore, along with piety, a true foundation is to be laid in childhood in order that all may act wisely in life, wherever God may place them."

METHODS AND STUDIES.—In the following interesting passage, which touches upon methods and studies, the practical spirit of Francke is clearly manifest. He would not overtask the student. "Youth," he says, "needs pleasure and recreation. This it finds partly in physical exercise, partly in pleasant and at the same time useful employments, especially in mechanical employments; partly in the examination of new and interesting objects of nature and art. In all instruction we must keep the pupil's station and future calling in mind, but to all classes alike is piety necessary. Hence, it must remain in all schools the chief matter, the principal lesson. In the instruction of those who are destined to unprofessional employments and trades, the most important thing after religion is an acquaintance with the indispensable arts of reading, writing, and reckoning; but the elements of other branches of knowledge should not be neglected, especially the elements of natural science, geography, history, and government, which, however, are to be brought forward incidentally and later."

DISCIPLINE.—The following rules are taken from Francke's instructions to his teachers upon the manner of exercising school-discipline. They exhibit his clear pedagogical insight, his piety, and his sympathy and love for children:

1. In exercising discipline, which is necessary and conformable to the will of God, the teacher should pray God first of all to give him the necessary wisdom.

2. As most teachers seek to correct children by rigorous punishment rather than by gaining their love through patience, forbearance, and affection, and as young teachers in particular are lacking in paternal solicitude and Christian gentleness, they ought to supplicate the Lord, without ceasing, to fill them with love for the young who are confided to them, and to deliver them from all harshness and carnal sufficiency.

3. The teacher should learn to govern himself, without which he can not properly govern others.

4. A teacher should maintain discipline over his pupils, and should exhort and punish them when necessary; nevertheless, education should not be hard and severe, but gentle and paternal.

5. A teacher ought never to punish a child in anger.

6. A teacher ought not to be ill-humored, but cordial and kind, like a father.

7. Children ought not to be punished for little faults inherent in their age, but should be encouraged to be more careful.

8. A Christian teacher should beware of becoming the occasion of disorder which he is to punish.

9. Children should not be abused with harsh epithets. It is contrary to the spirit of Christianity.

10. A child ought never to be scolded because it can not understand. If it is dull of comprehension, the teacher should redouble his efforts in its behalf.

11. A teacher should study the disposition of his pupils, as delicate and gentle natures are not to be treated like coarse and hardened natures.

12. In avoiding too great severity the teacher should not fall into the opposite extreme, and become the sport of the children.

13. With youth over fifteen years of age the teacher should abstain from harsh words, threats, and blows, by which they may become embittered. It is better to take them separately, talk to them kindly—sometimes even pray with them. If these means are fruitless, let them be brought before the school board, or punished in the presence of a colleague.

6. ABSTRACT HUMAN EDUCATION

A NEW MOVEMENT.—The eighteenth century witnessed a new movement which has been characterized as abstract human education. In general, it ignores or rejects revealed religion, and bases its educational principles on the purely natural. Though as one-sided as the theological tendency, it has the great merit of stimulating a careful study of man in the interests of correct educational methods. In this way it rendered invaluable service to the cause of educational progress.

TWOFOLD TENDENCIES.—This movement exhibited two entirely different tendencies—the realistic tendency, which emphasized the study of Nature, and the humanistic tendency, which emphasized the study of words. Both of these tendencies, which had been in conflict to a greater or less degree during the preceding century, agreed in eliminating revealed religion from education.

This dual movement admits of an easy explanation. In the great process of human development extremes tend to beget extremes. The path of human progress is zigzag. Throughout the seventeenth century, which we have just considered, a mere formal religion remained in the ascendency. It continued the controlling factor in education, in spite of the attacks of pietists and educational reformers. It long thwarted the confident expectations of Comenius. But a religion which has lost its vital power can not hold a permanent ascendency over the world. Its weakness exposes it to attack.

DEISM.—A skeptical movement, known as Deism, arose in England, and gradually extended over the whole of Europe. It was a religion of nature—based, as its adherents thought, on common sense. It rejected the supernatural. From the deistic or skeptical standpoint, the education of the time, unduly controlled by narrow ecclesiastical influences, was judged defective. Educational reformers representing the deistic tendency arose, and new movements were inaugurated.

A. Rousseau

BIOGRAPHICAL.—There are few men who have exerted
a greater influence upon education than the celebrated
author, Jean-Jacques Rousseau. He was born at Geneva,
in 1712, the son of a poor watchmaker. As a child he was
feeble in body and shy in disposition, but at the same time
he was endowed with remarkable vivacity in thought and
feeling. He was exceedingly fond of reading, in which he
was encouraged by his father; and, among other works,
many of which were worthless, he early devoured Bossuet,
Ovid, and Plutarch. "Thus began to be formed within
me," he says, "that heart, at once so proud and so tender,
that effeminate but yet indomitable character which, ever
oscillating between weakness and courage, between indulgence and virtue, has to the last placed me in contradiction with myself, and has brought it to pass that abstinence and enjoyment, pleasure and wisdom, have alike
eluded me."

INCONSISTENCIES.—It is not worth while to follow him
through the unimportant events of his life. His boyhood
was by no means worthy of imitation; and in his Confessions, a work written with the utmost frankness late in
life, he does not attempt to conceal theft and lying. He
ran away from an engraver to whom he had been appren-
ticed, and during the remainder of his life he was a wan-
derer who enjoyed but temporary seasons of repose. His
life was a singular paradox. He possessed extraordinary
genius, and his books are filled with the noblest sentiments
and the most stirring eloquence; but his life frequently
fell into unpardonable baseness. While he wrote splendid
pages on the beauty of domestic life, he placed his own

children in a foundling hospital. "I do evil," he confessed, "but I love good. My heart is pure."

ÉMILE.—Rousseau has exerted his influence upon education through a single work, half treatise and half romance. It is, as he himself says, "a collection of thoughts and observations, without order and almost without connection." It is entitled Émile, or Concerning Education. In many respects a radical book, it is flung defiantly in the face of prevalent usage. "Go directly contrary to custom," he says, "and you will nearly always be right." The work abounds in mingled truth and error, and needs to be read with great discrimination; but many of its truths are fundamental, and ever since their publication they have been gradually forcing an entrance into educational practise. "Not Rousseau's individual rules," says the great German Richter, "many of which may be erroneous without injury to the whole, but the spirit of education which fills and animates the work, have shaken to their foundations and purified all the schoolrooms and even the nurseries in Europe. In no previous work on education was the ideal so richly and beautifully combined with actual observation as in his."

FUNDAMENTAL PRINCIPLES.—Rousseau was largely indebted to his predecessors, especially to Locke, whom he frequently quotes. The two fundamental truths which have perhaps exerted the widest influence are these: 1. Nature is to be studied and followed; 2. Education is an unbroken unity, extending from early childhood to maturity. It is true that both of these principles had been advocated by Comenius, but it was through the charm of Rousseau's work that they made the widest impression upon the educational thinking of Europe. Along with positions wholly indefensible, Rousseau urges, in admirable style, many of the reforms with which we are already familiar, and which have won our hearty approval. His standpoint, as presented in the opening sentence of Émile, is undoubtedly wrong. " Everything is good," he says, " as it comes from the hands of the Creator; everything degenerates in the hands of man."

RETURN TO NATURE.—Rousseau is thus seen to be hostile to the established order of things. Society at the French capital had become exceedingly artificial and corrupt. Its shallow conventionalities and irrational customs irritated Rousseau, and with an exaggeration natural to him he made society at large the object of indiscriminate attack. He maintains that civilization fosters vice, that the arts and sciences have been born of sin, and hence he seeks a sovereign remedy for existing evils in a return to a state of nature. " Rousseau did not understand," says Paroz, " or rather he did not believe, that the evil reigning among mankind was anterior to civilization, and that civilization is dangerous only as it departs from the vivifying and elevating principles of Christianity. It is from the heart, and not from civilization, that the bad thoughts and bad actions which trouble humanity have their issue; and to elevate man we need a principle which renews and changes the heart. Every other means is insufficient; after having taken civilization from man to keep him from doing evil, it would still be necessary to deprive him of his limbs, and at last of life itself."

PERIODS OF DEVELOPMENT.—With the intention of following Nature, Rousseau carries Émile, his hero, through five periods of development: the first embraces his infancy, the second extends to his twelfth year, the third to his fifteenth, the fourth to his twentieth, and the fifth includes his marriage. To each of these periods a book is devoted,

19

setting forth the matter and method of training in detail. He recognizes three educational agencies. "We are born weak," he says, "we have need of strength; we are born without anything, and need assistance; we are born without intelligence, and need judgment. All that we have not at birth, and shall need at maturity, is given us by education. This education comes to us either from nature, or from men, or from things. The internal development of our faculties and organs is the education of nature; the use which we are taught to make of this development is the education of men; and the acquirements of our own experience from the objects that affect us is the education of things."

THE STUDY OF CHILDREN.—Rousseau maintained that child-nature should be investigated as the basis of all correct training. "People," he says, "do not understand childhood. With the false notions we have of it, the further we go the more we blunder. The wisest apply themselves to what it is important for men to know without considering what children are in a condition to learn. They are always seeking the man in the child, without reflecting what he is before he can be a man." "Nature," he says again, "requires children to be children before they are men. If we wish to pervert this order, we shall produce forward fruits, having neither ripeness nor taste, and certain soon to decay; we shall have young professors and old children. Childhood has its manner of seeing, perceiving, and thinking peculiar to itself; nothing is more absurd than our being anxious to substitute our own in its stead."

CHILDHOOD TRAINING.—In his views regarding early childhood, Rousseau reminds us strongly of Locke. He lays it as a sacred duty upon parents to care for their children. The mother ought to be the nurse; and as to the father, " there is no poverty, nor labor, nor human consideration that can exempt him from the obligation to support his children and to educate them himself." Children should not be too tenderly reared, but accustomed to cold, hunger, thirst, and fatigue. They should not be dosed with medicine; " temperance and toil are the two genuine physicians of man." As the memory and imagination are still inactive, sensations are the only materials of knowledge. But the child should be allowed to discover the relation between its sensations and the objects that cause them. " He wishes to touch everything, to handle everything: do not oppose this restlessness; it is suggesting a very necessary apprenticeship. It is thus that he learns to feel heat, cold, hardness, softness, weight, the lightness of bodies; to judge of their size, shape, and all their other sensible qualities, by observing, feeling, hearing, especially by comparing the sight with the touch, and by estimating by the eye the sensation which they would make under his fingers."

EARLY BOYHOOD.—The next step in Rousseau's system takes the child to the age of twelve. This period should be given up to a strengthening of the body and a training of the senses. The only text-book to be employed is nature; and the method of learning is experience. Suffering, which is the lot of man, should be one of the first lessons acquired. In morals the child needs to learn nothing more than not to do harm to others. There should be no cruel restraint on the part of the parents or tutors—no imposition of tasks that crush out the buoyant happiness natural to childhood. Listen to his eloquent words, which contain a message for to-day. " Love childhood," Rousseau exclaims; " encourage its plays, its pleasures, its instincts for happiness! Who of us has not sometimes regretted that age when a smile was always on the lips, and the soul was always at peace? Why do you wish to deprive these little innocent ones of the enjoyment that will so soon escape them, and of a precious blessing that they can not abuse? Why do you wish to fill with bitterness and sorrow those early fleeting years, which will no more return for them than for you? Fathers, do you know the moment when death awaits your children? Do not lay up regrets for yourself by depriving them of the few moments which Nature gives them. As soon as they can feel the pleasure of existence, let them enjoy it; and at whatever hour God may call them away, do not let them die without having tasted the sweetness of life."

LATER BOYHOOD.—The third book of Émile gives directions for his education from the age of twelve to fifteen. His intellectual training begins, not with languages, but with the physical sciences, which give an opportunity for observation. Rousseau distrusted the knowledge obtained merely from books. "The abuse of books," he says, "is destructive to knowledge. Imagining ourselves to know everything we read, we believe ourselves released from learning it. Too much reading serves only to make us presumptuous blockheads. Of all the ages in which literature has flourished, reading was never so universal as in the present, nor were men in general ever so ignorant." There is one book, however, which Emile is to read, and which for a long time is to compose his entire library. It is an admirable treatise on the education of nature. "What, then, is this marvelous book? Is it Aristotle? is it Pliny? is it Buffon? No; it is Robinson Crusoe."

ACTIVITY OF PUPIL.—Rousseau assailed the practise of imparting knowledge to the passive pupil by the weight of authority. He wished the learner to exercise his own powers. "Another advantage," he says, "resulting from this method of learning for ourselves is, that we do not accustom ourselves to a servile submission to the authority of others; but, by exercising our reason, grow every day more ingenious in the discovery of the relation of things, in connecting our ideas and inventing instruments; whereas, by adopting all that is told us, the mind grows dull and indifferent, as a man, who is always dressed and served by his servants and drawn by his horses, loses at length the activity and use of his limbs."

END OF EDUCATION.—With Rousseau the end of education was to develop a complete man. Life is more than any particular calling; and to prepare the young for living seemed to him the first duty of the educator. "In the order of nature," he says, "all men are equal, their common vocation is the estate of man; and whoever is well brought up for that will not fail in anything belonging to it. It is a matter of little importance to me whether my pupil be destined for arms, for the Church, or for the bar. Before the vocation assigned him by his parents, Nature calls him to human life. To live is the business I wish to teach him. When he leaves my hands I acknowledge that he will be neither magistrate, soldier, nor priest; he will be first of all a man—all that a man ought to be he can be; and, though fortune change, he will be prepared for every condition."

MORAL AND RELIGIOUS CULTURE.—The moral and religious culture of Émile forms the subject of the fourth book, which covers the period from his sixteenth to his twentieth year. He is now to learn his relations to his fellow men, and to develop the sentiment of benevolence. In this moral training, the practise of virtue is to count

for more than lectures on ethics. " Nurses and mothers,"
Rousseau says, " become fond of children through the care
they bestow upon them; the practise of the social virtues
begets in the heart a love for humanity. It is by doing
good that one becomes good; I do not know any exercise more certain in its results. Occupy your pupil with
all the good actions that are in his reach; let the interests
of the poor always be his; let him assist them not only
with his purse, but with his personal attentions; let him
serve them, protect them, and consecrate to them his person and his time; let him be their advocate: he will never
have a nobler employment."

The religion Émile is to learn is based on Nature. A
study of the world, as the honest Savoyard vicar shows,
reveals the existence and character of God. This faith
is to be held with sincerity and courage. " A proud philosophy," says Rousseau, " leads to skepticism, as a blind
devotion leads to fanaticism. Avoid these extremes; always remain steadfast in the way of truth, or of what seems
to be so in the simplicity of your heart, without ever turning from it through vanity or weakness. Dare to confess
God among philosophers; dare to preach humanity to the
intolerant. You will be alone in your views, perhaps; but
you will have within yourself a witness, which will render
that of men unnecessary. Whether they love you or hate
you, whether they read or despise your writings, matters
not. Speak what is true, do what is good; that which is
important to man is to fulfil his duties on the earth."

EDUCATION OF WOMAN.—In the fifth book of Émile
Rousseau presents his views of woman's education. So
noble and independent in many of his views elsewhere, it
is disappointing to find him here echoing the narrow sentiments of his day. He thinks of woman merely as an ap-

purtenance of man; and consequently she is to be educated, not as a human being, but as a housewife. " On the good constitution of mothers," says Rousseau, " depends that of children; on the care of women depends the first education of men; on women depends again their manners, passions, tastes, pleasures, and goodness even. Thus the whole education of women ought to be relative to men. To please them, to be loved and honored by them, to bring them up when they are little, to care for them when they are grown up, to counsel them, to console them, to render their lives agreeable and pleasant—such have been the duties of women in all ages, and what they ought to learn from childhood."

CONCLUSION.—It is not easy to resist the temptation unduly to multiply quotations from Émile, for almost every page has something striking or suggestive. And yet, as we have seen, the teachings of this brilliant book can not be blindly followed. The general scheme of education that Rousseau proposes is entirely Utopian. It is neither possible nor advisable to isolate the child in the manner he recommends. In this matter Nature—to use the word he conjures with—is wiser than the Frenchman. His conception of childhood, in spite of much shrewd observation, bears the marks of fallibility. The reasoning powers are developed much earlier than he believes; and all the faculties of the child, both physical and mental, develop in simultaneous growth. The successive periods, into which he divides the education of Émile, are purely arbitrary divisions, and strangely underrate the needs and capacities of the growing boy. Nor can we approve of the utter neglect of literature and history in the course of study. These reveal to us the achievements of man, and give us a deeper insight into life. But, in spite of numerous defects, Émile abounds in the wealth and inspiration of genius, making it a book that will never lose its interest for thoughtful parents and teachers.

B. Philanthropin

LEADING REPRESENTATIVES.—Rousseau was only a theorizer in education. He did not undertake to put his views into practise. This was left for a group of educators who, from the name of the first school, are known in educational history as Philanthropinists. Most prominent of these were Basedow, Salzman, and Campe. Recognizing the defects of existing schools, they all sought to carry out practically the reforms proposed by Comenius, Locke, and above all by Rousseau. In this undertaking they had the sympathy of a number of eminent men, among whom the philosopher Kant deserves especial mention.

SCHOOLS OF THE PERIOD.—The current training of children has been thus portrayed by Raumer: " Youth was then, for most children, a sorrowful period ; the instruction hard and heartlessly severe. Grammar was beat into the memory, and likewise portions of Scripture and poetry. A common punishment at school was to learn by heart the one hundred and nineteenth Psalm. Schoolrooms were gloomily dark. No one thought that youth could find pleasure in work, or that they had eyes for anything but reading and writing. The profligate age of Louis XIV imposed upon the poor children of the higher classes hair curled by the barber and smeared with powder and pomade, laced coats, knee-breeches, silk stockings, and a dagger at the side—for active, lively children the severest torture."

ACCORDING TO NATURE.—The Philanthropinists set themselves against these evils. The keynote of their system was *everything according to nature.* Some of its fundamental ideas, evidently drawn from Rousseau's work, are thus set forth by Basedow: "You should attend to nature in your children far more than to art. The elegant manners and usages of the world are, for the most part, contrary to nature. These come of themselves in later years. Treat children like children, that they may remain the longer uncorrupted. A boy, whose acutest faculties are his senses, and who has no perception of anything abstract, must first of all be made acquainted with the world as it presents itself to the senses. Let this be shown him in Nature itself, or, where this is impossible, in faithful drawings and models. He can thus, even in play, learn how the various objects are named. Comenius alone has pointed out the right road in this matter. By all means reduce the wretched exercises of the memory."

BASEDOW.—Basedow, as the founder of the Philanthropin, is worthy of some consideration. He was born at Hamburg, in 1723. His youth was somewhat irregular. He studied theology at Leipsic, but his skeptical views prevented his ordination to the ministry. He turned to teaching. Having advocated educational reform in a work published in 1771, from which the extract above is taken, he was received under the patronage of the Prince of Dessau, and placed in charge of a school in which he was to exemplify his theories. His purpose is announced in the following appeal made in 1776, two years after the founding of the Philanthropin. "Send your children," he says, "to a happy youthful life in successful studies. This affair is not Catholic, Lutheran, or Reformed, but Christian. . . . We are philanthropists, or cosmopolites. The sovereignty of Russia or Denmark is not, in our teaching and judgment, placed after the freedom of Switzerland."

END OF EDUCATION.—" The end of education must be to form the European, whose life may be as harmless, useful, and contented as education can make it. It must, therefore, be provided (1) that little vexation, pain, and disease await him, and (2) that he accustom himself to the careful enjoyment of the good. . . . The art of all arts is virtue and contentment. But few exercises for the virtues, as they should be employed in education, have yet been invented. Hear, ye wise and philanthropic authors! A plan for the methodical exercise of the virtues in families and schools is one of the few weighty books to benefit all mankind. If we were rich, we would offer a prize of ten thousand dollars for the best book of this kind appearing within two years."

RELIGIOUS TRAINING.—" For the paternal religion of each pupil, the clergy of the place will provide; but natural religion and morality is the chief part of philosophy, which we will see to ourselves. In the Philanthropin faith in God as the Creator, Preserver, and Lord of the universe is first inculcated. . . . Little memorizing is done with us. The pupils are not forced to study, not even by reproof. Yet we promise, by the excellence of our method and its agreement with the philanthropinistic education and mode of life, to make double the progress in study that is common in schools and gymnasia. And especially do we promise much culture of sound reason through the use of a truly philosophical mode of thinking."

THE PHILANTHROPIN.—The following extract, taken from an account of a visit to the Philanthropin, will give us some idea of the novelty and freedom of the methods pursued. The pupils were plainly dressed; their hair was cut short; their throats were quite open, the shirt-collar falling back over the coat. " The little ones," says the writer of the account in question, "have gone through the oddest performances. They play at 'word-of-command.' Eight or ten stand in a line like soldiers, and Herr Wolke * is officer. He gives the word in Latin, and they must do whatsoever he says. For instance, when he says, '*Claudite oculos*,' they all shut their eyes; when he says, '*Circumspicite*,' they look about them; '*Imitamini sartorem*,' they all sew like tailors; '*Imitamini sutorem*,' they draw the waxed thread like the cobblers. Herr Wolke gives a thousand different commands in the drollest fashion.

THE HIDING GAME.—"Another game, 'the hiding game,' I will teach you. Some one writes a name and hides it from the children—the name of some part of the body, or of a plant, or animal, or metal—and the children guess what it is. Whoever guesses right gets an apple or a piece of cake. One of the visitors wrote *intestina*, and told the children it was a part of the body. Then the guessing began. One guessed *caput*, another *nasus*, another *os*, another *manus*, *pes*, *digiti*, *pectus*, and so forth, for a long time; but one of them hit it at last. Next Herr Wolke wrote the name of a beast, a quadruped. Then came the guesses—*leo*, *ursus*, *camelus*, *elephas*, and so on, till one guessed right; it was *mus*. Then a town was written, and they guessed Lisbon, Madrid, Paris, London, till a child won with St. Petersburg.

" They had another game, which was this: Herr Wolke gave the command in Latin, and they imitated the noises of different animals, and made us laugh till we were tired. They roared like lions, crowed like cocks, mewed like cats, just as they were bid."

---

* One of Basedow's assistants.

FAILURE OF PHILANTHROPIN.—The Philanthropin acquired a wide reputation, and it was visited by persons interested in education from various parts of Europe. The impression generally made was favorable, yet the results, somehow did not answer to Basedow's confident manifesto. It seems that he himself was poorly adapted to carry on such an institution. His methods, well suited to young children, were prolonged into the period when more advanced and more systematic work should have been done. His teaching did not keep pace with the development of his pupils, and hence failed to fulfil the promise it had made in the beginning. The Philanthropin, which had naturally many opponents, was closed before the end of the century, yet not without leaving several similar institutions to survive it, through which it continued to exert a salutary influence upon education.

OPINION OF KANT.—Kant, who had at first predicted great results from the Philanthropin, was sadly disappointed; and in his Pädagogik he refers to it in an interesting passage. "One fancies indeed," he says, "that experiments in education would not be necessary, and that we might judge by the understanding whether any plan would turn out well or ill. But this is a great mistake. Experience shows that often in our experiments we get quite opposite results from what we had anticipated. We see, too, that, since experiments are necessary, it is not in the power of one generation to form a complete plan of education. The only experimental school which, to some extent, made a beginning in clearing the road was the Institute at Dessau. This praise at least must be allowed it, notwithstanding the many faults which could be brought up against it—faults which are sure to show themselves when we come to the results of our experiments, and which merely prove that fresh experiments are necessary. It was the only school in which the teachers had liberty to work according to their own methods and schemes, and where they were in free communication both among themselves and with all learned men throughout Germany."

C. The Humanists

DISTINGUISHING CHARACTERISTICS.—It is now time to consider the humanistic movement of the eighteenth century, which made the study of classical antiquity the basis of all culture. It was a reaction in part against the ecclesiasticism which fostered the ancient languages only for the sake of theology, and in part against the realistic school represented by Comenius, Rousseau, and especially the Philanthropinists.

The distinguishing characteristic of the humanists is the prominence which they give to Latin and Greek. These languages are made the basis of education; and the attempt is made to justify this prominence by their value as a means of culture, and also as studies of practical utility. It is maintained that the study of the ancient languages is unequaled in disciplinary worth, and that the literatures of Greece and Rome contain incomparable models of style. Hence, the study of Latin and Greek gives strength to the faculties and cultivation to the taste. It is further claimed that the study of Latin and Greek possesses great practical worth, inasmuch as it furnishes a valuable acquaintance with English etymology and general grammar, leads to a vast storehouse of knowledge, and gives a better understanding of the present, which has its roots in the past. The humanists are unsympathetic with the present; they depreciate the science, literature, and culture of modern times, and scarcely allow to Christian civilization any superiority over that of paganism in literary productions.

SCHMIDT'S SUMMARY.—The fundamental principles of the humanists have been given by Karl Schmidt: " 1. The ancient languages are the foundation of all true culture; a knowledge of them makes the scholar; hence they must lie at the basis of all instruction, especially in the higher education. In itself considered, the study of language is a means of mental culture, and hence has disciplinary value. But it is also related to all departments of human learning. Greek and Latin writings are the sources of all learning, and whoever would go to the fountain-head must be acquainted with these languages. The original documents of religion, Roman jurisprudence, the correct principles of medicine, philosophy, the principles and examples of rhetoric and poetry, history—all have come to us from Greece and Rome. . . . 2. The study of grammar must precede that•of philosophy, history, æsthetics. Grammar is necessary to a thorough knowledge of language. The method used in teaching the modern languages does not suit with the ancient languages. A dead language is well spoken only by a few. This ability is far from being possessed by all good philologians. . . . 3. A too early pursuit of the natural sciences is unfavorable to a thorough acquisition of languages, for the time given to the latter must be brief and dependent—adequate studies in them being deferred to riper years. The languages belong to the schools, the sciences to the universities. 4. It is a mistake to suppose that the study of the ancient languages is hurtful to practical knowledge. The broadest scholars have the greatest respect for the ancients. It is not easy to name, in any nation, a distinguished author or scholar who is not indebted to the Greeks and Romans for his superior attainments. The too early pursuit of all possible sciences at school results in shallow minds that are thorough in nothing. There is no thorough, scientific culture apart from the study of language."

HUMANISM AND PHILANTHROPINISM.—The contrast between humanism and philanthropinism has been sharply drawn by Niethammer, a prominent humanist of the latter part of the eighteenth century: 1. Humanism aims at general culture; philanthropinism, at utility. 2. Humanism seeks to exercise and strengthen the mind; philanthropinism, to fill it with useful knowledge. 3. Humanism demands but few subjects of study; philanthropinism, many. 4. Humanism exercises the mind with ideas; philanthropinism, with things. 5. Humanism deals with the true, the beautiful, and the good, the elements of human culture; philanthropinism, with matter. 6. Humanism finds its subjects of study in classical antiquity; philanthropinism, in the present. 7. Humanism regards learning as a serious employment; philanthropinism makes it, as far as possible, an amusement. 8. Humanism leads to thoroughness in a few things; philanthropinism, to superficiality in many. 9. Humanism cultivates the memory, the repository of knowledge; philanthropinism neglects it.

LEADING HUMANISTS.—The leading representatives of the humanistic tendency in the eighteenth century were Gesner, Heyne, Ernesti, and Wolf. They pursued the study of the ancient classics with great enthusiasm and success, and succeeded in giving Greek a place by the side of Latin in the higher education. They raised Germany to the leadership in classical learning—a position it has held ever since. The college curriculum of England and America has been largely influenced by the humanists.

REACTION.—Within the past few years a strong reaction has set in and forced a partial readjustment of the college course. The fundamental principles of humanism have been brought into question, and subjected to both scientific and practical tests. Many of them are found to be in part or wholly fallacious. Our knowledge of the ancient world is not dependent upon an acquaintance with Latin and Greek. It is best obtained in the exhaustive labors of great historians who have embodied the results of their investigations in our own and other modern tongues. The treasures of ancient literature—the immortal works of Virgil and Homer, of Cicero and Demosthenes, of Horace and Æschylus—are accessible in scholarly translations, which we can read with the same satisfaction we enjoy in perusing the records of Moses, the songs of David, or the arguments of Paul. And the knowledge thus gained of ancient authors is far more satisfactory than that obtained by college students, who struggle through inconsiderable fragments with grammar and dictionary. While there may be question as to the comparative excellence of style in ancient and modern writing, it is a fact beyond reasonable doubt that the vast extension of the field of knowledge in modern times—the development of science, the marvels of invention, the truths of Christianity—has made the literature of the past two hundred and fifty years greatly more valuable than that of antiquity. The current of thought, like a river, grows broader and deeper as it flows farther from its source. In view of the fact that the ancient languages are not the parents of German and English, but rather elder children of the same Aryan family, it is coming to be recognized that Latin and Greek have no monopoly of general grammar, and that the principles underlying the structure of language can be readily learned from the modern tongues. As the modern languages are not necessarily subject to the abuse of illegitimate helps, and as they call into active exercise every faculty of the student's mind in the threefold work of translating, speaking, and hearing, they do not appear to be at all inferior to the ancient languages as disciplinary studies.

MODERN STUDIES.—It is now felt, too, that the modern world, in which we are to play our parts, should not be ignored in our courses of instruction. Considered in its external relations, the end of education is to prepare us for useful living. Great nations are moving upon the stage of the twentieth century; investigators are at work in all Christian lands; international relations are becoming closer each year; the whole earth, bound together by telegraphs and commercial interests, daily challenges our thought. In view of these facts, many hold that it is not wise to require a young man to spend his best years in Greece and Rome as a preparation for intelligent living in the twentieth century—the grandest that the world has seen. It leaves too large a gap between the college and practical life. Hence Latin and Greek, notwithstanding the stubborn resistance of the humanists, are being gradually retired from their former prominence to make way for the mother-tongue, the natural sciences, and the modern languages.

7. EDUCATION IN THE NINETEENTH CENTURY

GENERAL FEATURES.—The nineteenth century gathered within its embrace the fruits of all the labors, struggles, and sufferings of the past. The field of knowledge was not only widened, but it was brought within the reach of the masses. Mighty forces of nature were brought into subjection to the will of man, and made obedient servants in the cause of progress. The seeds of human liberty, sown in blood at the close of the eighteenth century, sprang up into a beautiful harvest. The sentiment of humanity was awakened, and a serious calamity in any quarter of the world instantly awakened a general and fruitful sympathy. Reason learned to assert its rights in society and state, in science and art, while the law of love began to prevail more and more in all the relations of life.

EDUCATIONAL PROGRESS.—This great expansion of knowledge, with its broader outlook upon life, could not remain without influence upon education. The century is without parallel in its educational progress. Near its beginning a few great thinkers and educators, who will presently call for consideration, laid the foundations of educational science. More rational methods were devised. The principles of human dignity and equality, as proclaimed by the American and French revolutions, called for popular education. The state assumed control of education, and to a greater or less degree established schools of every grade. The worth of the individual, as proclaimed in the teachings of Christianity, was recognized, and female education received a degree of attention unknown in the past. Teaching was recognized as a profession that requires special training; and to this end a new class of fitting schools was established in large numbers. Better schoolhouses were built; and, for more efficient instruction, libraries, laboratories, and apparatus of various kinds, were provided. In no other particular, perhaps, was the nineteenth century—so remarkable in many ways—more distinguished than for its progress in education.

A. Richter

BIOGRAPHICAL.—Jean Paul Friedrich Richter, commonly known as Jean Paul, was born in Bavaria in 1763. He studied at the University of Leipsic, and acquired through miscellaneous reading a vast amount of information. Poverty drove him to literature, in which he displayed great originality and power. Though unappreciated for many years, he at length became one of the most distinguished and popular authors of his time, and enjoyed the friendship of Herder, Wieland, and other illustrious contemporaries. He was a private teacher for a time, but it was from his own children, as he tells us, that he derived the clearest insight into the principles of education. He was acquainted with the best educational literature of his time, but was most largely indebted to Rousseau's Émile. Like that celebrated work, Richter's Levana is not a thorough, systematic treatise, but it is irradiated with the splendor of a great brain and heart.

PURPOSE OF EDUCATION.—Richter esteemed the spirit of education above individual or mechanical rules. Within every child there is an ideal manhood, like the statue in the crude block of marble, which is to be liberated by the artistic touch of education. It is not the separate faculties, but the whole being that is to be cared for and developed. " Do not, like the ordinary educator," he says, " water the individual branches, but the roots, and they will moisten and unfold the rest. Wisdom and morality are no ants' colonies of separate, cooperating workmen, but organic parents of the mental future which only require life-giving nourishment. We merely reverse the ignorance of the savages, who sowed gunpowder instead of making it, when we attempt to compound what can only be developed."

REGARD FOR CHILDHOOD.—The hopes of the future rest in childhood. Each generation of children begins the history of the world anew. The people who have reached maturity are fixed in their opinions and characters; it is difficult to reach and change them. But " by education we can sow upon a pure, soft soil the seeds of poisonous or of honey-bearing flowers; and as the gods stooped to the first men, so do we, physical and spiritual giants to children, descend to these little ones, and form them to be great or small. . . . Let a child be more holy to you than the present, which consists of things and matured men. By means of the child—although with difficulty—by means of the short lever-arm of humanity, you set in motion the long one, whose mighty arc you can scarcely define in the height and depth of time."

FAITH OF CHILDREN.—The faith or trustfulness of children, which is the basis of education, is to be jealously guarded and preserved. The sciences rest on faith, for we have to accept the statements of others. An upright character in the teacher should answer to the natural confidence of the child. " Holily preserve childlike trust," Richter says, " without which there can be no education. Never forget that the little inexperienced child looks up to you as to a lofty genius, an apostle full of revelations, whom he trusts altogether more absolutely than his equals, and that the lie of an apostle destroys a whole moral world. Wherefore never bury your infallibility by useless proofs, nor by confessions of error: the admission of your ignorance comports better with you. Power and skepticism the child can sufficiently early, and at your charges, polemically and protestantly exercise and strengthen on the declared opinions of strangers."

RELIGION AND MORALITY.—Richter presents religion as

an irrepressible need of the soul, and the purest distinction between man and the lower animals. It is based on faith; but the child is to be led to religion, not by arguments, but by intuition. "We arrive there by wings, not by steps." Religion he defines as belief in God. "Without God," he continues, "we are lonely throughout eternity; but if we have God we are more warmly, more intimately, more steadfastly united than by friendship and love. I am then no longer alone with my spirit. Its great first Friend, the Everlasting whom it recognizes, the inborn Friend of its innermost soul, will abandon it as little as it can do itself, and in the midst of the impure or empty whirl of trifles and of sins, on the market-place and battle-field, I stand with closed breast in which the Almighty and All-holy speaks to me, and reposes before me like a near sun, behind which the outer world lies in darkness."

The teacher of religion should be religious, for a man can not impart what he does not possess. Children are to be taught religion less by precept than by example; and hence, in parents and teachers, they should see devotional and holy sentiments. Favorable occasions are to be seized to impress the young mind with the manifestations of divine power. "The younger a child is," Richter says, "the less let him hear the Unspeakable named, who only by a word becomes to him the speakable: but let him behold His symbols. The sublime is the temple step of religion, as the stars are of immeasurable space. When what is mighty appears in nature—a storm, thunder, the starry firmament, death—then utter the word God before the child. A great misfortune, a great blessing, a great crime, a noble action, are building sites for a child's church."

REALISTIC STUDIES.—Richter sides with the realistic reformers of the eighteenth century. He holds that it is impossible for the immature student to grasp and appreciate the beauties of the classic literature of Greece and Rome. "Is it not madness to think it ever possible," he exclaims, "that a boy of fourteen or sixteen, however great his abilities, can comprehend the harmony of poetry and deep thought contained in one of Plato's dialogues, or the worldly persiflage of Horace's satires?" The mind should be prepared by the study of native literature to appreciate the literary beauty of foreign tongues. "At home and at school," he says, "let the native poets be first placed on the altar as gods of the household and the country; let the little child rise from the lesser to the greater gods. What love of country must not that hanging on the lips of native poets inspire!" And in reference to the natural sciences he says: "Give natural philosophy and natural history, astronomy and geometry, and abundant supplies of 'bread studies,' a place in the schoolrooms and lecture-rooms of your gymnasiums; and in so doing you will give the boys ten times more pleasure than they receive from the unfolding of the mummy bandages of the ancient graces; thus, too, you impart the common nourishment needed by both the future divisions of your pupils into sons of the muses and sons of labor."

EDUCATION OF GIRLS.—Richter's view in regard to the education of girls marks a distinct advance over the opinions generally held in his day. While recognizing the home as the peculiar sphere of woman's activity, he goes beyond Rousseau in clearly grasping the idea of the human being back of the wife and mother. The thought of woman's sphere must not be ignored in her training; but, at the same time, her education must aim "to make the whole nature complete." "Before and after being a mother," Richter says, "a girl is a human being; and neither

motherly nor wifely destination can overbalance or substitute the human, but must become its means, not end.
As above the poet, the painter, or the hero, so above the
mother does the human being rise preeminent." It naturally follows from this view that the education of girls
should be of a comprehensive and substantial character.
Botany, geography, astronomy, history, geometry, and a
foreign language should be included in their course of
study. But Richter did not think much of mere accomplishments. "The so-called ladylike accomplishments,"
he says, "are at most but garlands of flowers by which
Cupid may be bound; but Hymen, who breaks through
these, and garlands of fruit too, is best guided and held
by the golden chain of domestic capability."

B. Kant

BIOGRAPHICAL.—Immanuel Kant, one of the greatest
speculative philosophers of all time, was born at Königsberg in 1724. He was educated at the university of his
native town, and in 1770 was appointed professor of logic
and metaphysics there. His life was devoted to philosophy
with great singleness of purpose. He never traveled more
than forty miles from his native city, but during the
thirty years of his professorship gave himself to his speculative studies with mechanical regularity. He carried philosophy to greater depths than it had before attained, in
his Critique of Pure Reason. But it is with his educational views, as embodied in his Pädagogik, that we are
here concerned. Naturally, however, his pedagogy rests
upon his psychology.

EDUCATION AS DEVELOPMENT.—Kant conceives of education as a development of the native powers of the child.

Man alone of all creatures needs education. The ideal toward which he is to be developed is a higher self or perfect manhood. "There are many undeveloped powers in humanity," he says, "and now it is our business symmetrically to develop these dormant capacities, and unfold the humanity within us, so that man may attain his destiny. Animals fulfil their destiny of themselves and unconsciously. But man must make an effort to attain it; and this he can not do unless he has a conception of its nature." But it will require generations to perfect a system of education. The individual can not arrive at perfection without a corresponding development of the human race. "Education," he says, "is an art, the practise of which must be perfected through many generations. Each generation, equipped with the knowledge of its predecessor, can bring forth an education that will more symmetrically and fittingly develop all the native powers of man, and so lead the entire human race to its destiny."

EDUCATION DIFFICULT.—Education, in the true sense of the word, is a difficult problem. It has not yet been fully solved. Upon its right solution depends the future of our race. There is nothing more important than this development of the individual and of mankind. "Man," Kant says, "must develop his native capacities for good. Providence has not bestowed them already formed; they are simply capacities, and without ethical difference. To make himself better, to cultivate his faculties, and if he is evil, to establish morality in his life—that is the work man has to do. But when we consider the matter carefully, we find that this is a very difficult task. Hence, education is the greatest and most difficult problem that can be laid upon man. For intelligence depends upon education, and education in turn depends upon intelligence.

Hence, education can progress only by degrees; and a correct conception of the method of education can arise only as one generation after another bequeaths its knowledge and experience to its successor. What a knowledge and experience this conception presupposes! It can arise only at a distant day, and we ourselves have not yet settled it."

A WEIGHTY PRINCIPLE.—Kant naturally sought to base educational practise on a broad and solid foundation. Merely practical or temporary ends could not satisfy his philosophical spirit. He found fault with parents and princes for considering only utilitarian and selfish ends. " A principle of educational science," he says, " that should be especially considered by men who devise systems of education, is this: children should not be educated for the present condition of the human race, but for the future and better condition that is possible; that is to say, in conformity with the idea of humanity and its entire destiny. The principle is of great weight. Parents usually educate their children to conform to the present state of the world, though it be degenerated. But they should educate them better, in order that a future better condition be brought forth. But we find two hindrances here: 1. Parents are commonly solicitous only that their children get on in the world; and 2. Princes consider their subjects only as instruments to subserve their own ends."

FOURFOLD EDUCATION.—In education there is a negative and a positive side. In the educational process there are tendencies that need to be repressed, as there are others that need to be drawn out. In the entire work of education the nature and the relations of man are to be taken into account; and as a result, the world is to be made better for it. Kant distinguishes four parts or factors in education:

" 1. In education man must be disciplined. To discipline means to attempt to prevent the animal side of our nature, in the individual and in society, from doing harm. Thus discipline is merely taming the wildness of our nature.

" 2. Man must be cultivated. Culture includes information and instruction. It is the attainment of skill, or the possession of an ability, that is adequate for all desired ends. It does not determine ends, but leaves that to circumstances. Some kinds of skill are good in all cases, as reading and writing; others only for particular ends, as music, in order to make us beloved.

" 3. It must be seen to that man also becomes *prudent*, that he is adapted to human society, that he be esteemed, and that he have influence. For this purpose we need a certain kind of culture which is called civilization. To this belong manners, politeness, and a certain prudence, by which one can use all men for his purposes. It conforms to the changing taste of every age. Thus, a few decades ago, people loved ceremony in society.

" 4. We must have regard to ethics. Man is not merely to become skilful in all things, but he is also to acquire the state of mind in which he will choose only what is good. Good aims are those that are necessarily approved by every one, and that can at the same time be adopted by every one."

MORAL CULTURE.—Kant was a man of strict integrity of character and a profound sense of right and wrong. He understood the importance of character, without which all other education must fail of its highest end. He laid. stress, therefore, on moral instruction and training, which he would not have left to the church. " People practically educate their children," he says, " in such a manner that morals are left to the preacher. But how infinitely important is it, to teach children from youth up to detest vice, not alone because God has forbidden·it, but because it is in itself detestable. Otherwise they easily come to the thought that they can practise it, and that it is permissible if God has not expressly forbidden it, and that God therefore might indeed make an exception. God is the holiest Being, and wills only what is good, and desires that we practise virtue on account of its inner worth, and not because He desires it."

MORAL MAXIMS.—Kant would not have character developed merely by a training in the exercise of virtue. Laws and maxims are necessary, in order to bring before the mind of the child a correct conception of what he should do and become. Character-building must not be a matter of mere training; it must be grounded in a recognition of the truth, and in a free conformity to it. " The maxims," he says, " must spring out of the human being himself. In moral culture we should seek early to bring before children conceptions of what is good or evil. If we wish to establish morality, we must not inflict punishment. Morality is something so holy and exalted that one dare not place it in the same rank with discipline. The chief thing in moral education is to form a character. Character consists in readiness to conform to maxims. At first it is the maxims of the school, and afterward the maxims of mankind. In the beginning the child obeys laws. Maxims are also laws, but subjective; they spring out of the understanding of mankind. No transgression of school regulations, however, must go unpunished, though the punishment should be commensurate with the transgression."

RELIGIOUS CULTURE.—To moral culture is to be added religion. Religion consists, not in a system of dogmatic beliefs, but in obedience to God. It is morality brought into relation with the Supreme Being. "But what is religion?" Kant inquires. "Religion is the law within us, in so far as it receives sanction from a Lawgiver and Judge over us; it is a morality based on the knowledge of God. If we do not unite religion with morality, then religion becomes merely a suing for divine favor. Praise, prayers, public worship should only give new strength and courage for improvement, or be the expression of a heart animated by a sense of duty. These exercises are only a preparation for good works, but are not themselves good works, and we can not otherwise become acceptable to the Supreme Being than by becoming better men."

TRAINING FOR WORK.—Kant maintains that it is of the greatest importance that children learn to work. He regards labor as a blessing of heaven. If Adam and Eve had remained in Paradise with nothing further to do than to sit together, sing Arcadian songs, and admire the beauties of nature, they would have suffered ennui. "Man must be so occupied," Kant says, "that he is not conscious of himself, and the most agreeable rest is that after toil. Hence the child should be accustomed to labor. And where else shall the inclination to work be cultivated but in the school? The school is a compulsory culture. It is extremely hurtful when the child is accustomed to regard everything as play. There must be a time for recreation, but there must also be a time for work. Though the child do not at once see the use of compulsion, he will later become conscious of it. It would only be pampering the idle curiosity of children, always to answer their question, 'What is that for?' 'Of what use is it?' Education must be compulsory, but it should not on that account be slavish."

Conclusion.—Through Kant education entered into relations with philosophy. Henceforth it became common to ground the science of education upon principles derived from psychology and ethics, and attempts were made to define it in comprehensive and philosophic terms. Thus Niemeyer, the author of an able work on the science of education, who died in 1828, says that "education is the conscious physical and mental influence exerted on man in childhood and youth, in order to bring him to a higher consciousness, and to develop all his faculties and powers." Schwarz, an educational writer of distinction, who died in 1837, says that "to educate a man means to develop him; that is, to work upon him according to his nature and destiny, so that he reaches perfection, and represents his type in full realization." Stephani, a school official and educational author of some note in Germany, who died in 1850, lays down the following injunction as the guiding principle of education: "Treat your pupil as a free human being, who is to learn to use spontaneously his will as his highest destiny demands." These philosophic definitions of education, and many others, are directly traceable to the influence of Kant.

C. Pestalozzi

Relation to Popular Education.—In the long line of educational reformers since the Reformation, there is perhaps no other that has done so much for popular education as Pestalozzi. The devotion of his life, as well as the truth of his pedagogic principles, has been a power in the educational world. He was not distinguished for learning or ability; his were the higher talents of a noble enthusiasm for the elevation of our race, and an inexhaustible love for man. Following the example of our divine Master, he gave himself for the good of others. His labors and self-sacrifices were not in vain. Through the noble devotion of his endeavors, he became the medium through which all that was best in educational theory up to his time obtained permanent recognition.

CONDITION OF SCHOOLS.—The labors of previous educational reformers were not altogether fruitless. Here and there might be discerned improvement in the schools. Some enlightened rulers directed their attention to the subject of popular education; and, as early as 1717, Frederick William I, of Prussia, published an edict of compulsory education. But, in general, it may be said that the primary schools of the eighteenth century remained in a wretched condition. The teachers were unsuccessful students, disabled workmen, discharged soldiers, and common servants. They were held in light esteem, and received but little pay. Schools were by no means general, and those that were opened were not regularly attended. The common people were lacking in educational interest, and looked upon the schools as a burden. While the clergy generally regarded themselves as the legitimate custodians of education, they paid no adequate attention to its interests. Many princes, believing that general intelligence would increase the difficulty of ruling, were unfavorable to the education of the masses. A vast work yet remained to be accomplished.

EARLY LIFE.—John Henry Pestalozzi, who was to contribute so largely to this work, was born January 12, 1746, in the beautiful town of Zürich. At six years of age he lost his father. His mother was an excellent woman, but her tenderness was unfavorable to the development of strength of character. " I grew up," he says, " by the side of the best of mothers, as a mother's child. Year after year I never came out from behind the stove. In short, all means and stimulus for the development of manly strength, manly experience, manly ways of thinking, and manly practise, were wanting to me just in proportion as I needed them by the peculiarity and weakness of my individual character."

SCHOOL-DAYS.—He did not distinguish himself at school; on the contrary, he became the butt of fun for his companions. " In all games," he says, " I was the most awkward and most helpless of all my schoolmates, and yet I wished to excel in them above the rest. That often gave them occasion to laugh at me. One of them gave me the nickname of Harry Queer, of Follyville. Most of them were pleased with my good temper and serviceableness, but they knew my one-sidedness and want of skill, and my thoughtlessness in everything which did not interest me much."

STRONG SYMPATHY.—His sympathies were very strong —at once a source of weakness and of strength. Feeling predominated over judgment; and as a result, his life was not regulated by the dictates of practical wisdom. He was thoroughly injudicious. This fact was understood by an intimate friend named Bluntschli, who upon his death-bed gave Pestalozzi, then a young man, the following advice: " I die," he said; " and, when you are left to yourself, I warn you never to embark in any career which, from your good-natured and confiding disposition, might become dangerous to you. Seek for a quiet, tranquil career; and, unless you have at your side a man who will faithfully assist you with a calm, dispassionate knowledge of men and things, by no means embark in any extensive undertaking, the failure of which would in any way be perilous to you."

NEUHOF.—Pestalozzi first studied theology, but, breaking down in his first sermon, he gave up the ministry for law. To this pursuit he did not long remain constant. In 1767 he purchased a farm of about one hundred acres, to which he gave the name Neuhof, and turned his attention to agriculture. As might be expected from what we already know of his character, the enterprise was a failure. At an earlier period he had perused Rousseau's Emile, which made a profound impression upon him. Unmindful of his own financial embarrassment, moved by sympathy for the suffering ones around him, he opened an industrial school for the poor. He soon had fifty children under his charge to provide for. His plan was to combine study with remunerative labor. But after five years the school was closed, in 1780, leaving Pestalozzi heavily involved in debt, but greatly enriched in educátional experience. This was his consolation: "The Christian in the strength of faith and love," he says, "considers his property not as a gift but as a trust, which has been committed to his hand, that he may use it for the good of others."

AT STANZ.—The next few years were devoted chiefly to authorship as a means of obtaining subsistence. He produced several works in which he advanced his educational ideas, and through which he has exerted a lasting influence upon education. But we follow him in his work as a practical educator. In 1798 Stanz, a town on Lake Lucerne, was burned by the French. The whole surrounding district was laid waste, and a number of orphans were left destitute and homeless. Upon the recommendation of the Swiss directors, Pestalozzi went thither to look after them. With only one servant he established himself in an unfinished convent, and soon had eighty children under his care. They composed a heterogeneous mass that would have been appalling to any one with less enthusiasm than Pestalozzi. He addressed himself with almost superhuman zeal to the work of improving their condition. " Every assistance," he says, " everything done for them in their need, all the teaching that they received, came directly from me; my hand lay on their hand, my eye rested on their eye. My tears flowed with theirs, and my smile accompanied theirs. Their food was mine, and their drink was mine. I had nothing, no housekeeping, no friends, no servants; I had them alone. I slept in their midst; I was the last to go to bed at night, and the first to rise in the morning. I prayed with them, and taught them in bed before they went to sleep." This is an unselfish devotion that makes us forget many defects of character.

" His schoolroom," says a biographer, " was totally unprovided with books, and his apparatus consisted of himself and his pupils. He was forced to adapt these means to the accomplishment of his end. He directed his whole attention to those natural elements which are found in the mind of every child. He taught numbers instead of figures; living sounds instead of dead characters; deeds of faith and love instead of abstruse creeds; substance instead of shadow; realities instead of signs."

Success and Failure.—In the space of a few months Pestalozzi wrought a great change in the physical, mental, and moral condition of his pupils. They no longer seemed the same beings. The high hopes of the noble enthusiast, however, were again doomed to disappointment. In less than a year the French army returned to Stanz, and unceremoniously took possession of the convent. No choice was left Pestalozzi. He was obliged to relinquish his

21

labors, and parted from his children with tears and sobs. "Imagine," he writes to a friend, "with what sensations I left Stanz. Thus might feel a shipwrecked mariner, who sees land after weary and restless nights, and draws the breath of coming life, but is again thrown into the immensity of space. This was my own condition. Think of the fulness of my heart, the greatness of my plans, my success and my ruin, the trembling of my disordered nerves, and my mute agony."

AT BURGDORF.—In the course of a few weeks he entered a school at Burgdorf as assistant teacher. He carried with him his old enthusiasm and his old disregard for stereotyped methods. Ramsauer, then a pupil in the school and afterward a faithful assistant of Pestalozzi's, has given us an account of the Burgdorf school. He says: "I got about as much regular schooling as the other scholars—which, in fact, was none at all; but Pestalozzi's sacred zeal, his devoted love, which caused him to be entirely unmindful of himself, his serious and depressed state of mind, which struck even the children, made the deepest impression on me, and knit my childlike and grateful heart to his forever." Though he was the subject of envy and intrigue, Pestalozzi's labors at Burgdorf were not left wholly without recognition. The school committee of that town expressed themselves in a report as follows: "He has shown what powers are hidden in the feeble child, and in what manner they can be developed. The pupils have made astonishing progress in some branches, thereby proving that every child is capable of doing something, if the teacher is able to draw out his talent, and awaken the powers of his mind in the order of their natural development."

AT YVERDUN.—In 1805 he opened a school at Yverdun.

Here he attained his greatest triumphs. He achieved a European reputation, and kings and philosophers united in showing him regard. Yverdun became a place of pilgrimage for philanthropists and educators from all parts of Europe. In 1809 Pestalozzi had under him fifteen teachers and one hundred and sixty-five pupils, besides thirty-five adult students, who were there to learn his methods. The spirit animating the institution has thus been described by an eye-witness: " The teachers and pupils were united by that unaffected love which Pestalozzi, who in years was a man verging on the grave, but in heart and mind a genuine child, seemed to breathe out continually and impart to all who came within his influence. The children forgot that they had another home, and the teachers that there was any other world than the institution. Not a man claimed a privilege for himself, not one wished to be considered above others. Teachers and pupils were entirely united. They not only slept in the same rooms, and shared the labors and enjoyments of the day, but they were on a footing of perfect equality. The same man who read a lecture on history one hour would, perhaps, during the next sit on the same form with the pupils for a lesson in arithmetic or geometry, and without compromising his dignity would even request their assistance and receive their hints."

HIS ESTIMATE OF THE WORK.—In reference to his work here, Pestalozzi himself writes: " The difficulties that opposed my enterprise in the beginning were very great. Public opinion was wholly against me. Thousands looked upon my work as quackery, and nearly all who believed themselves competent judges declared it worthless. Some condemned it as silly mechanism; some looked upon it as mere memorizing, while others contended that it neglected the memory for the sake of the understanding; some accused me of a want of religion, and others of revolutionizing intentions. But, thank God, all these objections have been overcome. The children of our institution are full of joy and happiness; their innocence is guarded; their religious feelings are fostered; their minds are cultivated; their knowledge increased; their hearts inspired with a love of virtue. The whole is pervaded by the great spirit of home-union; a pure fatherly and brotherly spirit rules all. The children feel free; their activity is incited by their occupations; affection and confidence elevate and guide their hearts."

SELF-FORGETFULNESS.—In the midst of his success, Pestalozzi still retained his touching simplicity and self-forgetfulness. On one occasion " a poor young man had traveled on foot a long distance to pay his tribute of respect and admiration to Pestalozzi; but, upon arriving at Yverdun, he found himself so reduced that he could not pay for a night's lodging at the hotel. Pestalozzi, not wishing to disturb the household, offered his own bed to the wearied guest. Some friends, calling at his room soon after, were astonished to see his bed occupied by a stranger. Alarmed by his absence they went in search of him, and found him at last stretched on one of the hard benches of the schoolroom in sound sleep, and totally unconscious that he had done anything but his duty."

HIS DEATH.—The sun of Pestalozzi's life, which had shone brightly for a little while in the afternoon, was to set in clouds. Discord broke out at length among the teachers at Yverdun. After disturbing the peace and prosperity of the school for a long time, it led at last, in 1825, to its suspension. Pestalozzi returned to Neuhof, where he was prostrated with a fever. He died February

17, 1827. During his last hours he said: " I forgive my enemies; may they find peace, now that I go to my rest. I should have been glad to live another month, in order to complete my last work; but I also thank God for calling me away from this life. My beloved family, remain attached to one another, and seek your happiness in the quietness of your domestic circle." Subject to disappointment all his days, his life was still a great triumph. It was spent in unselfish devotion to the good of others; and, like that of the blessed Master who went about doing good, it has borne a rich fruitage for the world.

EDUCATIONAL PRINCIPLES.—The object of our study thus far has been chiefly to gain a clear knowledge of the man. We now turn to a brief examination of some of his educational principles, as embodied in his leading works, viz.: Evening Hour of a Hermit, Leonard and Gertrude, and How Gertrude Teaches Her Children. He rejected the current humanistic word-teaching. " A man," he says, " who has only word-wisdom is less susceptible to the truth than a savage. The use of mere words produces men who believe that they have reached the goal, because their whole life has been spent in talking about it, but who never ran toward it, because no motive impelled them to make the effort; hence, I come to the conviction that the fundamental error—the blind use of words in matters of instruction—must be extirpated before it is possible to resuscitate life and truth."

EDUCATION AS DEVELOPMENT.—The educational conception that lies at the basis of Pestalozzi's system is that of a natural, progressive, and symmetrical development of all the powers and faculties of the human being. This is the completest and grandest conception of education. " Sound education," says Pestalozzi, " stands before me symbolized by a tree planted near fertilizing waters. A little seed, which contains the design of the tree, its form and proportions, is placed in the soil. See how it germinates and expands into trunk, branches, leaves, flowers, and fruit! The whole tree is an uninterrupted chain of organic parts, the plan of which existed in its seed and root. Man is similar to the tree. In the new-born child are hidden those faculties which are to unfold during life. The individual and separate organs of his being form themselves gradually into an harmonic whole, and build up humanity in the image of God."

EDUCATION BY DOING.—Pestalozzi beautifully emphasizes in reference to the higher exercises of the mind the principle of Comenius that "things to be done should be learned by doing them." "The moral, intellectual, and executive powers of man," he says, "must be nurtured within himself, and not from artificial substitutes. Thus, faith must be cultivated by our own act of believing, not by reasoning about faith; love, by our own act of loving, not by fine words about love; thought, by our own act of thinking, not by merely appropriating the thoughts of other men; and knowledge, by our own investigation, not by endless talk about the results of art and science."

NATURAL ORDER OF STUDIES.—A natural order is to be observed in education. "Men, fathers!" Pestalozzi exclaims, "force not the faculties of your children into paths too distant before they have attained strength by exercise, and avoid harshness and over-fatigue. When this right order of proceedings is neglected, the faculties of the mind are weakened and lose their steadiness, and the equipoise of their structure. This you do when, before making them sensitive to truth and wisdom by the real knowledge of actual objects, you engage them in the thousand-fold confusions of word-learning and opinions, and lay the foundation of their mental character and of the first determination of their powers, instead of truth and actual objects, with sounds and speech—and words."

FUNDAMENTAL PRINCIPLES.—The fundamental principles of Pestalozzi, most of which are contained in the extracts already given from his writings, have been summarized by Joseph Payne substantially as follows:

1. The principles of education are to be sought in human nature.

2. This nature is organic, consisting of physical, intellectual, and moral capabilities, ready and struggling to develop themselves.

3. The function of the educator is both negative and positive. He must remove impediments to the learner's development, and he must also stimulate the exercise of his powers.

4. Self-development begins with sensations received through the senses. These sensations lead to perceptions which, registered in the mind as conceptions or ideas, constitute the basis of knowledge.

5. "Spontaneity and self-activity are the necessary conditions under which the mind educates itself, and gains power and independence."

6. Practical aptness depends more on exercise than on knowledge. "Knowing and doing must, however, proceed together. The chief aim of education is the development of the learner's powers."

7. All education must be based on the learner's own observation—on his own personal experience. "This is the true basis of all knowledge. The opposite proceeding leads to empty, hollow, delusive word-knowledge. First the reality, then the symbol; first the thing, then the word."

8. What the learner has gained by his own observation has become an actual possession which he can explain or describe in his own words. His ability to do this is the measure of the accuracy and extent of his knowledge.

9. The learner's growth necessitates advancement from the near and actual to the more remote; hence, from the concrete to the abstract, from particulars to generals, from the known to the unknown.

D. Froebel and the Kindergarten

BIOGRAPHICAL.—One of the most illustrious disciples of Pestalozzi was Frederick Froebel, who was born in Thuringia in 1782. He was the son of a Lutheran clergyman, who was so occupied in caring for a large parish that he neglected his son. His religious instruction in the village school made a deep impression upon him; it became, as he tells us, " the birth to a higher spiritual life." He learned to enter into deep sympathy with nature. " The plant and flower world became," he says, " so far as I could see and touch it, an object of my contemplation and thought." At ten years of age he went to live with an uncle, and entered the town school of Stadt-Ilm. The teacher, " a regular driller of the old, time-honored stamp, had not the slightest conception of the inner nature of his pupil," says Joseph Payne, " and seems to have made no effort to discover it. He pronounced the boy to be idle (which, from his point of view, was quite true) and lazy (which certainly was not true)—a boy, in short, you could do nothing with. And, in fact, the teacher did nothing with his pupil, never once touched the chords of his inner being, or brought out the music they were fitted, under different handling, to produce. Froebel was indeed, at that time, a thoughtful, dreamy child, a very indifferent student of books, cordially hating the formal lessons with which he was crammed, and never so happy as when left alone with his great teacher in the woods."

FINDS HIS LIFE-WORK.—At the age of fifteen he became a forester's apprentice, and adopted a " religious life in nature," living entirely in and with plants. In 1799 he entered the University of Jena, where he attended lectures on mathematics, botany, natural history, physics, chemistry, the science of finance, forest matters, and architecture.   After he had tried several employments with but little satisfaction, Gruner, the principal of a model school just established at Frankfort, said to him : " Give up architecture; it is not for you.   Become an educator.   We need a teacher in our school.   Make up your mind, and you shall have the place."   After some hestitation he accepted the position ; and the ecstasy he felt, as he stood for the first time in the presence of the school, convinced him that he had found his place.   To use his own expression, " The fish was in the water."

WITH PESTALOZZI.—In 1808 he went to Yverdun, and spent two years with Pestalozzi.   He took with him three pupils, of whom he had charge as tutor.   " Thus it happened," he says, " that I was there both as teacher and scholar, educator and pupil.   In order to be fully and perfectly placed in the midst and heart of Pestalozzi's work, I wished to reside with my pupils in the building of the institution, in the castle so called.   We wished to share everything with the rest; but this wish was not granted us, for strange selfishness interfered.   Yet I soon came to dwell as near the institution as possible, so that we shared dinner, afternoon lunch, and supper, the instruction adapted to us, and the whole life of the pupils.   I for

myself had nothing more serious to do than to allow my
pupils to take a full share of that life, strengthening spirit
and body. With this aim we shared all instruction, and
it was a special care to me to talk with Pestalozzi on every
subject from its first point of connection, to learn to know
it from its foundation." He thus became thoroughly acquainted with Pestalozzi's system, which in its essential
features he cordially adopted, but which he also supplemented and improved.

AT KEILHAU.—Afterward feeling the necessity of increasing his store of knowledge, he studied at the Universities of Göttingen and Berlin. In 1813 he joined the Prussian army, and took an active part in the campaign against
Napoleon. After the close of the war he established a
school at Keilhau in 1817, in which he followed "the
principle of cultivating the self-activity of the pupil by connecting manual labor with every study." He was opposed
by the Prussian government, which distrusted the political
and religious character of his work. This opposition led
to the inspection of the school by Superintendent Zech,
whose report is at once a splendid vindication and exposition of Froebel's work. "The object of the institution,"
he said, "is by no means mere knowledge, but the free,
self-active development of the mind from within. Nothing
is added from without except to enlighten the mind, to
strengthen the pupil's power, and to add to his joy by
enhancing his consciousness of growing power."

EDUCATION OF MAN.—While at Keilhau Froebel published in 1826 his great work entitled The Education of
Man. In this work he shows himself a philosopher, and
lays the foundation of his pedagogy deep and firm. Pestalozzi accentuated sense-perception; starting from the same
standpoint, Froebel emphasizes self-activity. He felt the

inner connection or unity of all things in God. On the
one hand, education should "lead man to see and know
the divine, spiritual, and eternal principle which animates
surrounding nature, constitutes the essence of nature, and
is permanently manifested in nature"; on the other hand,
it should lead man to "the realization of a faithful, pure,
inviolate, and hence holy life." Again, in comprehensive
definition, he says: *"Education should lead and guide
man to clearness concerning himself and in himself, to
peace with nature, and to unity with God;* hence it should
lift him to a knowledge of himself and of mankind, to a
knowledge of God and of nature, and to the pure and
holy life to which such knowledge leads."

THE PRINCIPLE OF METHOD.—There is one great fundamental principle of method in education, namely, free and
cheerful obedience to truth and right. What is mandatory
or compulsory should be accepted in a spirit of freedom
because of its recognized righteousness. Teacher and pupil
are equally bound to this willing and cheerful submission
or obedience to the omnipotent law of reason, right, or
truth. "All true education," Froebel says, "in training
and instruction should, therefore, at every moment, in
every demand and regulation, be simultaneously double-
sided—giving and taking, uniting and dividing, prescrib-
ing and following, active and passive, positive yet giving
scope, firm and yielding; and the pupil should be similarly
conditioned: but between the two, between educator and
pupil, between request and obedience, there should invisibly
rule a third something to which educator and pupil are
equally subject. This third something is the *right*, the *best*,
necessarily conditioned and expressed without arbitrariness
in the circumstances. The calm recognition, the clear
knowledge, and the serene, cheerful obedience to the rule

of this third something is the particular feature that should be constantly and clearly manifest in the bearing and conduct of the educator and teacher, and often firmly and sternly emphasized by him. The child, the pupil, has a very keen feeling, a very clear apprehension, and rarely fails to distinguish whether what the educator, the teacher, or the father says or requests is personal or arbitrary, or whether it is expressed by him as a general law and necessity."

THREE FIELDS OF KNOWLEDGE.—There are three departments of knowledge—man, nature, and God; but in them all there is an ever-living unity. The purpose of education is to bring the student into harmony with this unified diversity. Through clear volition he must proceed to the attainment of his destiny. " The school and instruction," Froebel says, " are to lead the boy to the threefold, yet in itself one, knowledge—to the knowledge of himself in all his relations, and thus to the knowledge of man as such; to the knowledge of God, the eternal condition, cause, and source of his being and of the being of all things; and to the knowledge of nature and the outer world as proceeding from the Eternal Spirit, and depending thereon. Instruction and the school are to lead man to a life in full harmony with that threefold, yet in itself one, knowledge. By this knowledge they are to lead man from desire to will, from will to firmness of will, and thus in continuous progression to the attainment of his destiny, to the attainment of his earthly perfection."

CHILDREN'S PLAY.—Froebel saw a profound significance in the play of children. He regarded it as the self-active representation of their inner being. In a beautiful paragraph he says: " Play is the purest, most spiritual activity of man at this stage, and, at the same time, typical of

human life as a whole—of the inner hidden natural life
in man and all things. It gives, therefore, joy, freedom,
contentment, inner and outer rest, peace with the world.
It holds the sources of all that is good. A child that
plays thoroughly, with self-active determination, perse-
veringly until physical fatigue forbids, will surely be a
thorough, determined man, capable of self-sacrifice for the
promotion of the welfare of himself and others. Is not
the most beautiful expression of child-life at this time a
playing child?—a child wholly absorbed in his play?—a
child that has fallen asleep while so absorbed?"

THE KINDERGARTEN.—This brings us to the Kindergarten, upon which the fame of Froebel chiefly rests.
Though the idea was not developed for a dozen years, the
germ of it lay in The Education of Man. Carefully considering the ways of children, Froebel saw that they delight
in movement; that they use their senses; that they observe;
that they invent and construct. All this activity he proposed to turn to account in the interest of education. He
said: " I can convert children's activities, energies, amusements, occupations, all that goes by the name of play, into
instruments for my purpose, and therefore transform play
into work. This work will be education in the true sense
of the term. The conception of it as such I have gained
from the children themselves. They have taught me how
I am to teach them."

The Kindergarten is a school which receives children
at a very early age, and by systematizing their plays, directing their activity, and giving order to their ideas, develops
their faculties harmoniously, and prepares them for the
work of the ordinary school. The object of the Kindergarten, as expressed by Froebel himself, is as follows: " It
shall receive children before the usual school age, give them

employment suited to their nature, strengthen their bodies, exercise their senses, employ the waking mind, make them acquainted judiciously with nature and society, cultivate especially the heart and temper, and lead them to the foundation of all living—to unity with themselves."

The physical nature of the child is developed by calisthenic exercises; its social instincts are strengthened by association with companions in amusements and work; its senses are cultivated by means of playthings, called gifts, such as balls, cylinders, cones, variously dissected cubes, quadrilateral and triangular tablets, sticks, and mats for weaving; and its mind is exercised by the imitative or inventive uses it is taught to make of these objects.

EDUCATION AS DEVELOPMENT.—Froebel accepted the great body of Pestalozzi's educational principles. He held that education is a harmonious development of the human faculties; that its principles are to be found in a study of nature; that development depends upon the self-activity of the learner; and that observation is the basis of knowledge. In reference to education as a development, he says with vehemence: " All that does not grow out of one's inner being, all that is not one's own original feeling and thought, or at least awakens that, oppresses and defaces the individuality of man instead of calling it forth, and nature becomes thereby a caricature. Shall we never cease to stamp human nature, even in childhood, like coins, to overlay it with foreign images and foreign superscriptions instead of letting it develop itself and grow into form according to the law of life planted in it by God the Father, so that it may be able to bear the stamp of the Divine, and become an image of God? For hundreds of years we Germans especially, through imitation of foreign nations, have worn these fetters, which do not allow the deepest nature of the people or of individuals to move and unfold freely."

SUPPLEMENTS PESTALOZZI.—In several points, however, Froebel has supplemented the principles of Pestalozzi. He recognizes the impracticability of the domestic training for early childhood which Pestalozzi so warmly advocated. Most mothers have neither the time nor qualifications to give this training. And, appreciating the importance of it, Froebel devised the Kindergarten, which supplies a veritable want in education.

. He further placed more emphasis on the productive self-activity of the child than Pestalozzi did. All knowledge gained is utilized at once in some form of productiveness. In the language of Dr. W. N. Hailman: " Every new intuition is to be used in new forms of expression, and to be combined in every possible manner with previous acquisitions, in more and more complicated, more and more directly useful productions. He keeps the learner ever busy, imitating and inventing with the ever-increasing stock of knowledge, and ever increasing the stock of ideas with the aid of imitations and inventions."

WOMEN AS TEACHERS.—Froebel was also the first to appreciate fully the value of women as educators. In many respects women are better fitted for instructing children than men are. They have greater tenderness, a deeper sympathy, a keener perception, greater adaptability to childish ways, and at the same time they are more graceful and winning. " The destiny of nations," Froebel often repeated, " lies far more in the hands of women—the mothers—than in the possessors of power, or of those innovators who for the most part do not understand themselves. We must cultivate women, who are the educators of the human race, else the new generation can not accomplish its task." He regarded women as his natural allies in his educational reforms, and to his appeals they have responded nobly. It is chiefly through their agency that his reforms have been promoted in both America and Europe. Fortunate is the cause that enlists the hearty interest and support of women!

SUMMARY OF PRINCIPLES.—The leading ideas in Froebel's educational system have been summed up as follows:

" 1. The task of education is to assist natural development toward its destined end. As the child's development begins with its first breath, so must its education also.

" 2. As the beginning gives a bias to the whole after-development, so the early beginnings of education are of most importance.

" 3. The spiritual and physical development do not go on separately in childhood, but the two are closely bound up with each other.

" 4. Early education must deal directly with the physical development, and influence the spiritual development through the exercise of the senses.

" 5. The right mode of procedure in the exercise of these organs is indicated by nature in the utterances of the child's instincts, and through these alone can a natural basis of education be found.

" 6. The instincts of the child, as a being destined to become reasonable, express not only physical but also spiritual wants. Education has to satisfy both.

" 7. The development of the limbs by means of movement is the first that takes place, and therefore claims our first attention.

" 8. Physical impressions are at the beginning of life the only possible medium for awakening the child's soul. These impressions should, therefore, be regulated as systematically as is the care of the body, and not be left to chance."

FROEBEL'S SPIRIT.—It is interesting to look behind a great work to discover the spirit of the author, and it is also important to examine the principles upon which it rests. Froebel, like his illustrious master, Pestalozzi, was animated by a profound love for humanity. This gave to his endeavors an exalted. character. "The fame of knowledge," it was said over his grave, " was not his ambition. Glowing love for mankind, for the people, left him neither rest nor quiet. After he had offered his life for his native land in the wars of freedom, he turned with the same enthusiasm which surrenders and sacrifices for the highest thought, to the aim of cultivating the people and youth, founded the celebrated institution at Keilhau among his native mountains, and talked and planted in the domain of men's hearts. And how many brave men he has educated, who honor his memory and bless his name!"

E. Herbart

BIOGRAPHICAL.—John Frederick Herbart, a distinguished philosopher and educator, was born at Oldenburg, Germany, in 1776. He was a student under Fichte at the University of Jena, though he later discarded the views of that great metaphysician. In Switzerland he became tutor in a private family, and made the acquaintance of Pestalozzi, whose views he adopted and subsequently improved. In 1800 he delivered a course of pedagogical lectures in Bremen, and two years later became a lecturer at Göttingen. In 1809 he was called to the University of Königsberg, where he filled the chair previously occupied by the illustrious Kant. The following year he established

22

a pedagogical seminary, or normal school, in which young teachers were to impart instruction under his direction and according to his educational principles.

PEDAGOGY AND PSYCHOLOGY.—With Kant, Fichte, Hegel, and other great German philosophers, pedagogy was incidental and secondary in their investigations. With Herbart it was different. Pedagogy was the ultimate aim of his philosophical inquiries. " For my part," he says, " I have devoted every energy for twenty years to metaphysics, mathematics, self-contemplation, experiments, and trials, in order only to find the basis of true psychological insight. And the prime motive of these laborious investigations was and is above all my conviction that a large part of the huge gaps in our pedagogical science proceeds from a lack of psychology, and that we must first have this science, yea, must beforehand get rid of the mirage that is nowadays called psychology, before we can determine with some degree of certainty what is right and what is wrong in a single hour of instruction."

HERBART AND PESTALOZZI.—In an important sense Herbart may be said to supplement or complete the work of Pestalozzi. The great Swiss educator laid stress upon sense-perception. He accomplished a great work in pedagogy by insisting on clearness and definiteness in our observation of the external world. The whole fabric of knowledge is based on the ideas that come to us from our senses. But Pestalozzi made no adequate provision for system in sense-perception, and failed to consider fully the upbuilding of knowledge and soul-power through mental digestion and assimilation. It is this phase of education, neglected by Pestalozzi, that Herbart emphasizes. " He teaches," as Dr. W. T. Harris well says, " that the chief object of instruction is to secure the reaction of the mind upon what is offered to sense-perception. We must understand what we see. We must explain it by what we know already. Herbart would secure the assimilation of all our new perceptions by the total amount of experience already stored in our minds. Pestalozzi, on the other hand, made no account of previous experience and of this process of digesting our intellectual food. Pestalozzi wished to have us learn by seeing and hearing and the use of our other senses. In his mental physiology, the process of eating is everything, and the process of digestion is ignored."

APPERCEPTION.—This brings us to the great word of the Herbartian system, namely, apperception. By this term is meant the active contribution of the mind to the ideas received in sense-perception. In perceiving a house, for example, we recognize or identify it as that of a friend, or we classify it as a factory or a place of worship. This identification or classification is what the mind, from its previous knowledge, adds or contributes to the sense-perception. When we identify or classify an object, we apperceive it. Or, to borrow the lucid explanation of Dr. Harris, " In perception we have an object presented to our senses; but in apperception we identify the object or those features of it which were familiar to us before; we recognize it; we explain it; we interpret the new by our previous knowledge, and thus are enabled to proceed from the known to the unknown, and make new acquisitions; in recognizing the object we classify it under various general classes; in identifying it with what we had seen before, we note also differences which characterize the new objects and lead to the definition of new species or varieties. All this and much more belong to the process called apperception, and we see at once that it is the chief business of school instruction to build up the process of apperception. By it we reenforce the perception of the present moment by the aggregate of our own sense-perception, and by all that we have learned of the experience of mankind."

COURSE OF STUDY.—The importance he attached to apperception led Herbart to a careful consideration of the best order of studies. In education it is of the first importance to seize and hold the pupil's attention. Not only must the teacher gain his respect and obedience, but the studies pursued, by their progressive and logical connection, should arouse his interest. There must be a conscious unfolding of mental power, by which the pupil's attention is secured and maintained. This result mathematics attains, Herbart thinks, better than any other study. " Every self-deception," he says, " pretending to understand what it does not understand, to be conversant with that with which it is not conversant, may thus come to light. The weakness of his logic must be plainly evident to the pupil; but not only his weakness, also his strength and his capacity for development such an instruction must show him. It must lead him to demonstrate them to himself by his deeds. That which seemed incomprehensible, unattainable, that before which his mental powers stood still, must become perfectly clear, and clearness must lead to perfect ease of execution."

It is different, Herbart argues, with geography, natural history, and linguistic studies. These are matters of memory. They supply additions from without, but do not develop the understanding from within. " It is true," Herbart says, " that the names are gradually fixed in memory, but the fixation is not a sensible gain. Knowledge does not by this means grow. It does not push on. It does not reach out round about it. It unriddles nothing. It does not enchance the fulness of thought as is done by mathematical insight, which increases even by mere dwelling upon the problem." Chemistry alone, he thinks, approaches mathematics in pedagogical value.

MATHEMATICS THE BASIS OF KNOWLEDGE.—Herbart makes mathematics, that is, number and form, the basis of all knowledge. He associates mathematics, in trigonometrical forms, with sense-perception. This is the burden of his treatise on the A B C of Sense-Perception. But mathematics is not confined to this early stage of knowledge. With Pythagoras, Herbart finds number and form throughout the universe. The invisible forces of nature and the laws of the physical world all operate in accordance with mathematical forms and relations. The planets describe ellipses and gravity attracts according to the square of the distance. Nothing goes by chance; everything proceeds by law. " Habituate the youth," he says, " to look upon the things of this world as only gradually capable of conformation to the good. Habituate him to look upon them as magnitudes and upon their changes as functions of the motor forces, or, in other words, as necessary results of efficient causes, absolutely accordant to law, despite all apparent irregularity, and perfectly definite in every step of their progress. Show him that wherever knowledge has penetrated, the phantom of irregularity has vanished, and that knowledge has progressed successfully wherever it has sought for magnitude and measure. Lay bare to him the ridiculous conceit of ignorance, inclined in the past and inclined to-day, to deny the existence of law unless it be manifestly obvious."

MORAL EDUCATION.—The end of education, as Herbart conceives it, is morality. The teacher who confines himself only to information and neglects morality, abandons the most important part of his office. Morality can not be reduced, as some philosophers have taught, to a single comprehensive principle, such as the useful or the agreeable. The right and the good are to be learned from a large acquaintance with experience, society, and history. The student learns what he should do from an " esthetic presentation of the universe." What is morality? It is goodness of will, the determination to follow the law of righteousness from whatever source revealed. It includes the force with which the individual resists what he recognizes as evil. " As the highest purpose of man," Herbart says, " and consequently of education, we universally recognize morality. He who should deny this could not really know what morality is." In its highest ascent morality mounts to God. " God, the real center of all moral ideas and of their limitless efficacy, the Father of man, and the head of the world," Herbart says, " should fill the background of memory as the oldest, the first percept, to which all recollections of the mind, returning out of the confusion of life, must invariably come at last that it may rest as in its very self in the holding of faith."

TWOFOLD ASCENT.—There is a twofold path by which the pupil must ascend to the supreme idea of God. The one is cognition, which begins in sense-perception. Through the marvels of creation—the moon and the stars which He has ordained—we gradually climb to the conception of God. The other path Herbart calls progressive sympathy. He would lay the foundation of this sympathy in a study of the Homeric poems, which appeal to the boyish imagination. With his interest thus awakened, the boy passes to a clearer comprehension of humanity and society, and at last he sees and feels their dependence on a Supreme Being. This result, as he imagined it, made Herbart an ardent advocate of Greek learning. " The time series of history ends in the present," he says, " and in the beginnings of culture among the Greeks a luminous point is fixed for every subsequent generation by the classical presentations of an ideal boyhood era in the Homeric poems. If one is not afraid to let the noblest among languages precede in instruction the accepted learned language, there will be avoided, on the one hand, innumerable false incidents and displacements in whatever pertains to insight into literature, the history of man, of opinions, of arts, etc.; and, on the other hand, we are sure to offer to the interest of the boy events and personalities he can completely master, and whence he can make a transition to infinitely manifold reflections on humanity and society, and on the dependence of both on a higher Power."

MECHANICAL ROUTINE.—The development of the individual for his own sake is the purpose of Herbart's educational system. He makes this principle the criterion for judging of studies and methods. Not utilitarian ends outside of the student, but his subjective growth and culture are to determine the subjects pursued. Because of their subjective educative value, as he conceives, " mathematics and ancient languages will always necessarily remain the two trunk lines of instruction." The ends of education are not attained by a mechanical grind on the part of teacher and pupil. There must be interest, self-activity, a joyous diligence in the school before the best results can be obtained. He condemns what he calls " the machine-like diligence of teachers and pupils, tormenting each other simply that both may be able to say that they have done their duty. By this method the teachers in reality do not do their duty; their occupations are not of a sort that can be despatched and done with. Where the joyous diligence of the scholars does not proclaim everywhere that they are fond of working, that has not been done which ought to have been done, even though the examinations for promotion and graduation furnish forth the most brilliant results."

Conclusion.—It is evident from the foregoing survey that Herbart has made important contributions to pedagogy. He avoids two evils which, as we have seen, extend almost through the entire course of educational history, namely, the memorizing of words and the unsystematic employment of sense-perception. He accentuates inward growth, to which all subjects of study and all methods of teaching are to be conformed. The characteristic feature of Herbart's pedagogy, to adopt the words of Dr. Eckoff, " can be condensed into a watchword—Educative Instruction. Its cardinal affirmation is twofold. Education of man by man is impossible except through instruction. That instruction is valueless in the acquisition of which no education—or, in psychologic language, no apperception —occurs."

F. Jacotot

Biographical.—Joseph Jacotot, the inventor of the method known as Universal Instruction, was born at Dijon, France, in 1770, and studied at the college of his native city. At the age of nineteen he was made professor in the department of arts. He had a rare aptitude for study, and distinguished himself no less in mathematics than in letters. He ardently espoused the principles of the French Revolution, and became a captain of artillery. When the Polytechnic School was founded, he became director of studies, and afterward filled chairs in other colleges. After the second Restoration, he was exiled from France, and in

1818, after a year or two spent in private teaching, he obtained the chair of French literature in the University of Louvain in Belgium. It was there that he was led by circumstances to devise his new method of instruction.

UNIVERSAL INSTRUCTION.—In the lecture-room Jacotot discovered, to his great dismay, that three-fourths of his youthful auditors did not understand French, and he himself knew nothing of Dutch. What was to be done. Chance placed before him a copy of Fénelon's Télémaque, containing the French on one page and the Dutch translation on the other. He placed this book in the hands of his students, requiring them to learn the French by heart and to puzzle out the meaning from the Dutch translation. He made them repeat constantly what they had learned, and daily to make new acquisitions. From memorizing he proceeded to narration, conversation, and writing. By questions and comparisons the students were skilfully led to see and correct their own mistakes. To his great surprise Jacotot found that his students, without any explanations on his part, were able, in a comparatively short time, to speak and write the French language correctly. Hence he concluded that the explanations of teachers are not necessary; and after he had tried the same plan in teaching mathematics,.Hebrew, and other studies, he came to the conviction that merely by directing the student's activities, a person can teach anything to others, even what he does not understand himself. To this directive method, the details of which will be pointed out later, he gave the name of Universal Instruction.

SUCCESS AND OPPOSITION.—This method and its phenomenal results in the hands of Jacotot soon attracted attention. A commissioner of the government made an investigation and submitted a favorable report. " My observations," said Baron Kinker, "have thoroughly convinced me that by it a pupil makes, in a shorter time than is usually allotted to study, such progress as must convince the most skeptical unbeliever of its superior merits, and as would appear miraculous, were it not that by a little attention to the mode of studying, we are enabled to trace the pupil's steps." Prince Frederick of Holland in 1827 called Jacotot to the head of a military academy which had been established at Louvain. The results appear to have been remarkable; but the innovator encountered criticism and opposition, and in 1830 he returned to France, where he died ten years later. The last years of his life he gave to the development and propagation of his method. He had the confidence of an enthusiastic innovator, and sometimes assumed the air of a self-constituted reformer; but he was at heart a gentle and candid man, whose charitable feelings went out to all mankind.

INTELLECTS EQUAL.—There are certain principles or axioms which Jacotot placed at the basis of his system which require consideration. These principles, without being absolutely true, contain elements of truth and were fruitful in results. The first principle is that " all intellects are equal." The differences that are seen actually to exist proceed, he contended, from the will. " Hope everything from your own efforts," he says, " for there is no innate superiority. You can all learn to write like great authors, not only in your mother-tongue, but even in a foreign language. Whatever study you may choose, you shall have no other teachers than ourselves. But we can teach you all the languages and all the sciences, even those which we do not understand." Every one can accomplish what he wills to do. This principle, which recognizes the power of resolute determination, tends, on the one hand, to repress all pride of intellect, and, on the other, to stimulate the efforts of the dull and discouraged.

" ALL IS IN ALL."—The next principle lying at the basis of Jacotot's method is " All is in all." This axiom, which recognizes the close correlation of all knowledge, is to be taken in a general sense; it is not true in particulars. The basis of all grammar, literature, history, and philosophy is found in any book that may be taken up. " No one doubts," Jacotot says, " that he would be very wise who should know one book and all the connections to which it might give rise. It is true that this supposition is abused under the old method; such a result can be obtained only by years of toil; it is the fruit of the continual efforts of a memory which constantly breaks down under the weight of a prodigious number of facts and new reflections, *scattered, without order,* and consequently *without relation.* But what appears impossible becomes a play when one begins by knowing one book. It is easy to perceive that all other books are nothing else than the commentary and development of the ideas contained in the first. Learn nothing, therefore, without referring it in thought to the first subject of your study; *this exercise ought to last through life.* Thus there are formed intimate relations among your ideas; they help one another, they are developed and clarified by one another; although they touch at all points, they are not confused."

This extract shows us the spirit of Jacotot's method. It consists in requiring the student to learn one book thoroughly, and to make all possible combinations with its facts, ideas, and words, and to accustom himself to refer all that he sees elsewhere to this touchstone of first knowledge. The principle *All is in all* has as its practical corollary, *Know one thing thoroughly, and refer all the rest to that.* This method has the merit of being based on a foundation of solid attainment, and, furthermore, it introduces a spirit of organization or unity into knowledge.

REPETITION.—Jacotot insisted on *repetition* as the only means of retaining what one has learned. Not what we learn, but what we retain makes us learned. The memory is, therefore, to be assiduously cultivated, for it supplies material for the imagination and judgment. But in laying the foundation of any language or science, the memory is not to be mechanical in its operation. What is remembered must be thoroughly understood and readily employed in new intellectual processes. This is an achievement of the pupil's own effort; every scholar is self-made. The office of the teacher is to direct, stimulate, question, but it is left for the student to do all the work. These facts explain the real meaning of Jacotot's principles, which have been severely criticized, namely, " No teacher is needed to explain "; " Everybody can teach "; " One can teach what he does not understand himself."

TELEMACHUS.—The book with which Jacotot began in teaching the mother-tongue was Fénelon's Telemachus. He began, not with letters and syllables, but with words. The pupil repeated after the teacher:

Calypso

Calypso could

Calypso could not

Calypso could not console

Calypso could not console herself

Calypso could not console herself for

Calypso could not console herself for the departure

Calypso could not console herself for the departure of Ulysses.

This sentence was then written by the pupil after the

teacher's copy, and the latter *verified,* by means of questions, the former's knowledge of all the words, syllables, and letters. "Beware of proceeding too rapidly at the start," says Jacotot; "keep the pupil at the first lesson until he knows it thoroughly. There are so many new acquisitions for him to make in a single sentence; it is necessary to be so attentive in order to avoid confusion, and to repeat so often in order not to forget anything." Thus the student proceeded till he had memorized six books. Writing, spelling, conversation, repeating from memory were constant accompaniments. Under the principle that "all is in all," Jacotot, according to the pupil's advancement, developed from what had been thoroughly memorized the principles of grammar, rhetoric, criticism, and oratory.

CONCLUSION.—The method, it will be observed, calls into play the student's own activity. All his faculties are wide awake; there is continual investigation, comparison, and exercise of the creative faculties of the mind. The pupils acquire a manly self-confidence. In the hands of a skilful and enthusiastic teacher, the method may be made a powerful educational instrument, and in many cases, in the heyday of its popularity, it frequently gave surprising results. It was applied indifferently to foreign languages, mathematics, and the sciences. It was introduced in Philadelphia in 1831, and Roberts Vaux, president of the Board of Education, pronounced the success "almost incredible." "From this experiment," he said, "I am induced to believe that a new era is about to dawn upon our country, as it regards the facilities for imparting useful knowledge by the method under notice; and I would recommend it to the especial observation of the friends of universal education."

G. Horace Mann

BIOGRAPHICAL.—The most distinguished of American educators, perhaps, during the nineteenth century was Horace Mann, of Massachusetts. He may be regarded as the organizer of the public-school system as it exists to-day in this country. The idea of popular education was almost as old as the Massachusetts colony; but Horace Mann, more than any other, was the educational statesman who gave it comprehensive organization and thorough efficiency. He was specially endowed by nature for the work which he was called to do. To an intellect of rare penetration and brilliancy he added a profound moral sense; he was gifted with the eloquence of tongue and pen; and above all, perhaps, he had the enthusiasm and determination that mark the reformer and martyr in every age.

He was born at Franklin, Massachusetts, May 4, 1796, and grew up in an atmosphere of poverty and toil. He regarded it as an irretrievable misfortune that his childhood was not a happy one. He had an unquenchable desire for knowledge; and after acquiring the elements of learning in a poor district-school, which he attended a few weeks every winter, he read through the library of old histories and theologies which Benjamin Franklin had donated to the town. Getting a start in Latin and Greek from an itinerant school-teacher, he entered the sophomore class of Brown University at twenty, where he graduated at the head of his class. He studied law, and at the age of twenty-seven was admitted to the bar. His ability soon gained recognition. In 1823 he was elected to the Legislature of Massachusetts, in which he served a number of terms. In 1848 he was elected to Congress to fill the vacancy caused by the death of John Quincy Adams. Everywhere he showed himself a strong and fearless advocate of reform, progress, and humanity.

BOARD OF EDUCATION.—In 1837 the Legislature of Massachusetts appointed a Board of Education to reorganize and improve the common schools of the State. This Board, consisting of the Governor, Lieutenant-Governor, and eight other men of prominence, called Horace Mann to act as secretary—a position that practically made him the State Superintendent of Education. His duty, as officially defined, was to " collect information of the actual condition and efficiency of the common schools and other means of popular education, and diffuse as widely as possible throughout every part of the Commonwealth information of the most approved and successful methods of arranging the studies and conducting the education of the young, to the end that all children in this Commonwealth who depend upon the common schools for instruction may have the best education which these schools can be made to impart." The salary was one thousand dollars a year. To accept this onerous and responsible position Horace Mann gave up a lucrative law practise and bright political prospects. Why did he make this great sacrifice? He looked upon his new position as an opportunity to render a great service in the cause of humanity; for he regarded the public schools, as he afterward said, " as the way that God has chosen for the reformation of the world."

CONDITION OF THE SCHOOLS.—In spite of the beautiful regulation promulgated by the early colonists, the common schools of Massachusetts in 1837 were exceedingly defective. There was no State supervision; and in the separate districts, each of which controlled its educational interests, a class spirit, to a greater or less degree, prevailed. The wealthier part of the community patronized private schools; and as a result, the public schools too frequently degenerated into makeshifts for the poorer classes. The teachers were poorly equipped for their work; the schoolhouses were neglected and shabby; the school term for each year covered only a few months. It was this unfortunate and undemocratic condition of things that Horace Mann heroically undertook to improve. He wished " to restore the good old custom," as his wife tells us, " of having the rich and the poor educated together; and for that end he desired to make the public schools as good as schools could be made, so that the rich and the poor might not necessarily be coincident with the educated and the ignorant." It was this democratic idea—upon which the welfare of the people and the perpetuity of our institutions depend—to which Horace Mann gave the next twelve laborious years of his life.

METHODS OF WORK.—To bring about the reform that he ardently desired both as a philanthropist and patriot, Horace Mann had to form public opinion. It was necessary to win or conciliate men of influence, and especially to inform and arouse the great body of the Commonwealth. To this end he devised judicious and comprehensive, but at the same time laborious plans. He annually published abstracts showing the actual condition of the schools; he prepared elaborate annual reports in which he discussed the principles and methods of education; he established and edited the Common School Journal; he carried on an enormous correspondence with educators and others throughout the State; and he traveled from town to town delivering educational addresses, the matter of which was as solid as the phrasing and delivery were eloquent. His Annual Reports, of which there are twelve, form a valuable and interesting contribution to American pedagogy. Their wide dissemination, along with his other activities, gradually wrought a change in public sentiment, and in his eleventh Report he was able to speak of the great changes that had taken place. The rural schools had been improved; the graded system was being adopted in the towns and cities; the appropriations for school purposes had been increased; normal schools had been established and more competent teachers provided; the school term had been lengthened and the attendance of pupils increased.

DIFFICULTIES AND CONTROVERSIES.—No work of reform that tends to unsettle existing arrangements will go unchallenged. There are always selfish interests, apart from the natural conservatism of humanity, to resist innovations. The moral enthusiasm of Horace Mann, as well as his official position, made him polemic in spirit and method. "The feeling which springs up spontaneously in my mind," he said in an educational address, "and which I hope springs up spontaneously in your minds, my friends, in view of the errors, and calamities, and iniquities of the race, is *not* to flee from the world, but to remain in it; *not* to hie away to forest solitudes or hermit cells, but to confront selfishness, and wickedness, and ignorance, at whatever personal peril, and to subdue and extirpate them, or to die in the attempt."

He encountered ecclesiastical prejudices, and at an early period in his work a strong effort was made in the Legislature to abolish the Board of Education. But his most famous controversy was with the grammar-school masters of Boston. In 1843, on the occasion of his second marriage, he made a trip to Europe, and devoted his bridal tour to an inspection of the schools of Great Britain and

23

the Continent. He was especially pleased with the personnel, spirit, and methods of the teachers in Prussia. He embodied the results of his observations in his famous Seventh Annual Report. "On reviewing a period of six weeks, the greater part of which I spent in visiting schools in the north and middle of Prussia and in Saxony, entering the schools to hear the first recitation in the morning, and remaining till the last was completed at night, I call to mind three things about which I can not be mistaken. In some of my opinions and inferences I may have erred, but of the following facts there can be no doubt:

"1. During all this time, I never saw a teacher hearing a lesson of any kind (excepting a reading or spelling lesson), *with a book in his hand.*

"2. I never saw a teacher *sitting* while hearing a recitation.

"3. Though I saw hundreds of schools, and thousands of pupils, *I never saw one child undergoing punishment, or arraigned for misconduct. I never saw one child in tears from having been punished, or from fear of being punished.*"

The effect of this Report in Boston is best given, perhaps, in the author's own words in a letter to a friend. "My Report," he says, "caused a great stir among the Boston teachers: I mean those of the grammar schools. The very things in the Report which made it acceptable to others made it hateful to them. The general reader was delighted with the idea of intelligent, gentlemanly teachers; of a mind-expanding education; of children governed by moral means. The leading men among the Boston grammar-school masters saw their own condemnation in this description of their European contemporaries,

and resolved, as a matter of self-preservation, to keep out
the infection of so fatal an example as was afforded by
the Prussian schools." Accordingly they united in the
publication of a large pamphlet in criticism and dispar-
agement of Horace Mann's statements and opinions. This
provoked a severe Reply to the Boston Masters, which
in turn called forth a Rejoinder, till the controversy
prolonged itself for nearly two years. The issue was in
favor of the indomitable secretary and "the new education"; the Boston schools were overhauled, incompetent
masters were dismissed, and a more humane discipline
was introduced.

NORMAL SCHOOLS.—Horace Mann early recognized the
need of normal schools to train competent teachers. Soon
after he entered upon his work as secretary, he directed
his attention to the establishment of these schools of training. A private gift of $10,000, to which the Legislature
added an equal sum, enabled him to open at Lexington in
1839 the first normal school in America. In due course
of time other similar institutions, all admirably conducted,
were established in different parts of the State. At the
dedication of the normal school at Bridgewater in 1846,
Horace Mann gave very strong expression to his views on
the subject. "I believe normal schools," he said, "to be
a new instrumentality in the advancement of the race.
I believe that, without them, free schools themselves would
be shorn of their strength and their healing power, and
would at length become mere charity schools, and thus
die out in fact and in form. Neither the art of printing,
nor the trial by jury, nor a free press, nor free suffrage,
can long exist, to any beneficial and salutary purpose,
without schools for the training of teachers; for, if the
character and the qualifications of teachers be allowed to

degenerate, the free schools will become pauper schools, and the pauper schools will produce pauper souls, and the free press will become a false and licentious press, and ignorant voters will become venal voters, and through the medium and guise of republican forms, an oligarchy of profligate and flagitious men will govern the land; nay, the universal diffusion and ultimate triumph of all-glorious Christianity itself must await the time when knowledge shall be diffused among men through the instrumentality of good schools."

AN EDUCATIONAL REFORMER.—In 1852, the same year he was nominated for Governor of Massachusetts, he accepted the presidency of Antioch College, Ohio. There, as in his work as Secretary of the Board of Education, he showed his adhesion to the educational reformers of Europe. He looked upon education as mind-growth, the two great laws of which were symmetry and self-activity. He held that religion and morality are central in life. " We ought to do and feel right because it is right, not because God commands it." In school life he exorcised the spirit of emulation and sought to substitute the spirit of courtesy and love. He was favorable to the coeducation of the sexes, which was adopted at Antioch, and he especially valued women as teachers. He held that " woman's teaching, other things being equal, is more patient, persistent, and thorough than man's," and of a higher moral quality. The spirit that animated his whole life is embodied in the closing words of his baccalaureate address in 1859, the year of his death: " I beseech you to treasure up in your hearts these my parting words: *Be ashamed to die until you have won some victory for humanity."*

H. Herbert Spencer

BIOGRAPHICAL.—No other English philosopher of recent times has shown a larger intellectual grasp and a keener analytic power than Herbert Spencer. His system of philosophy, though based on the theory of evolution, is largely inductive in its method of treatment. In support of his various views or leading up to them, he marshals an enormous array of facts drawn from almost every department of knowledge. No other man, perhaps, has exerted so profound an influence upon English philosophic thought during the past fifty years. Though fiercely assailed in his earlier career, his philosophic system has at length gained wide acceptance.

Herbert Spencer was born at Derby, England, April 27, 1820. Through the influence of his father, who was a man of strong character and wide culture, he developed a spirit of independent scientific investigation. He early showed a fondness for natural history, and in his boyhood made considerable entomological collections. Later he became a civil engineer; but in 1848 he took up his residence in London and devoted himself to literary and philosophical pursuits. He became a contributor to the Westminster and Edinburgh Reviews. In 1855 he published The Principles of Psychology, which may be regarded as the beginning of his philosophical system, to the elaboration of which he devoted the rest of his long life.

TREATISE ON EDUCATION.—In 1860 he published a work entitled " Education: Intellectual, Moral, and Physical," which has provoked much discussion and changed, to a greater or less degree, the educational studies and methods of Great Britain and America. At the time of its appearance it was little less than revolutionary, running counter at almost every point to the prevailing system in the secondary and higher institutions of learning. It is written out of large resources of fact and observation; and however much we may differ from its principles and conclusions, it must be recognized as a masterly contribution to modern pedagogy. In general principles and methods Herbert Spencer stands in line with Comenius, Locke, Rousseau, and Pestalozzi; but his philosophical range and acumen enabled him to lay broader and deeper foundations.

RELATIVE VALUE OF STUDIES.—The first chapter of this great work seeks to determine "what knowledge is of most worth." It is impossible to include in a school curriculum all branches of knowledge; a selection, therefore, becomes necessary, and to this end, their relative values should be antecedently determined. "Before there can be a rational curriculum," Spencer says, "we must settle which things it most concerns us to know; or, to use a word of Bacon's, now unfortunately obsolete, we must determine the relative values of knowledges."

To determine this question he recurs to the end of education, and formulates a definition that has since become well known. "How to live," he says, "that is the essential question for us. Not how to live in the mere material sense only, but in the widest sense. The general problem which comprehends every special problem is, the right ruling of conduct in all directions under all circumstances. In what way to treat the body; in what way to treat the mind; in what way to manage our affairs; in what way to bring up a family; in what way to behave as a citizen; in what way to utilize all these sources of happiness which nature supplies—how to use all our faculties to the greatest advantage of ourselves and others—how to live completely? And this being the great thing needful for us to learn, is, by consequence, the great thing which education has to teach. To prepare us for complete living is the function which education has to discharge; and the only rational mode of judging of any educational course is to judge in what degree it discharges such function."

LEADING ACTIVITIES.—Looking at life we discover leading classes or departments of activity. There are physical, mental, and social needs, all of which must be provided for in a rational system of education according to their relative importance. Herbert Spencer classifies the leading kinds of activity as follows: " (1) those activities which directly minister to self-preservation; (2) those activities which, by securing the necessaries of life, indirectly minister to self-preservation; (3) those activities which have for their end the rearing and discipline of offspring; (4) those activities which are involved in the maintenance of proper social and political relations; (5) those miscellaneous activities which make up the leisure part of life, devoted to the gratification of the tastes and feelings."

These different classes of activity, which broadly make up the sum of life, naturally demand such studies as physiology, mathematics, physics, chemistry, biology, and social science. In short, in opposition to the humanists, Spencer would make natural science the basis of education. " Thus to the question," he says, " with which we set out, What knowledge is of most worth? the uniform reply is—science. This is the verdict in all the counts. For direct self-preservation or the maintenance of life and health the all-important knowledge is—science. For that indirect self-preservation which we call gaining a livelihood, the knowledge of greatest value is—science. For the due discharge of parental functions the proper guidance is to be found only in—science. For that interpretation of national life, past and present, without which the citizen can not rightly regulate his conduct, the indispensable key is—science. Alike for the most perfect production and highest enjoyment of art in all its forms, the needful preparation is still—science. And for purposes of discipline—intellectual, moral, religious—the most efficient study is, once more—science."

CRITICISM OF CURRENT SYSTEM.—The current system of education, as Herbert Spencer thought, was devoted almost exclusively to that part of life which is concerned chiefly with elegant leisure and esthetic tastes. It did not aim at the utilitarian side of life as involved in the leading kinds of activity. It neglected the plant for the sake of the flower; in anxiety for elegance it forgot substance. "However fully we may admit," he says, "that extensive acquaintance with modern languages is a valuable accomplishment, which through reading, conversation, and travel, aids in giving a certain finish, it by no means follows that this result is rightly purchased at the cost of that vitally important knowledge sacrificed to it. Supposing it true that classical education conduces to elegance and correctness of style, it can not be said that elegance and correctness of style are comparable in importance to a familiarity with the principles that should guide the rearing of children. Grant that the taste may be greatly improved by reading all the poetry in extinct languages, yet it is not to be inferred that such improvement of taste is equivalent in value to an acquaintance with the laws of health. Accomplishments, the fine arts, *belles-lettres,* and all those things which, as we say, constitute the efflorescence of civilization should be wholly subordinate to that knowledge and discipline in which civilization rests. *As they occupy the leisure part of life, so should they occupy the leisure part of education."*

INTELLECTUAL EDUCATION.—The second chapter of Spencer's work is devoted to intellectual education. He agrees with Herbart that educational practise should be based on a sound psychology. From this standpoint he lays down and ably defends the following principles with which we have been made familiar in the writings of other educational reformers: (1) in giving instruction we should proceed from the simple to the complex; (2) the concrete should precede the abstract; (3) the education of the child should accord with the educational development of the race; (4) the empirical should go before the rational or philosophical; (5) the true process of education is self-development; and (6) pleasurable excitement on the part of the student must be the criterion of any educational method. With Comenius and Rousseau, Spencer holds that nature must be our guide. In reference to the principles of self-activity and of pleasure in learning, " the most important and the least attended to," he says, " if progression from simple to complex, and from concrete to abstract, be considered the essential requirements as dictated by abstract psychology, then do these requirements that knowledge shall be self-mastered, and pleasurably mastered, become the tests by which we may judge whether the dictates of abstract psychology are being fulfilled. If the first embody the leading generalizations of the *science* of mental growth, the last are the chief canons of the *art* of fostering mental growth. For manifestly if the steps in our curriculum are so arranged that they can be successively ascended by the pupil himself with little or no help, they must correspond with the stages of evolution in his faculties; and manifestly if the successive achievement of these steps is intrinsically gratifying to him, it follows that they require no more than a normal exercise of his powers."

HARSH METHODS.—The methods of instruction and of discipline should not be unduly exacting and harsh. When the acquisition of knowledge is made repugnant to the student, he will be likely to develop a distaste for it, and to give up his education as soon as the coercion of parents and teachers is withdrawn. "These results," Spencer says, "are inevitable. While the laws of mental association remain true—while men dislike the things and places that suggest painful recollections, and delight in those which call to mind bygone pleasures—painful lessons will make knowledge repulsive, and pleasurable lessons will make it attractive. The men to whom in boyhood information came in dreary tasks along with threats of punishment, and who were never led into habits of independent inquiry, are unlikely to be students in after years; while those to whom it came in the natural forms, at the proper times, and who remember its facts as not only interesting in themselves, but as the occasions of a long series of gratifying successes, are likely to continue through life that self-instruction commenced in youth."

MORAL EDUCATION.—The third chapter of the work under consideration treats of moral education. It is less comprehensive and satisfactory than the chapters we have already considered. Morality is not associated either with religion or with general ethical principles. It is made chiefly a matter of training. Spencer believes neither in the absolute goodness nor the total depravity of children. Consequently he is less sanguine than Horace Mann about the immediate regeneration of society by means of popular education. "We are not among those," he says, "who believe in Lord Palmerston's dogma that 'all children **are** born good.' On the whole, the opposite dogma, untenable as it is, seems to us less wide of the truth. Nor do we agree with those who think that, by skilful discipline, children may be made altogether what they should be. Contrariwise, we are satisfied that though imperfections of nature may be diminished by wise management, they can not be removed by it. The notion that an ideal humanity might be forthwith produced by a perfect system of education is near akin to that shadowed forth in the poems of Shelley, that would mankind give up their old institutions, prejudices, and errors, all the evils in the world would at once disappear; neither notion being acceptable to such as have dispassionately studied human affairs."

MORAL DISCIPLINE.—Herbert Spencer argues with great force against arbitrary punishments. He would have the punishment for any fault or transgression to come in the form of a natural consequence or retribution. He advocates what he calls "natural penalties." "Is it not manifest," he asks, "that, as 'ministers and interpreters of nature,' it is the function of parents to see that their children habitually experience the true consequences 'of their conduct—the natural reactions; neither warding them off, nor intensifying them, nor putting artificial consequences in place of them?" No unprejudiced reader will hesitate in his assent. For example, if a child litters a room, it should be required to put it in order again; or if it neglects to get ready in time for a walk, it should be left at home. This "measure would be more effective," he thinks, "than that perpetual scolding which ends only in producing callousness."

SELF-GOVERNMENT.—Inasmuch as like begets like, harshness naturally produces harshness; on the other hand, sympathy will as naturally produce confidence and love. Too high a standard of morality in children is not to be expected; we should, as parents and teachers, be satisfied with moderate results. "Be sparing of commands; but when you *do* command, command with decision and consistency." "Bear constantly in mind," Spencer continues, "the truth that the aim of your discipline should be to produce a *self-governing* being, not to produce a being to be *governed by others.* Were your children fated to pass their lives as slaves, you could not too much accustom them to slavery during their childhood; but as they are by and by to be free men, with no one to control their daily conduct, you can not too much accustom them to self-control while they are still under your eye."

PHYSICAL EDUCATION.—In the last chapter of his work, Herbert Spencer discusses physical education with great cogency. He finds fault with the fathers of England for being more concerned about the welfare of their horses and cattle than about the welfare of their children. With Huxley he holds that it is important for a man, first of all, to be "a good animal"—to have a sound physical constitution. Health he regards as a duty. "Few seem conscious," he says, "that there is such a thing as physical morality. Men's habitual words and acts imply the idea that they are at liberty to treat their bodies as they please. Disorders entailed by disobedience to nature's dictates they regard simply as grievances, not as the effects of a conduct more or less flagitious. Though the evil consequences inflicted on their dependents and on future generations are often as great as those caused by crime, yet they do not think themselves in any degree criminal. It is true that, in the case of drunkenness, the viciousness of a purely bodily transgression is recognized, but none appear to infer that, if this bodily transgression is vicious, so, too, is every bodily transgression. The fact is, that all breaches of the laws of health are *physical sins."*

CRAMMING SYSTEM.—Spencer is inclined to the belief that the English race is physically deteriorating. The causes he finds in the growing strenuousness of modern life, and in the overcrowded courses of study in the schools. Nature averages an undue taxing of the brain by a corresponding loss in general physical growth and strength. He sets forth the injurious effects of the cramming system in words that every parent and educator ought to heed. " If, as all who investigate the matter must admit," he says, " physical degeneracy is a consequence of excessive study, how grave is the condemnation to be passed upon this cramming system! It is a terrible mistake, from whatever point of view regarded. It is a mistake in so far as the mere acquirement of knowledge is concerned; for it is notorious that the mind, like the body, can not assimilate beyond a certain rate; and if you ply it with facts faster than it can assimilate them, they are very soon rejected again: they do not become permanently built into the intellectual fabric, but fall out of recollection after the passing of the examination for which they were got up. . . . But the mistake is still deeper. Even were the system good as a system of intellectual training, which it is not, it would still be bad, because, as we have shown, it is fatal to that vigor of *physique* which is needful to make intellectual training available in the struggle of life. Those who, in eagerness to cultivate their pupils' minds, are reckless of their bodies, do not remember that success in the world depends much more upon energy than upon information; and that a policy which, in cramming with information, undermines energy is self-defeating."

CRITIQUE.—Strong and convincing as Herbert Spencer's work is in many particulars, it seems to go somewhat astray on two fundamental points. In the first place, its conception of education lays undue stress on the objective side or purpose of school training. How to live, in what is made a material or utilitarian sense, is not the whole aim of education. There is a subjective side that is equally important and logically antecedent. It is found, not in *doing,* but in *being;* it consists in such an unfolding of the mental powers that we may readily enter into the intellectual heritage of our race, and in such a character that we habitually choose and follow what is right. No amount of physiology, chemistry, and biology; no equipment for the mechanical or practical relations of life, can take the place of culture and character, which after all are the essential requisites for " complete living." What Spencer relegates to a subordinate place in his system seems, on the basis of a humanity of intrinsic and infinite worth, to deserve the foremost consideration.

In the second place, he seems to err in the educative and disciplinary value he assigns to the natural sciences. Though his presentation of the matter is at times eloquent, his views are not borne out by the decisive test of experience. It is generally found that students who pursue merely scientific studies somehow lack insight and sympathy with what is finest in the intellectual achievements of the race. There appears to be a certain dulness or unresponsiveness of sensibilities. The reason is, perhaps, not far to seek. Inasmuch as language and literature embody the thoughts and feelings of humanity—the soul-life of our race—it is evident that the best way to climb to the summits of its intellectual achievement is through a patient mastery of the elements in which the

highest culture finds expression.   There is more mental
uplift in one of Shakespeare's plays or in the Sermon
on the Mount than in the most learned treatise on digestion or the ablest discussion of the lever.

8. CONTEMPORARY EDUCATION

GENERAL SURVEY.—There can be no doubt that education is receiving far more attention at present than at any
period in the past.   It is rapidly becoming universal.
Popular intelligence is everywhere reckoned an element
of national power and wealth, and the stability of repub-
lics is recognized as resting upon the knowledge and
virtue of the people.   Woman is no longer held in the base
subjection of Oriental countries, but enjoys, in all enlightened nations, excellent facilities for education.   New
spheres of activity are open to her; and with cultivated
mind she takes a place of wider influence in society and
of greater dignity in the home.   The science and art of education are receiving increased attention; and in addition
to a large number of normal schools for the training of
teachers, our universities are establishing chairs of pedagogy.   Illiteracy is being rapidly diminished, and in a
few countries it has been practically annihilated.

IN THE ORIENT.—No civilized nation now fails to make
provision, to a greater or less degree, for the instruction
of the people.   Even the unprogressive nations of the
Orient are affected by the Christian education of the West.
China, with its strange conservatism, is relaxing its former
rigor against foreign institutions.   Many schools have
been established by Christian missionaries, especially of
the Catholic Church; and, besides a workshop at Shang-
hai, and a polytechnic school in the province of Futs-

chien conducted by foreign teachers, a university on the European plan was opened at Peking in 1868 under imperial patronage. Japan has been thoroughly modernized in education. Since 1872 that country has had a comprehensive school system, including primary schools, academies, normal schools, colleges, and universities. These schools, modeled chiefly after those of America, are supplied with modern furniture and apparatus, and are conducted upon scientific methods. Both sexes have the same educational advantages up to the normal school. The courses of instruction are substantially the same as in schools of corresponding grade in Europe and America, save that English and other modern languages take the place of Latin and Greek.

Under the sovereignty of England, the system of education in India has been transformed and modernized. Public instruction now forms a department of the government, and a network of schools of various grades is being extended over the whole country. Some institutions are entirely supported by the Government, while others, established by local effort or missionary zeal, receive grants in aid. The efficiency of schools of every kind is maintained by a careful system of inspection. In spite of strong national prejudice, the education of girls, especially in the regions where Christian missionaries are influential, is making progress. The apex of the educational system of India is found in the Universities of Calcutta, Madras, Bombay, and Lahore. These universities, after the model of London University, are examining bodies; and, though not giving academic instruction, they control, by means of their examinations, the entire course of higher education. It may be safely predicted that sooner or later India will be transformed by Western civilization.

IN THE OCCIDENT.—But it is in Europe and America that the tendencies toward universal education have manifested themselves most fully, and accomplished the greatest results. Though some countries are more advanced than others, every Christian nation now provides with tolerable completeness for popular instruction. Greece and Italy adopted during the past century systems of education more comprehensive and useful than were ever contemplated by Plato and Quintilian. Germany, France, Belgium, Denmark, Norway, Sweden, Spain, Portugal— all have at present some system of popular education; and most of them have adopted the system of compulsory attendance. During the past few decades England has shown great interest in popular education, and granted annually, in connection with a system of thorough inspection, ever-increasing subsidies to public schools. The educational systems of several of these countries will later be considered more in detail.

NOTEWORTHY TENDENCIES.—There are certain great tendencies to-day that are expanding and modifying the processes of education. They are not confined to a single country, but are almost world-wide in their extent. The changes they have wrought, as will be seen, are very important.

1. It may be fairly claimed that the *scientific spirit* dominates our age. Investigation—systematic, minute, and prolonged—has in large measure supplanted metaphysical speculation. Tradition has lost much of its power; and with their growing intelligence men are less willing to be guided by the dicta of mere authority. Careful and patient toilers are at work in every department of learning; and Nature, questioned as never before, is gradually yielding up her secrets. The same patient methods of in-

24

vestigation are applied to the study of the mind, the origin of man, and the history of the past. The theory of evolution, sometimes with greater or less modification, has generally been accepted, and, like the law of gravitation or the Copernican system, has greatly changed our views of nature and of history. Many old beliefs have been modified or destroyed; but the general result of the scientific spirit has been to give us greater breadth of thought and a clearer insight into the works of God.

As a natural consequence of this vast enlargement of the field of human knowledge, the courses of study in schools of all grades have been expanded and modified. In the primary schools we have what are called nature studies, through which the children are made acquainted with the elements of science. In the secondary schools and colleges the curricula have been made to include such studies as physics, chemistry, botany, geology, astronomy, and physiology; and in order to make room for them, the elective system or parallel courses have been adopted. And in the universities the natural sciences and related subjects have been divided and distributed among specialists who push their investigations to the remotest confines of knowledge. These innovations upon the traditional courses of study have encountered stout resistance; but slowly and surely the scientific spirit of the age has proceeded with its conquests.

2. The *moral and religious spirit* of the time is worthy of special note. The conflict between dogma and science, which at times has been sharp, has not been prejudicial to genuine Christianity. Superstition is rapidly becoming a thing of the past, and the emphasis of religious teaching is now laid upon fundamental and practical truths. The gospel is looked upon as a rule of life for the present

world, and the unselfish benevolence of Christ is becoming more and more the conscious ideal of men. The ascetic spirit has given place in larger measure to an active spirit, which finds the highest service of God in bravely meeting the duties of every-day life. The asperities of religious sects are softening, and the illness and death of a pious pope touch the sympathies, not only of the Roman Catholic, but also of the Protestant part of Christendom. The Evangelical Alliance and the Young Men's Christian Association are the practical manifestations of the general tendency toward closer union and cooperation among Christian people.

In harmony with the practical tendencies of the period, religion has become more benevolent in its activities. The fatherhood of God and the brotherhood of man are appreciated as never before. The sense of stewardship weighs more and more upon the consciences of men of wealth. The Church is active in missionary work at home and abroad. It is prominent in every work that seeks to relieve the unfortunate and reclaim the lost. The treatment of the unfortunate and criminal classes is more humane; and the effort is made to bring a just and benevolent spirit to the settlement of the great social and political problems of the day.

This moral and religious sense of the people is far more potent in education than is commonly supposed. It manifests itself in many ways—sometimes through the individual, sometimes through the Church, and sometimes through the State. In this country the examples of private munificence to education are without parallel. The endowments of a large majority of the colleges come from individual gifts. A few of our great universities, among which may be mentioned Cornell, Chicago, Leland Stanford, Johns Hopkins, and the Carnegie Institution, are due to individual munificence. Notable among such benevolent contributions are those of George Peabody and John F. Slater, the former in aid of white schools in the South, and the latter in aid of colored schools. The sum annually contributed by persons of wealth to education reaches many millions. The spirit in which most of these gifts are made has been well expressed by Andrew Carnegie: " Surplus wealth is a sacred trust to be administered during life by its possessor for the best good of his fellow men, and I have ventured to predict the coming of the day—the dawn of which, indeed, we already begin to see—when the man who dies possessed of available millions which were free, and in his hands to distribute, will die disgraced."

The influence of ecclesiastical and moral organizations upon education takes various forms. Prominent among these is the Sunday-school, which is maintained by almost every religious body in this country. The object of the Sunday-school is to impart religious instruction to the young. The main subject of study is the Bible; and, as organized at present, the Sunday-school is a powerful instrumentality for the moral and religious training of the people. The number of Sunday-schools in the United States at present is something more than a hundred thousand, with nearly a million officers and teachers, and about nine million scholars. These schools are numerous also in Great Britain; but on the Continent religious instruction is usually imparted in the public schools.

The denominational colleges of our country are at present, as they have been from the beginning of our educational history, the principal means of higher education. They far exceed in number, though not in wealth and equipment, the State and non-sectarian institutions, and, in not a few instances, they have been multiplied beyond actual needs and the possibility of the highest efficiency. Protestants generally patronize the public schools for elementary and secondary instruction; but the Roman Catholics generally, as also a part of the Lutheran Church, are building up a system of parochial schools coextensive with their needs. In addition to their twenty-six hundred parochial schools, the Roman Catholics maintain also six hundred academies and nearly a hundred colleges and universities.

At the present time there seems to be a growing feeling in this country that education is being unduly intellectualized; and as a result, we find an increasing demand for moral and religious instruction. It is being recognized that knowledge ought to be guided by an enlightened conscience, and that our educational system ought to be strengthened on the moral side of its work. The subject has been discussed in the National Educational Association; and the past year (1903), an association of prominent educators was organized in Chicago for the purpose of " unifying, stimulating, and developing all those forces which together can secure to religion and morality their true place and their proper influence." The Bible has recently been introduced into the courses of many colleges as a regular study. The growing temperance sentiment in Christendom makes use of the public school to fight alcoholism. By means of lectures and text-books, the evils of strong drink are impressed on the minds of the children. In this country the Woman's Christian Temperance Union has been very active in this work, and largely through its efforts temperance physiologies have been introduced into the schools of nearly all the States.

The moral and religious sentiment has manifested it self in eleemosynary legislation. This is seen, first of all, in the provision made for what are known as the defective classes, namely, the blind, the deaf, and the feeble-minded. There is no State in the country that does not make provision for the training of these unfortunates. There are at present in the United States thirty-nine schools for the blind, one hundred and eighteen schools for the deaf, and twenty State schools for the feeble-minded. Similar institutions, which were unknown to the ancient world, are supported in other parts of Christendom.

In the same spirit an effort is made to reclaim vicious young persons by means of reform schools. Idle and vicious habits are overcome by salutary instruction and discipline. Useful trades—sewing, cooking, carpentry, shoemaking, bricklaying, and others—are skilfully taught. There are ninety-two reform schools in the United States, the majority of which are State and municipal, with six hundred and ninety-six teachers, and twenty-two thousand inmates. Similar institutions are found in Great Britain and on the Continent.

But the moral and religious sentiment of the country has not found, perhaps, a more striking manifestation than in the efforts to educate the negro. Throughout the South, the negro equally shares in the advantages of the public schools. It is estimated by the Commissioner of Education, Dr. W. T. Harris, in his Report for 1901, that the South had spent, during the previous thirty-one years, $121,000,000 for the education of the colored race. Nearly all of this large amount came from the white people, and a considerable part of it was contributed out of the poverty that followed the civil war. The people of the North have felt, to a greater or less degree, the responsibility they incurred in liberating five million illiterate slaves and investing them with American citizenship. With a large philanthropic and Christian sentiment, which has not always been judicious in its methods, individuals, ecclesiastical organizations, and the national Government have made gigantic efforts for the education and social betterment of the negro. Liberal contributions, of which the Slater gift of $1,000,000 is most noteworthy, have been made for the establishment and support of various schools. Missionary organizations, of which the American Missionary Association and the Freedmen's Aid Society of the Methodist Episcopal Church may be taken as types, have expended millions in promoting negro education. The Freedmen's Bureau, established by the national Government in 1865, expended more than $5,000,000 on schools for the colored race during the five years of its existence. As a result of these united efforts, springing chiefly from the moral and religious sentiment of the land, the negro race enjoys educational advantages in the South scarcely inferior to those of the whites. In addition to the public schools, it has one hundred and thirty-eight institutions for secondary and higher education.

3. The third great tendency to be noted is *the practical, commercial, or utilitarian spirit.* Its object is some form of material gain. It has been strongly advocated in England by Huxley and Spencer, and in Germany by no less a person than the Emperor himself. It springs out of the wonderful mechanical inventions of the past few decades, by which the power of man has been vastly increased, and the great opportunities for acquiring wealth, which industrial development and world-wide commerce have offered. The building of railroads has created a demand for civil engineers; the manifold applications of

electricity have called for electrical experts; the enlargement of business houses and the establishment of great industrial enterprises have produced a need for skilful bookkeepers, stenographers, architects, and mechanics; and agricultural opportunity and competition have made scientific farmers a necessity. This great practical need, indifferent to all humanistic ideals of culture, demands an education that fits men for some industrial vocation or profession.

The effects of this practical or utilitarian tendency are seen, not only in the introduction of what are called " bread-winning studies " in the older kinds of schools, but also in the establishment and multiplication of new kinds of schools. In recent years business colleges have sprung up in great numbers in this country. They give comparatively short courses in bookkeeping, stenography, typewriting, business correspondence, commercial law, and related subjects. They generally offer a short road to business. The work of the business or commercial colleges in its relation to a liberal education has been thus set forth by Dr. Edmund J. James: " They have done and are doing and are destined to continue doing a great and useful work. But the training which they, with few exceptions, furnish, can scarcely be called a higher training at all. It has to do with facilities—indeed, chiefly with manual facilities—writing, reckoning, etc., those things that go to make a good clerk, things of great value in themselves, things which every business man would be the better for having, and yet things which after all are only facilities; they do not touch the essence of successful business management or tend to develop the higher sides of business activity; they bear little or no relation to those broader views characteristic of the business manager as distinct from the business clerk and are of course next to useless as a means of liberal education."

Though the idea of industrial or manual training was advocated by Locke, Kant, Pestalozzi, and other educational reformers, it is only in recent years that industrial schools have been established in large numbers. In Europe more or less manual training is given in the common schools. The training of eye and hand, the correlation of brain and muscle, and skill in one or more forms of manual labor are thought to be, not only a mental stimulus, but a valuable preparation for after life. In the manual-training schools of this country, one hundred and fifty-three in number, the student's time is about equally divided between academic studies and manual exercises, such as sewing, cooking, carpentry, farm or garden work, laundering, drawing, etc.

Technological schools are growing in numbers and importance. Their purpose is to impart a scientific knowledge and practical skill in the useful arts. It is recognized that the highest practical skill is usually attained only through a theoretical knowledge of principles. Institutions of technology are numerous in Great Britain and the Continental nations. In America the Agricultural and Mechanical Colleges usually supply technological instruction, including agriculture, architecture, the different kinds of engineering, forestry, horticulture, and kindred subjects. But other institutions, particularly the State universities, also have courses in technology.

Recent years have witnessed, not only great commercial expansion, but also keen international competition and rivalry. With the marvelous increase in its powers of production, every progressive nation finds it necessary to enter and cultivate foreign markets. The need of competent employees which has arisen in this manner, has called into existence what is known as a higher commercial education. In various countries we now find schools of commerce with courses of study extending over three or four years, and including a writing and speaking acquaintance with one or two foreign modern languages, commercial and international law, political and economic science, banking and exchange, and such other subjects as will qualify a young man for a responsible position in a large commercial business. The first school of this high commercial character in this country was the Wharton School of Finance and Economy of the University of Pennsylvania, which was established in 1881. Its purpose, as stated by the founder, was "to provide for young men special means of training and of correct instruction in the knowledge and in the arts of modern finance and economy, both public and private, in order that, being well informed and free from delusions upon these important subjects, they may either serve the community skilfully as well as faithfully in offices of trust, or, remaining in private life, may prudently manage their own affairs, and aid in maintaining sound financial morality." Since the establishment of the Wharton School, a number of our great universities—the University of California, the University of Chicago, New York University, and others—have provided courses of commerce and finance.

A. Germany

GENERAL SURVEY.—In no country has education received more attention, or produced, upon the whole, better results, than in Germany. Though in subjection to the social conditions belonging to a monarchical form of government, the German system embodies many points of excellence. In the science and history of education, the Germans are in the lead. The principles of Pestalozzi, which found able advocates in all parts of Germany, have permeated the primary schools, and given a great impulse to the professional training of teachers.

INTEREST IN PRIMARY EDUCATION.—The existing interest in primary education in Germany dates from the opening of the nineteenth century. Humiliated by the wars of Napoleon, Germany felt the necessity of developing greater internal strength. Frederick William III addressed the following wise words to the German people: " We have indeed lost in territory, and fallen in external power and splendor, but we must see to it that we gain in internal power and splendor; and hence it is my earnest desire that the greatest attention be given to the instruction of the people." He was nobly seconded by able ministers, and the present educational system, in its essential features, was devised.

GOVERNMENT CONTROL.—Education is an interest wholly in the hands of the Government. The general supervision of educational affairs is entrusted to a Minister of Public Instruction, who is assisted by school boards in the several provinces, regencies, and districts of the State. The course of study, the text-books used, the methods of instruction, the examination and appointment of teachers, the supervision of the schools—everything is directly or indirectly under the control of the general Government. The school buildings, many of which were constructed for other purposes, are generally massive structures of stone or brick. Defective in ventilation and light, and furnished only with plain and often uncomfortable desks, these buildings are not models of school architecture. The schools are well supplied with maps, charts, globes, and other apparatus, which the teacher employs judiciously in giving instruction.

PRIMARY SCHOOLS.—The educational system of Germany embraces, under various names, three grades of schools, all of which have received a high degree of development. The primary schools (*Volksschulen*), which are brought within reach of the whole population, give instruction in religion (catechism and Bible history), reading, writing, arithmetic, geography, natural history, singing, and gymnastics. The instruction, which is imparted in accordance with recent scientific methods, is very thorough. All children are required to enter school at seven years of age, and to continue their attendance till fourteen, at which time they are usually confirmed as members of the State Church. Through the successful enforcement of the compulsory system, the percentage of illiteracy is lower in Germany than in any other country of Europe. More than 99½ per cent of the recruits received into the army in 1893 were able to read and write.

SECONDARY SCHOOLS.—Secondary instruction is given in the gymnasia and the real-schools. The gymnasia, which give great prominence to Latin and Greek, are designed to prepare students for the university and the professions. The real-schools, which attach importance to the mother-tongue, mathematics, natural sciences, and modern languages, aim to fit their students for the ordinary business callings of life. As the gymnasia are humanistic and the real-schools practical, they have been the occasion of a warm conflict between educators of these two tendencies. The conflict is still going on; but meanwhile, in accordance with the practical spirit of the age, the real-schools have been constantly increasing in number and popularity. In a recent order the Emperor of Germany has thrown the weight of his authority on the side of the real-schools. "With reference to the privilege of students of abridging their military service to one year," he says, "the three kinds of schools—the Gymnasia, the Realschulen of the first order, and the Realgymnasia—shall be considered of equal value in general education. . . . I lay especial weight upon the importance which knowledge of the English language has gained of late, and desire, therefore, that English be introduced as an optional study everywhere of equal rank with Greek."

The studies in these two classes of schools vary somewhat in different parts of Germany; but the courses pursued at present in the Prussian gymnasia and real-schools are fairly representative:

PRUSSIAN GYMNASIUM

STUDIES	Sexta	Quinta	Quarta	Unter-Tertia.	Ober-Tertia	Unter-Secunda	Ober-Secunda	Unter-Prima	Ober-Prima	Total
Religion	3	2	2	2	2	2	2	2	2	19
German	3	2	2	2	2	2	2	3	3	21
Latin	9	9	9	9	9	8	8	8	8	77
Greek or English	..	..	..	7	7	7	7	6	6	40
French	..	4	5	2	2	2	2	2	2	21
History and geography	3	3	4	3	3	3	3	3	3	28
Mathematics	4	4	4	3	3	4	4	4	4	34
Natural history	2	2	2	2	2	..	..	..	..	10
Physics	..	..	..	..	..	2	2	2	2	8
Writing	2	2	..	..	..	..	..	..	..	4
Drawing	2	2	2	..	..	..	..	..	..	6
Hours per week	28	30	30	30	30	30	30	30	30	..

PRUSSIAN REAL-SCHOOL

STUDIES	Sexta	Quinta	Quarta	Unter-Tertia	Ober-Tertia	Unter-Secunda	Ober-Secunda	Unter-Prima	Ober-Prima	Total
Religion....................	3	2	2	2	2	2	2	2	2	19
German.....................	3	3	3	3	3	3	3	3	3	27
Latin	8	7	7	6	6	5	5	5	5	54
English	..	..	..	4	4	3	3	3	3	20
French.....................	..	5	5	4	4	4	4	4	4	34
History and geography	3	3	4	4	4	3	3	3	3	30
Mathematics	5	4	5	5	5	5	5	5	5	44
Natural history	2	2	2	2	2	2	..	..	..	22
Physics	..	..	..	..	..	3	3	3	3	12
Chemistry..................	..	..	..	..	..	..	2	2	2	6
Writing.....................	2	2	..	..	..	..	..	..	..	4
Drawing	2	2	2	2	2	2	2	2	2	18
Hours per week..........	28	30	30	32	32	32	32	32	32	..

The course of instruction in both the gymnasia and
the real-schools extends through nine years. Pupils enter
at nine years of age, and complete the course at eighteen
or nineteen; but many give up their studies at fourteen.
As a rule, they do not room or board in the school buildings; and, when coming from a distance, they are placed
under the care of some trustworthy resident of the town
or city, who watches over their studies and conduct out
of school hours. The secondary schools usually charge a
tuition fee, which varies from about five dollars to twenty-
seven dollars, according to class.

TEACHING AND WOMAN'S EDUCATION.—Germany has,
perhaps, the best trained teachers in the world. With very
few exceptions, they are graduates of normal schools, and
have had a practical training before entering upon their
work. Only after repeated examinations in the science
and art of education, as well as in academic studies, are

they finally enrolled in the teaching force of the Government. Henceforth they are officers of the State, and enjoy the respect and confidence which they have fairly earned by their academic and professional training. Only about fifteen per cent of the teachers are women. In reference to woman's higher education Germany has remained very conservative. The German Government is loath to consider women otherwise than in her domestic relations. Hence the secondary and higher education of women is left chiefly to private institutions. A few of the German universities, by way of special and limited privilege, have been opened to women.

TECHNICAL INSTRUCTION.—Germany has awakened to a new industrial and commercial life. Its energetic and far-seeing Emperor is ambitious to make Germany a great world-power. In close sympathy with the practical spirit of the age, he is seeking to acquire for his people a prominent place in the markets of the world. He is interested in German colonization. For the protection of German interests abroad, he is persistently building up a great navy. But at home he is using his influence in favor of technological education, upon which, as he discerns, the industrial and commercial success of the country must ultimately rest. If German products are to compete successfully in the markets of the world, they must excel in mechanical and artistic quality. This feeling is widespread in Germany, and is gradually modernizing its education. Professor A. Riedler, rector of the Polytechnic Institute of Berlin, recently said: " The demands made by present conditions of life upon education are different from those of former times, and they are determinative. Powerful forces and influences have changed conditions of life, and education, to be correct, must be in harmony with these conditions. Public education is not meant only to serve certain classes of society, but must promote national and political interests by stimulating productive activity." As a result of this sentiment, the traditional courses of study are being modified; and numerous technological schools, notably the Polytechnic Institute of Berlin, and many commercial institutions have been established.

THE UNIVERSITIES.—The universities, both for comprehensiveness and thoroughness of instruction, stand preeminent. Their large number is due mainly to the former subdivisions of Germany into separate States, each of which was ambitious to maintain an institution for superior instruction. Many of the universities possess a considerable endowment; but most of them receive large subsidies from the State. The studies are arranged under the four faculties of theology, law, medicine, and philosophy, the latter comprising, besides philosophy proper, natural science, mathematics, political economy, history, geography, literature, and philology. A rector, elected annually by the professors, is charged with the administration of the affairs of the university. German students can not become full members without having completed the course of a gymnasium or real-school. The universities founded during the nineteenth century are as follows: Berlin, 1810; Munich, 1826; Breslau, 1811; Bonn, 1818; and Strasburg, 1872. The University of Berlin is the largest, with a faculty of more than two hundred professors, and a yearly attendance of about five thousand students.

B. France

THE REVOLUTION.—The interest in popular education in France dates from the Revolution of 1789. The leaders of that movement were inspired with democratic ideas, and at the same time they believed that popular intelligence was necessary for the perpetuity of the Republic. Hence, the Convention in 1793 not only ordered the establishment of elementary schools throughout France, but also made attendance upon them compulsory. But discord at home and wars abroad, during the years immediately succeeding, prevented the execution of this wise decree.

NAPOLEON'S SYSTEM.—Having crowned himself emperor, Napoleon did not remain indifferent to the subject of general education. In 1806 he established a system of great compactness, which forms the basis of the excellent laws now in operation. He united all the teaching forces of the country into one body, which he called the University of France. This university, whose affairs were administered by a grand master, assisted by a university council, was divided into three branches: Primary instruction, provided in the elementary schools; secondary instruction, provided in the lyceums and colleges; and superior instruction, given by the faculties of arts, medicine, law, and theology. France was divided into a number of large districts called academies, which were presided over by a rector, assisted by an academic council. Schools under local supervision were to be established in each community. But Napoleon became too much absorbed in ambitious schemes of conquest to put his system into complete operation.

THE RESTORATION.—Under the Restoration, popular education languished. Though the system of Napoleon

25

was retained in its essential features, it was administered with a narrow sectarian and monarchical spirit. Under the cover of zeal for moral and religious instruction, education was placed in large measure in the hands of priests. A priest, M. de Freyssinous, was called to the office of grand master of the university. In a circular announcing his appointment, he set forth the principles directing his administration: " In calling to the head of public education a man invested with a sacred character, his Majesty declares to all France how much he desires that the youth of his kingdom be brought up in religious and monarchical sentiments. . . . The true Frenchman never separates love of his king from love of his country, nor obedience to magistrates from attachment to the laws and institutions which the king has given his people." While Germany was making vigorous efforts to retrieve its fortune through the intellectual development of its people, France, in the hands of a reactionary Government, saw its educational progress effectually thwarted.

LOUIS PHILIPPE.—With the Government of Louis Philippe after the Revolution of 1830, there came a change for the better. The system of Napoleon, as transmitted from the Government of the Restoration, was administered with a vigorous and progressive spirit. The schools were emancipated from priestly control. Each district or commune was required to have a school, and, in order that qualified teachers might not be wanting, normal schools were encouraged and multiplied. Schoolhouses were erected; scientific methods of instruction were introduced; an educational interest was awakened among the people. The basis of popular education was firmly established. For the encouragement of primary teachers in their unappreciated labors, Guizot, as Minister of Public Instruction, addressed them the following beautiful words: " I know full well that the care of the law will never succeed in rendering the simple profession of district teacher as attractive as it is useful. Society can not make a sufficient return to him who is devoted to this work. There is no fortune to be won, there is scarcely a reputation to be acquired in the discharge of his onerous duties. Destined to see his life pass away in monotonous toil, sometimes even to encounter the injustice and ingratitude of ignorance, he would become disheartened, and perhaps succumb, if he did not draw his strength and courage elsewhere than in the prospect of an immediate and purely personal interest. It is necessary that he be sustained and animated by a profound sense of the moral importance of his labors; that the austere pleasure of having served men and contributed secretly to the public weal become the worthy reward which his conscience alone gives him. It is his glory to pretend to nothing beyond his obscure and laborious condition; to exhaust his strength in sacrifices scarcely noticed by those who profit by them; in a word, to labor for men, and expect his reward from God alone."

PRESENT SYSTEM.—Under the second republic, the school laws were subjected, in 1850, to a comprehensive revision which, with recent minor modifications, resulted in the system now in force. There is a graduated and thorough system of superintendence. The highest educational authority is the Superior Council, which is presided over by the Minister of Public Instruction. The eighty-seven departments or counties of France are divided into seventeen districts, or academies, in each of which an academic council, under the direction of the Minister of Public Instruction, has charge of educational affairs. In each department or county there is another council composed of the prefect, the inspector of the academy, the inspector of primary instruction, and several others; while in each canton or commune a local board, with the mayor at its head, has supervision over all the schools, both public and private. Each commune of five hundred inhabitants is required to have a public school in which the following subjects are taught: Moral and civil duties, reading, writing, the elements of the French language and literature, history and geography (particularly of France), arithmetic, the elements of natural science and its applications, the principles of designing, modeling, and music, gymnastics, military exercises for boys, and needlework for girls. The schools are entirely free, and in 1882 the instruction of children between the ages of seven and fourteen was made compulsory. Any Frenchman twenty-one years of age, who has passed a satisfactory examination, is allowed to teach. Each department is required to have two normal schools, one for male and one for female teachers, with a course of study extending through three years. Since the humiliating defeat of 1870–'71, the French Government has been making vigorous efforts to promote popular education; and in no other country has there been, during the last decade, such marked educational progress.

MORAL INSTRUCTION.—A very significant movement in French education is the present earnest effort to give greater prominence to moral instruction in the primary schools. Though moral and civic instruction has stood at the head of the course of study since 1882, the Government has been recently forced by external pressure, especially from the teaching orders of the Roman Catholic Church, to meet the charge of immorality and to establish moral teaching on a more effective basis. As a result, the scientific spirit, which for a time dominated the secular schools, has given way to the ethical spirit, and an elaborate scheme of moral instruction has been adopted. The official program says substantially that " moral instruction is intended to complete, to elevate, and to ennoble all the other instruction of the school. While each of the other branches tends to develop a special order of aptitudes or of useful knowledge, this study tends to develop the man himself; that is to say, his heart, his intelligence, his conscience; hence moral education moves on a different plane from the other subjects. Its force depends less upon the precision and logical relation of the truths taught than upon intensity of feeling, vividness of impressions, and the contagious ardor of conviction."

The carrying-out of this program is naturally in the hands of the teacher. He is to impart moral instruction apart from religion, but in harmony with it. He is to join his efforts to those of parents and the clergy " to make each child an honest man." " By his character, his conduct, his example," the program well says, " the teacher should be the most persuasive of examples. In moral instruction what does not come from the heart does not go to the heart. A master who recites precepts, who speaks of duty without convictions, without warmth, does much worse than waste his efforts. He is altogether wrong. A course of morals which is regular, but cold, commonplace, dry, does not teach morals, because it does not develop a love for the subject. The simplest recital in which the child can catch an accent of gravity, a single sincere word, is worth more than a long succession of mechanical lessons."

SECONDARY INSTRUCTION.—Secondary instruction is provided by the lyceums and communal colleges. Previous to 1852 the lyceums, which correspond to the German gymnasia, were exclusively literary, Latin and Greek being the chief subjects of instruction. Since that time they have undergone important changes which bring them into closer relation with the present age. The classes and studies of the lyceums are as follows:

PLAN OF STUDIES FOR LYCEUM

STUDIES	ELEMENTARY DIVISION			GRAMMAR DIVISION			SUPERIOR DIVISION				
	Preparatory	Eighth Class	Seventh Class	Sixth Class	Fifth Class	Fourth Class	Third Class	Second Class	Rhetoric	Philosophy	Total
French, nine years......	10	10	8	3	3	3	3	4	5	....	49
Latin, seven years......	..	..	..	10	10	6	5	4	4	⎰ 1 ⎱	39½
Greek, five years.......	..	..	..	..	..	6	5	5	4	⎰ ⎱	20½
History and geography, ten years	4	4	4	3	3	3	4	4	4	3	36
Mathematics and science, ten years	4	4	4	3	4	3	3	3	5	9	42
English or German, ten years................	4	4	4	3	3	2	3	3	3	1	30
Philosophy	..	..	..	..	..	..	..	..	..	8	8
Drawing...............	2	2	2	2	2	2	2	2	2	2	20
Hours per week	24	24	22	24	25	25	25	25	27	24	..

Beginning with the grammar group, or the sixth class, there is now a trifurcation, which provides three courses of study. Accordingly, the student may elect a course with Latin and Greek, or a course with Latin and a modern language in place of Greek, or a course with modern languages in place of both Latin and Greek. The three courses are of equal rank, and lead alike to the bachelor's degree. The communal colleges, which greatly outnumber the lyceums, differ from them only in having less extended curricula.

LAW OF ASSOCIATIONS.—As shown by the statistics of 1898 and 1899, the secondary instruction of France had in large measure passed into the hands of Catholic religious associations. The attendance of pupils in the State secondary schools for 1899 was 85,599; in the schools of the religious orders, 91,825. The Government believed that the influence of these associations was adverse to the Republic, and hence in 1901 it secured the passage of what is known as the Law of Associations. The avowed purpose of this law was to bring the religious orders into subordination to the civil authority, of which they had previously been independent. "The law requires that every association shall publish, through its founders, its title and object, the place of its establishment, and the names, professions, and domicile of those who are in any way concerned with its administration or management." The execution of the law, which brings all secondary education under State control, was attended with violent discussions and riotous outbreaks; but the Government has triumphed, and the refractory orders have been disbanded or driven from the country. Of 16,500 religious establishments, only 5,000 have conformed to the requirements of the law.

HIGHER EDUCATION.—Superior instruction is given by the five faculties of theology, law, medicine, philosophy, and science. Until recently they were not united in one body, as is the case in the universities of Germany and the United States, but maintained a separate existence as professional schools.

The faculties of theology were established at Paris, Aix, Bordeaux, Lyons, Rouen, Montauban; those of law at Paris, Toulouse, Aix, Caen, Dijon, Poitiers, Rheims, Bordeaux, Grenoble, Douai, Nancy; those of science at Paris,

Besançon, Rennes, Caen, Bordeaux, Clermont, Poitiers, Dijon, Grenoble, Lille, Nancy, Lyons, Marseilles, Montpellier, Toulouse; and those of literature at Paris, Aix, Besançon, Bordeaux, Caen, Clermont, Dijon, Douai, Grenoble, Lyons, Montpellier, Poitiers, Rennes, Toulouse, Nancy. In addition to giving instruction, these faculties conducted examinations, and conferred the degrees of bachelor, licentiate, and doctor.

In 1890 fifteen of the separate faculties were organized into State universities, named after the cities in which they are located. "A university," says the law creating them, "must comprise at least the four faculties of law, medicine, sciences, and letters; other establishments of superior instruction may also be incorporated with it at the instance of the minister." Increased appropriations have been made by the Government, and new life has been infused into this department of the educational system. Specially notable is the stress laid upon technological studies. "Invested with civil personality and endowed with financial autonomy," says M. Perreau, of the Chamber of Deputies, "the universities have created institutes, courses, and laboratories for instruction in industrial and agricultural chemistry, applied mechanics, electricity, bacteriology, and for analysis, experiments, and research, under the direction of distinguished masters." Besides the practical work of the universities, special higher technical schools exist, among which may be mentioned the Polytechnic School of Paris, the School of Higher Commercial Studies, and the National Conservatory of Arts and Trades.

C. England

GENERAL SURVEY.—In England popular education has made less progress than in any other Protestant country of Europe. The explanation of this fact is to be found in the conservative character of the people, and the aristocratic organization of society. It is only in recent years that the masses have become prominent. Hence, it has happened that, while popular education was left to individual effort and denominational zeal, the children of the wealthy and the noble have enjoyed the advantages of the great preparatory schools—Eton, Winchester, Westminster, St. Paul's, Merchant Taylors', Charterhouse, Harrow, Rugby, Shrewsbury, and Christ's Hospital.

PREPARATORY SCHOOLS.—These preparatory or endowed schools, which have been justly celebrated in English education, were founded, with three exceptions, in the sixteenth century. They are large boarding-schools, whose courses of study raise them to the rank of the French lyceum or the German gymnasium. In accordance with the conservative character of English institutions, it is but recently that these schools have been much affected by modern educational progress. At present they are losing their medieval character before the pressure for reform; and though Latin and Greek still remain the chief subjects of study, increasing attention is being paid to the mother-tongue, the natural sciences, and the modern languages. The methods of instruction are becoming less mechanical; and the principle of authority, which formerly repressed a spirit of independence, is now giving place to freedom of thought and investigation. Athletics are cultivated with great zeal. The system of fagging, which requires students of the lower classes to perform menial services for those of the upper classes, still exists.

In addition to these endowed schools, there are many other schools and colleges devoted to secondary instruction.

THOMAS ARNOLD.—Dr. Thomas Arnold, who became head master of Rugby in 1828, instituted numerous reforms there, and proved himself one of the greatest educators England has produced. He made promotion depend, not on a mechanical routine of work, but upon merit and scholarship as determined by examinations. Through his strong personality and vigorous appeals to the moral sense of his pupils, he greatly improved the moral and religious tone of the school. In place of the brutal fagging system that had previously prevailed, he introduced a system of responsible supervision by the upper-class men over the younger boys, and thus created an opportunity for the exercise of manly virtue. He was severely criticized and opposed, but he persisted in his reformatory plans. And, to use the words of an English writer, " he firmly established his system, and his successors, men differing in training and temperament from himself and from each other, have agreed in cordially sustaining it. His pupils and theirs, men in very different walks of life, filling honorable posts at the universities and public schools, or ruling the millions of India, or working among the blind and toiling multitudes of our great towns, feel daily how much of their usefulness and power they owe to the sense of high trust and high duty which they imbibed at school."

THE UNIVERSITIES.—The Universities of Oxford and Cambridge, whose origin is lost in the darkness of the middle ages, are among the most celebrated in the world. They are similar in organization; Oxford comprising twenty-three separate colleges, and Cambridge nineteen. Each college has a separate organization of its own, presided over by a president, rector, or provost, while all are under a central or university government administered by a chancellor, in conjunction with a council elected by the several colleges. The universities are maintained by munificent endowments, the gifts of benefactors and the founders of colleges. Candidates for graduation must reside in a college for three academic years; when, upon passing a satisfactory examination before the university examiners, they receive their degree. Oxford and Cambridge are both very conservative, and still merit in some degree the criticisms of Bacon and Milton. During the nineteenth century other institutions for superior instruction were founded, chief among which is the University of London, created by royal charter in 1836.

The most important event in the recent higher education of Great Britain is the rise of university colleges in the great centers of industry. These colleges exhibit the modern progressive spirit, and are characterized by their liberal courses in science and technical training, and also by their admission of women on the same terms as men. They are supported by private and public contributions, and the most noteworthy phase of their development is their ascent into university organization. Thus Owens College, Manchester (1851), Yorkshire College, Leeds (1874), and University College, Liverpool (1881), were incorporated as Victoria University in 1880. The three colleges of Wales—Aberystwyth, Bangor, and Cardiff—are comprised in the University of Wales, which was organized in 1893. Mason College, Birmingham, is the nucleus of Birmingham University, which was incorporated in 1900. This development has been stimulated by a parliamentary grant which, since 1889, has been shared by the university colleges of England on the condition that they submit reports to the Department of Education.

ROBERT RAIKES.—Prior to the beginning of the last century, the education of the masses of England was almost entirely neglected. To Robert Raikes, the founder of the Sunday-school, belongs the honor of having first awakened an interest in popular education. This he did partly through his paper, the Gloucester Journal, in which he maintained that ignorance was the principal source of vice among the people, and partly through his actual labors for the instruction of the neglected children of his town. His efforts led to the establishment of numerous Sunday-schools, which form the beginning of popular instruction. He died in 1811.

ANDREW BELL.—The labors of two other educators, following the efforts of Raikes, gave an additional impulse to popular instruction. These were Andrew Bell and Joseph Lancaster, who independently of each other invented the monitorial system of teaching. Bell, who was born at St. Andrew's, Scotland, in 1753, went to India in 1787, where he was appointed superintendent of a school for the orphan children of British soldiers. Unable to procure suitable teachers, he fell upon the plan, sometimes adopted in the native schools of India, of employing advanced pupils as instructors. As the plan succeeded beyond expectation, he published an account of it on his return to England, and in 1807 established in London a school in which the monitorial (or Madras) system was employed. The experiment was successful; and as many influential persons, especially among the clergy, became interested in the system, the National Society was formed in connection with the Church of England for the purpose of establishing schools throughout the British dominions. The work of this society, under the direction of Bell, was prosecuted with great vigor, and in less than a dozen years one thousand schools had been opened, with an attendance of more than two hundred thousand children.

JOSEPH LANCASTER.—This remarkable activity was due in part to the labors of Joseph Lancaster, a Quaker. Having established a school in London in 1798, he found it necessary to reduce his expenses; and, as a means of doing this, he hit upon the monitorial system which Bell had already employed at Madras. His school met with great popular favor, and soon numbered one thousand pupils. It was visited by the royal family, on which occasion the King said to Lancaster: " I wish that every child in my kingdom were able to read the Bible." In view of the popularity and success of the school, an association of Dissenters, known as the British and Foreign School Society, was organized for the promulgation of the system of Lancaster; and the rivalry between this and the National Society of the Established Church led to extraordinary efforts in founding popular schools.

POPULAR EDUCATION.—It was not till 1818 that the English Government concerned itself about education. At that time a committee was appointed to inspect the public schools for the upper and middle classes, and report upon their condition. Many evils were exposed, and the way opened for subsequent reforms. The first annual grant for education was made in 1833. The movement toward popular education received a noteworthy impulse from the educational conference held in London in 1857 under the presidency of the Prince Consort. In 1858 a commission was appointed by Parliament to report upon the state of popular education. The interest thus manifested by the Government in popular education culminated in 1870 in a statute which ordered that " there shall be provided for every school district a sufficient amount of accommodation in public elementary schools available for all the children resident in such district, for whose elementary education efficient and suitable provision is not otherwise made."

PRESENT SYSTEM.—School boards, elected by all taxpayers, including women, were established to carry out the provisions of this law; and they were further invested with authority to compel parents to send their children to school between the ages of five and thirteen. With this action began a new era of educational progress. To secure better qualified teachers, normal or training colleges, under government inspection, were established, of which there are now sixty with more than five thousand students. In 1890 provision was made for the teaching of science and drawing in the elementary schools, and the county councils are authorized to levy a tax not exceeding a penny to the pound for the support of technical schools.

At present there are two classes of schools known as Voluntary Schools and Board Schools. The former have been built up and are partly supported by voluntary contributions, and are under ecclesiastical control; the latter have been established and are maintained by local taxation and are controlled by elected school boards. More than half the children of England—fifty-three per cent— attend the Voluntary Schools; the rest—forty-seven per cent—attend the Board Schools. In reference to the denominational schools, Mr. Chamberlain said in 1891 : " To destroy denominational schools is now an impossibility, and nothing is more astonishing than the progress they have made since the Educational Act of 1870. I had thought they would die out with the establishment of the Board Schools, but I have been mistaken, for in the last twenty-three years they have doubled their accommodation, and more than doubled their subscription list." Since 1891 the elementary schools have been practically free.

EXISTING CONDITIONS.—There is at present great interest in education in England, but there are many problems yet to be solved. There are conflicting policies growing out of social and ecclesiastical conditions. The Government, fearing, as it seems, democratic tendencies, occupies a conservative attitude. There is no unity or solidarity of system. The smaller schools of the rural districts are suffering for lack of financial support. The situation has been forcibly summed up by Dr. Macnamara, a Member of Parliament. "The village schools," he insisted, "were being most shamefully neglected. The State did as little for them as it could, and the localities did less. Pinchbeck and shabby to a degree was the financial treatment accorded to these schools. The grants from the central exchequer were paid to all schools, town and rural, on the capitation principle. The plan might be all right where the number of children by which the capitation payment was to be multiplied was pretty large; but where the number of children was small, the capitation plan was disastrous. The small school must have a lump sum from the exchequer every year sufficient to meet its annual charges for maintenance and establishment. Without this the head teacher would remain scandalously underpaid and shamefully unaided in his labors." But sooner or later the existing defects will no doubt be remedied.

D. The United States

NEED OF EDUCATION.—In the United States the sovereignty is vested, not in the few, but in the many. The masses are called upon to consider every kind of social and political question affecting the welfare of the country. The principles of human liberty; schemes for internal improvement; questions of finance and education; our relations with other countries—these are some of the weighty matters brought before the popular mind. At the polls, where every man has an equal voice, the decisions are made, and the policy of the Government determined.

These facts necessitate a considerable degree of popular intelligence. The illiterate, clearly incapable of performing the high duties imposed on American citizens, remain ciphers in society, or become the dangerous tools of designing politicians. In some form, popular education is necessary both to a wise administration of the Government and to its perpetuity. " Promote," says Washington, in his Farewell Address, " as an object of primary importance, institutions for the general diffusion of knowledge. In proportion as the structure of a government gives force to public opinion, it is essential that public opinion should be enlightened."

TWO PERIODS.—The educational history of the United States naturally divides itself into the colonial and national periods. The New England and the Southern colonies present a striking difference in their educational development. This difference had its origin partly in the dissimilar character and antecedents of the colonists, and partly in the physical conditions of the two sections. In New England education early received attention, and produced excellent results; in the South it was neglected.

As a result, the Southern colonies, in proportion to population and natural advantages, exhibited a slower development, losing ground that has not yet been recovered. As was the case in Europe during the corresponding period, the theological influence in education was very strong; but, at the same time, the peculiar circumstances of establishing a home in an unsubdued wilderness, and of laying the foundation of a great republic, early gave the schools vigorous life and a practical bearing.

(1) *Colonial Period*

VIRGINIA.—In Virginia popular education was almost wholly neglected during the colonial period. This was owing partly to the aristocratic spirit which existed in the colony from the beginning, and partly to the scattered condition of the population. While in New England the people naturally collected in towns, in Virginia the colonists, devoted to agriculture and seeking to reproduce the conditions of the mother-country, settled on large plantations. For half a century after the foundation of Jamestown, schools were almost unknown. Education was confined to the parental roof, and successive generations grew up in comparative ignorance. Sir William Berkeley wrote in 1671: " I thank God there are no free schools nor printing, and I hope we shall not have these for a hundred years; for learning has brought disobedience, and heresy and sects into the world, and printing has divulged them and libels against the best government. God keep us from both ! "

WILLIAM AND MARY COLLEGE.—The apathy or hostility prevailing in regard to popular schools did not exist to the same degree in reference to the higher education. From an early date the question of establishing a college had

26

been repeatedly discussed. Finally, after the lapse of more than three-quarters of a century from the time the subject was first broached, the College of William and Mary was founded in 1692. When the enterprise began to assume definite form, a commendable interest, both at home and in England, was manifested in its success. The Lieutenant-Governor headed the subscription-list with a generous gift, and his example was followed by other prominent members of the colony. The sum of twenty-five hundred pounds having been raised, the Rev. James Blair was sent to England to solicit a charter for the institution. This was readily granted; and, as an additional evidence of royal favor, the quit-rents yet due in the colony, amounting to nearly two thousand pounds, were turned over to the college. For its further support, twenty thousand acres of land were set apart, and a tax of a penny a pound was laid on all tobacco exported from Virginia and Maryland to other American colonies.

The institution was located at Williamsburg, and the Rev. James Blair, who had been active in securing its establishment, was chosen as its first president. In the language of the charter, the college was founded " to the end that the Church of Virginia may be furnished with a seminary of ministers of the gospel, and that the youth may be piously educated in good letters and manners, and that the Christian faith may be propagated among the Western Indians to the glory of Almighty God." The course of study embraced divinity, language, and natural philosophy—" a divinity," says Howison, " shaped and molded at every point by the liturgy and creed of the English Church; languages which filled the college walls with boys hating Greek and Latin grammars; and natural philosophy, which was just beginning to believe that the earth revolved around the sun, rather than the sun round the earth." Such was the founding of the next oldest American college, from whose walls have gone forth many able men influential in molding the destinies of our country.

LITERARY DEVELOPMENT.—The conditions in Virginia were not favorable to literary development. Descended in good part from noble families, the colonists brought with them the aristocratic feelings and religious intolerance characteristic of the royalists in England. The isolated condition of the population was unfavorable to the kindling of mind; the absence of schools and printing-presses lowered the tone of popular intelligence; the concentration of power and influence in the hands of an aristocracy of wealthy landowners, occupied chiefly with pleasure and politics, was not suited to awaken a literary spirit. With few exceptions, the writers of the colonial period were born or educated abroad. Instead of literary men, Virginia produced sagacious politicians, impassioned orators, and elegant country gentlemen of boundless and gracious hospitality.

THE PURITANS.—If the early colonists of Virginia were largely adventurers, seeking their fortune in the New World, the Puritans of New England, fleeing from religious oppression, came to establish a permanent home. A deep earnestness, which often ran into the extravagance of a forbidding asceticism, characterized their early history. They counted no sacrifice too great to maintain the integrity of their religious convictions. Giving up comfort, wealth, home, they faced the dangers of a winter sea and the inhospitality of a barren shore. They were intelligent and brave men, daring to think for themselves, and to maintain their convictions at any cost. Many of them had enjoyed the advantages of Oxford and Cambridge, and brought with them the precious seed of learning. They had some consciousness of their mission as the founders of a mighty people, and, with their eye turned to future generations, they laid the foundations broad and well. We may smile at their weaknesses, their superstition, and their austerity of life, but, underneath these peculiarities, we discover a strength of character, depth of conviction, and sincerity of purpose, that command our respect and admiration.

HARVARD COLLEGE.—In view of these facts, it is not strange that education in Massachusetts received early attention. The action of the Puritans was prompt and vigorous. Within a few years after the landing of the Mayflower, when their number was yet small; when their homes were without comfort; when they were continually menaced by the scalping-knife of the savage, they established a system of schools that placed them in advance of the most enlightened portions of Europe. In 1636 the General Court voted an appropriation of four hundred pounds for the founding of a school, which, after its first private benefactor, the Rev. John Harvard, received the name of Harvard College. It was cheerfully and liberally sustained by the New England colonies. It was opened in 1638, and sent forth its first graduating class in 1642. The standard of scholarship was not low. The requirements for entrance, in 1643, were given as follows: " When any scholar is able to understand Tully, or such like classical author extempore, and make and speak true Latin in verse and prose; . . . and decline perfectly the paradigms of nouns and verbs in the Greek tongue, let him then, and not before, be capable of admission into the college."

COMMON SCHOOLS.—The most remarkable action, however, of the Massachusetts colony was in relation to common schools. In 1647 the General Court passed the following order, the preamble of which recalls the powerful words of Luther: "It being one chief project of the old deluder, Satan, to keep men from the knowledge of the Scriptures, as in former times by keeping them in an unknown tongue, so in these latter times by persuading from the use of tongues, that so at least the true sense and meaning of the original might be clouded by false glosses of saint-seeming deceivers; that learning may not be buried in the grave of our fathers in the Church and Commonwealth, the Lord assisting our endeavors—

"It is therefore *ordered,* that every township in this jurisdiction, after the Lord hath increased them to the number of fifty householders, shall then forthwith appoint one within their town to teach all such children as shall resort to him to write and read; whose wages shall be paid, either by the parents or masters of such children, or by the inhabitants in general, by way of supply, as the major part of those that order the prudentials of the town shall appoint; provided, those that send their children be not oppressed by paying much more than they can have them taught for in other towns; and it is further *ordered,* that when any town shall increase to the number of one hundred families or householders, they shall set up a grammar-school, the master thereof being able to instruct youth so far as they may be fitted for the university; provided, that if any town neglect the performance hereof above one year, that every such town shall pay five pounds to the next school till they shall perform this order."

OTHER COLONIES.—The other colonies of the North manifested the same interest in popular education shown by Massachusetts; those of the South, following the example of Virginia, left it to individual effort. A public school was established in Connecticut as early as 1639. The first code of laws for this colony, published in 1650, required " the selectmen of every town to have a vigilant eye over their brethren and neighbors, to see that none of them shall suffer so much barbarism in any of their families as not to endeavor to teach, by themselves or others, their children and apprentices so much learning as may enable them perfectly to read the English tongue." The colony of Rhode Island had a public school in 1640. By reason of their close political relations, Maine and New Hampshire had substantially the educational system of Massachusetts. The colonists of New Jersey were interested in schools from the beginning, though public action in reference to education was not taken till 1676. In that year the " town's men " of Newark were authorized to establish a school and employ a competent teacher for one year.

The educational history of Pennsylvania is praiseworthy. The first plan of proprietary government, drawn up by Penn, in 1682, makes mention of public schools. In 1683, the year Philadelphia was founded, the council of the province ordered the establishment of a school. A charter granted by Penn, in 1711, contains the following preamble: " Whereas, the prosperity and welfare of any people depend, in a great measure, upon the good education of youth, and their early introduction in the principles of true religion and virtue, and qualifying them to serve their country and themselves by breeding them in reading, writing, and learning of languages and useful arts and sciences, suitable to their sex, age, and degree—which can not be effected, in any manner, so well

as by erecting Public Schools for the purpose aforesaid."
Maryland seems to have made no provision for public
schools till 1723, when an act was passed "for the encouragement of learning, and erecting schools in the several counties in this province." The Constitution of North
Carolina, adopted in 1776, provided that "a school or
schools shall be established by the Legislature for the convenient instruction of youth, with such salaries to the masters, paid by the public, as may enable them to instruct at
low prices; and that all useful learning shall be encouraged
in one or more universities." No action was taken with
reference to public schools till 1819. South Carolina and
Georgia made no provision for popular education during
the colonial period.

(2) *National Period*

VIEWS OF LEADING STATESMEN.—When the independence of the United States had been achieved, and a Constitution adopted, education was left to the care of the
separate States. Yet the most influential leaders in the
formation of the new Government were outspoken advocates of education, and interpreted that clause of the Constitution empowering Congress "to lay and collect taxes,
. . . and provide for the common defense and general
welfare of the United States," as authorizing the General
Government to encourage the establishment of schools. In
a message to Congress, in 1790, Washington, after making
sundry other recommendations touching military organization, uniformity in currency, weights and measures,
etc., continued: "Nor am I less persuaded that you will
agree with me in opinion, that there is nothing which can
better deserve your patronage than the promotion of science and literature. Knowledge is in every country the

surest basis of public happiness. In one, in which the measures of government receive their impression so immediately from the sense of the community, as in ours, it is proportionately essential."

In his inaugural address, John Adams said: " The wisdom and generosity of the Legislature in making liberal appropriations in money for the benefit of schools, academies, and colleges, is an equal honor to them and their constituents; a proof of their veneration for letters and science, and a portent of great and lasting good to North and South America, and to the world. Great is truth—great is liberty—great is humanity—and they must and will prevail ! "

Thomas Jefferson was a friend to popular education. " I look to the diffusion of light and education," he said, " as the resources most to be relied on for ameliorating the condition, promoting the virtue, and advancing the happiness of man. And I do hope, in the present spirit of extending to the great mass of mankind the blessings of instruction, I see a prospect of great advancement in the happiness of the human race, and this may proceed to an indefinite although not an infinite degree. A system of general instruction, which shall reach every description of our citizens, from the richest to the poorest, as it was the earliest, so it shall be the latest of all the public concerns in which I shall permit myself to take an interest. Give it to us, in any shape, and receive for the inestimable boon the thanks of the young, and the blessings of the old, who are past all other services but prayers for the prosperity of their country, and blessings to those who promote it."

A NATIONAL UNIVERSITY.—The establishment of a national university, to be located at the seat of General Government, was earnestly advocated by Washington. He repeatedly refers to the subject, not only in his official communications to Congress, but also in his private correspondence with Hamilton, Jefferson, and others. He conceived that such an institution would guard American youth from the dangers of education abroad, and have a tendency to banish local and State prejudices from the national councils. In his last will he bequeathed fifty shares in the Potomac Company " toward the endowment of a university to be established within the limits of the District of Columbia."

LAND GRANTS.—The plan of granting a certain portion of the public lands for educational purposes had its beginning in 1785. In the ordinance for the government of the Northwest Territory, the sixteenth section (one square mile) in every township of thirty-six square miles was set apart for the maintenance of public schools. The principle governing this action was stated as follows: " Religion, morality, and knowledge being necessary to good government and the happiness of mankind, schools, and the means of education shall be forever encouraged." Two years later an additional grant of two townships or seventy-two square miles was made to each State for the support of a university. As this action was confirmed in 1789, after the adoption of the Federal Constitution, every State organized since that time has received, in addition to the grant for common schools, at least two townships for the promotion of higher education. In 1848 the thirty-sixth section of each township was added to the sixteenth for the support of common schools. Special grants have been made at different times. The land granted by the General Government for educational purposes between 1785 and 1862 amounts to nearly 140,-000,000 acres.

AGRICULTURAL COLLEGES.—In the dark days of 1862

Congress was not unmindful of the material progress of the country. The need of a more practical education than that furnished by the ordinary classical college was felt. With the view of bringing education into closer relation with the mechanic arts and the agricultural development of our vast domain, Congress made a grant of land-scrip to the amount of 30,000 acres for each senator and representative for the establishment of what are known as agricultural colleges. The leading object of these colleges, as the bill stated, "should be, without excluding other scientific and classical studies, and including military tactics, to teach such branches of learning as are related to agriculture and the mechanic arts, in order to promote the liberal and practical education of the industrial classes in the several pursuits and professions of life." The amount of land thus donated to the several States was 9,510,000 acres. All of the States have accepted the grant; and, in accordance with the provisions of the act, they have either established independent institutions, or have connected an agricultural department with an existing college or university. Supplemented by State appropriations and in a few cases by individual munificence, this donation by Congress is beginning to realize the expectations of its friends, and has led to the establishment of some excellent institutions.

BUREAU OF EDUCATION.—The Bureau of Education is an office in the Department of the Interior. It had its origin in the need of some central agency to collect, preserve, and distribute educational information. In 1866 a memorial emanating from the National Association of State and City School Superintendents was presented to the House of Representatives; and, substantially on the basis thus recommended, an act was passed March 2, 1867, establishing an agency " for the purpose of collecting such statistics and facts as shall show the condition and progress of education in the several States and Territories, and of diffusing such information respecting the organization and management of school systems and methods of teaching as shall aid the people of the United States in the establishment and maintenance of efficient school systems, and otherwise promote the cause of education." Since its establishment the Bureau of Education has collected a large amount of valuable educational intelligence, which by means of annual reports and circulars of information it has widely disseminated.

IN THE SOUTH.—By the Declaration of Independence the several colonies assumed the character of sovereign States. The States of the South continued to regard education, not as a public but as a private interest, to be left in the hands of parents or guardians. If here and there popular education found, as in the case of Jefferson, a strong advocate, it did not prevail. Primary education was supplied by means of subscription schools, which were maintained during the winter months in every community of sufficient population. For those unable to pay the cost of tuition, a public fund was provided. In the families of the wealthy, the custom of employing tutors generally prevailed. Private enterprise secured the establishment of numerous flourishing secondary schools, while denominational zeal multiplied the number of Christian colleges.

EFFECT OF CIVIL WAR.—By destroying the system of slavery, and leading, in some measure, to a reorganization of society, the civil war has brought the Southern States into harmonious relations with the rest of the country. The South has broken away from hurtful traditions; it is rapidly developing its material resources; it is looking to the future with a confident hopefulness that gives vigor and courage to every effort. In no particular has the change been more remarkable and significant than in education. Since the war every Southern State has adopted a system of free public instruction which, in spite of poverty, prejudice, and the scattered condition of the population, has made surprising progress. Opposition has been hushed or overcome; interest in popular education is profound and general; political parties vie with one another in befriending the public schools; young teachers, filled with the spirit of educational progress, have come to the front.

PRESENT CONDITIONS.—But there are serious difficulties in the way of a high degree of efficiency. Apart from the sparseness of population in many rural districts, and the lack of funds due to relative poverty, the problem is further complicated by the necessity of maintaining separate schools for the two races. The colored schools seem to need a larger infusion of the moral element in their work. The school terms are entirely too short, schoolhouse accommodations are inadequate, and the pay of teachers too meager to command, in many cases, the services of competent men and women. Politics enter too largely into the choice of State Superintendents of Education and other officers of the public-school system. There is, however, at present a brave facing of the situation. The "Ogden movement" (Southern Educational Board) is full of promise; and prominent educators and public men, notably Governor Montague, of Virginia, and Governor Aycock, of North Carolina, are emphasizing the importance of popular education. The latter said in his inaugural address: "I promised the illiterate poor man, bound to a life of toil and struggle and poverty, that life should be brighter for his boy and girl than it had been for him and the partner of his sorrows and joys. I pledged the wealth of the State to the education of his children. Men of wealth, representatives of great corporations, applauded eagerly my declaration. I have found no man who is unwilling to make the State stronger and better by liberal aid to the cause of education."

IN THE NORTH AND WEST.—The spirit of the North and West found fitting expression in the Constitution of Massachusetts, adopted in 1780. "Wisdom and knowledge," says this document, "as well as virtue, diffused generally among the body of the people, being necessary for the preservation of their rights and liberties; and as these depend on spreading the opportunities and advantages of education in the various parts of the country, and among the different orders of the people, it shall be the duty of legislators and magistrates, in all future periods of this Commonwealth, to cherish the interests of literature and the sciences, and all seminaries of them; especially the University of Cambridge, public schools, and grammar-schools in the towns; to encourage private societies and public institutions, rewards and immunities, for the promotion of agriculture, arts, sciences, commerce, trades, manufactures, and a natural history of the country; to countenance and inculcate the principles of humanity and general benevolence, public and private charity, industry and frugality, honesty and punctuality in their dealings; sincerity, good humor, and all social affections and generous sentiments among the people."

GENERAL SYSTEM.—Though differing in details, the system of popular instruction now adopted throughout the United States is everywhere substantially the same. It comprehends three grades of schools—the primary schools, in which reading, writing, arithmetic, geography, and English grammar are the principal subjects taught; the secondary schools, known as high schools, graded schools, grammar-schools, and academies, in which the higher mathematics, foreign languages, history, and natural science are introduced; and the colleges and universities, in which the curricula embrace the studies necessary to a liberal education and professional life. To these should be added the normal schools, which are designed to give teachers a scientific training for their vocation.

PRIMARY SCHOOLS.—The primary schools and, for the most part, the secondary schools, are supported by a tax levied on all assessed property, together with the income derived from any permanent fund created by special State appropriation or grant by the national Government. Though many States have one or more institutions for superior instruction maintained by annual appropriations from the public treasury, the majority of our colleges and universities are the fruit of denominational zeal and individual munificence. The State, usually through a Board of Education or Superintendent of Public Instruction, exercises a general supervision over the public schools, while the details of management are committed to local officers, consisting of county superintendents and district committees.

GENERAL INTEREST.—A strong interest in education exists in every section of our country; and, under the impulsion of this feeling, every effort is made to advance the public schools. Neat and well-furnished schoolhouses are rapidly supplanting the log huts and temporary makeshifts of the past; a better qualified class of teachers is being demanded by public sentiment; the various school officers are held more firmly to a faithful discharge of their duties; the school term is being lengthened; better courses of study and improved methods of teaching are being everywhere introduced. The French Commission to the Exposition of 1876 was correct in reporting that in the United States, " the great zeal for the education of the young, which grows as the population increases, penetrates into the public mind more and more, and manifests itself in more and more decided ways. What may have seemed at first a transient glow of enthusiasm, a generous impulse, has in time assumed all the force of a logical conviction, or rather of a positive certainty. It is no longer a movement of a few philanthropists or of a few religious societies, but it is an essential part of the public administration, for which the States, the cities, and townships appropriate every year more money than any other country in the world has hitherto devoted to the education of the people. Far from limiting this generosity as much as possible to primary instruction, it goes so far as to declare free for all not only primary but even secondary schools."

COMPULSORY EDUCATION.—The subject of compulsory education has naturally elicited considerable discussion. The opponents of the system say that it is essentially un-American; that it interferes with the rights of parents; that the difficulties of carrying it out are insuperable; and that its absence involves no danger to our institutions. The advocates of the system reply that ignorance is an evil which the State should remove; that the parent has no right to bring up his children in ignorance; that the State has a natural right to enact any laws that may be necessary for self-protection; and that the compulsory system, both in this country and in Europe, has produced beneficial results. The sentiment in favor of compulsory education is generally dominant; and as a result, thirty-two

States and Territories, of which only two or three are in the South, have adopted compulsory attendance.

COEDUCATION.—Another educational question that has evoked much discussion in recent years is the coeducation of the sexes in our colleges and universities. It is different from the question of the higher education of woman, about which there is a general agreement among the intelligent people of this country. In the primary schools and even in the secondary schools of this country, the young of both sexes have generally been educated together. Begun from considerations of economy and convenience, coeducation is now continued in these schools from a strong conviction of its excellence. But that the same system should apply to superior education has been stoutly denied. It is said that coeducation in our higher institutions of learning endangers the health of young women; that it does not give them a training suited to their destiny in life; that it develops a strong-minded type of womanhood; that it lowers the grade of scholarship; that it leads to personal attachments and matrimonial engagements; and, lastly, that it gives rise to scandals. These arguments are chiefly theoretical, and hence it happens that they are met by a series of counter-statements. The advocates of coeducation in our colleges, after a more or less extended observation of its workings, affirm that the system has not proved injurious to health; that it aims at individual development, which is the true end of education; that it makes young women more womanly, and young men· more manly; that it raises the standard of scholarship, since female students usually maintain a better average than their male competitors; that if it sometimes leads to matrimonial engagements, these are formed under the most favorable circumstances; that it does not give rise to more scandals than otherwise occur; that it elevates the moral tone of a college, and renders discipline less difficult; and that, by bringing about a communion of sympathy and taste between man and woman, it lays the foundation for greater domestic happiness. Whatever may be thought of the arguments on either side, coeducation has practically become the system in the United States. The primary schools are all coeducational; ninety-eight per cent of the secondary schools are coeducational; and about three-fourths of our universities and colleges admit women on the same conditions as men. Though a slight reaction has recently been noticeable, it probably springs from local and transient conditions.

E. Conclusion

The foregoing survey shows that education has not yet reached its final and ideal state. The educational world is still in the experimental stage of its development. Great problems in educational philosophy and educational practise remain to be solved. But able minds in all Christian lands are engaged upon these problems; and this fact, though it leaves education in an unsettled condition, promises well for the future. Within the past few decades, education has made great progress. More correct views of the nature and end of education have become generally prevalent. Beginning with Comenius, the educational reformers have been generally triumphant. In order that educational methods may have a scientific basis, the physical and mental constitution of man is being subjected anew to careful investigation. Childhood is made the subject of scientific study. The work of instruction is no longer left to novices, but is more and more committed to

27

teachers who have received a professional training. As a result of all this interest and activity we may confidently expect that in the course of time—it may yet be a long way off—there will come forth, through the law of development and the inherent power of truth, a system of education that will leave no part of man's nature neglected, but with supreme and unfailing effort will train the young to be strong, intelligent, and, above all, righteous men and women.

LIST OF AUTHORITIES

The following list contains the principal works that have been used in the preparation and revision of the present volume. The author has wished to avoid the use of frequent footnotes; but anyone interested in the quotations will be able, in nearly every instance, to locate and verify them in the books here given.

Alzog, J. B.: "Universal-Kirchengeschichte."

Ante-Nicene Fathers.

Aristotle: "Politics" and "Ethics."

Bacon, Francis: "Complete Works."

Bardeen, C. W.: "Orbis Pictus of Comenius."

Barnard, Henry: "American Pedagogy," "Normal Schools," "Journal of Education."

Boone, R. G.: "Education in the United States."

Bossuet, J. B.: "Variations of Protestantism."

Bréal, Michel: "Quelques Mots" sur l'Instruction Publique en France."

Browning, Oscar: "History of Educational Theories."

Bryce, James: "The Holy Roman Empire."

Cicero: "Offices," "Orations," and "De Oratore."

Coleman, Lyman: "Ancient Christianity Exemplified."

Comenius, John Amos: "Orbis Pictus" (Bardeen), "Great Didactic" (Keatinge).

Compayré, G.: "History of Pedagogy," "Abelard."

D'Aubigné, J. H. Merle: "History of the Reformation."

Davidson, Thomas: "Aristotle and the Ancient Educational Ideals."

De Guimps, R.: "Pestalozzi, His Life and Works."

Dictionnaire de Pédagogie (Buisson).

Dittes, F.: "Geschichte der Erziehung und des Unterrichts," "Grundriss der Erziehungs- und Unterrichtslehre."

Dyer, T. H.: "Life of John Calvin."

Eckoff, Wm. J.: "Herbart's A B C of Sense-Perception."

Edersheim, A.: "Life and Times of Jesus the Messiah."

Emerton, Ephraim: "Desiderius Erasmus."

Encyclopædia Britannica.

Falke: "Hellas und Rom."

Fénelon: "Oeuvres" (3 vols).

Ferté, H.: "Rollin: Sa Vie, Ses Oeuvres et l'Université de son Temps."

Fisher, George P.: "History of the Reformation."

Francke, A. H.: "Unterricht wie die Kinder zur wahren Gottseligkeit und Christlichen Klugheit anzuführen sind."

Froebel, Friedrich: "Education of Man" (Hailman).

Froude, James A.: "Life and Letters of Erasmus."

Geikie, C.: "Life of Christ."

Gibbon, Edward: "Decline and Fall of the Roman Empire."

Green, J. R.: "History of the English People."

Grob, Jean: "Life of Zwingli."

Grote, George: "History of Greece."

Hailman, W. N.: "History of Pedagogy."

Harris, Wm. T.: "Psychologic Foundations of Education," "Annual Reports."

Hegel, G. W. F.: "Philosophy of History."

Herbart, J. F.: "A B C of Sense-Perception" (Eckoff), "Text-Book in Psychology" (Smith).

Herodotus: "Complete Works" (Beloe).

Hughes, Thomas: "Loyola and the Educational System of the Jesuits."

Huxley, Thomas: "Lay Sermons."

Jackson, Samuel M.: "Huldreich Zwingli."

Jacotot, J.: "L'Enseignement Universel."

Jahn, J.: "Hebrew Commonwealth."

Johonnot, James: "Principles and Practice of Teaching."

Josephus, Flavius: "Works."

Kant, Immanuel: "Pädagogik."

Keatinge, M. W.: "Great Didactic of Comenius."

Kellner, L.: "Geschichte der Erziehung und des Unterrichts."

Kiddle and Schem, "Cyclopædia of Education."

Krüsi, H.: "Life, Work, and Influence of Pestalozzi."

Kurtz, J. H.: "Church History."

Lane, Frederick: "Elementary Greek Education."

Laurie, S. S.: "Comenius: His Life and Educational Work," "Rise and Early Constitution of the Universities," "Historical Survey of Pre-Christian Education."

Lewes, George H.: "History of Philosophy."

Library of the World's Best Literature.

Lindner, G. A.: "Encyklopädisches Handbuch der Erziehungskunde."

Literature of All Nations.

Locke, John: "Thoughts concerning Education."

Luther, Martin: "Schriften" (Leipsic Edition).

Mahaffy, J. P.: "Old Greek Education."

Mann, Horace: "Seventh Annual Report."

Mann, Mary: "Life of Horace Mann."

Marenholtz-Bülow: "Reminiscences of Friedrich Froebel."

Martin, W. A. P.: "The Chinese: Their Education, Philosophy and Letters."

Maspero, G.: "Egyptian Archæology."

Maurus, Rhabanus: "Von der Unterweisung der Geistlichen."

Merivale, C.: "History of the Romans."

Melanchthon, Philip: "Corpus Reformatorum."

Milton, John: "Tractate on Education."

Monroe, Paul: "Source-Book of the History of Education."

Montaigne, Michel de: "Essays."

Mosheim, J. L.: "Ecclesiastical History."

Neander, J. A. W.: "Church History."

Pachtler, G. M., S. J.: "Monumenta Germaniae Paedagogica" (Ratio Studiorum of Jesuits).

Painter, F. V. N.: "Luther on Education."

Payne, Joseph: "Lectures on the Science and Art of Education."

Paroz: "Histoire Universelle de la Pédagogie."

Pestalozzi, J. H.: "Wie Gertrud ihre Kinder lehrt."

Plato: "Protagoras," "Phædo," "Republic," and "Laws."

Plutarch: "Lives" and "Morals" (Goodwin).

Post-Nicene Fathers.

Quick, R. H.: "Educational Reformers."

Quintilian: "Institutes of Oratory."

Raumer, Karl von: "Geschichte der Pädagogik."

Rawlinson, George: "Five Great Monarchies," "Ancient Religions."

Richard, J. W.: "Philip Melanchthon."

Richter, Jean Paul: "Levana."

Ritter, H.: "History of Philosophy."

Rollin, Charles: "Method of Teaching and Studying the Belles-Letters" (4 vols.).

Rowe, A. D.: "Every-Day Life in India."

Sammlung der bedeutendsten pädagogischen Schriften aus alter und neuer Zeit. Herausgegeben von Dr. Bernh. Schulz.

Schmid, K. A.: "Geschichte der Erziehung von Anfang an bis unsere Zeit."

Schmidt, Karl: "Geschichte der Pädagogik."

Seebohm, F.: "The Protestant Revolution."

Seneca: "Morals."

Smith, Margaret K.: "Herbart's Text-Book on Psychology."

Spencer, Herbert: "Education: Intellectual, Moral, and Physical."

Staunton, Howard: "The Great Schools of England."

Thirlwall, C.: "History of Greece."

Thucydides: "Peloponnesian War" (Harpers).

Universal Classics.

West, Andrew F.: "Alcuin and the Rise of the Christian Schools."

Wilkinson, Sir J. G.: "Manners and Customs of the Ancient Egyptians."

Williams, S. W.: "The Middle Kingdom."

Wines, E. C.: "Laws of the Ancient Hebrews."

Xenophon: "Memorabilia," "Cyropædia," and "Economics."

INDEX

401

THE END